NEGOTIATING BOUNDARIES AT WORK

Talking and Transitions

Edited by Jo Angouri, Meredith Marra and Janet Holmes

EDINBURGH
University Press

Edinburgh University Press is one of the leading university presses in the UK. We publish academic books and journals in our selected subject areas across the humanities and social sciences, combining cutting-edge scholarship with high editorial and production values to produce academic works of lasting importance. For more information visit our website: edinburghuniversitypress.com

Edinburgh University Press Ltd
The Tun – Holyrood Road
12(2f) Jackson's Entry
Edinburgh EH8 8PJ

Typeset in 10/12 Ehrhardt by
Servis Filmsetting Ltd, Stockport, Cheshire,
and printed and bound in Great Britain by
CPI Group (UK) Ltd, Croydon CR0 4YY

A CIP record for this book is available from the British Library

ISBN 978 1 4744 0313 9 (hardback)
ISBN 978 1 4744 0314 6 (webready PDF)
ISBN 978 1 4744 1837 9 (epub)

Contents

Part II Transitions *within* a Profession

Notes on Contributors

Jo Angouri is Reader at the Centre for Applied Linguistics, University of Warwick, UK and Visiting Distinguished Professor at Aalto University, School of Business, Finland. Her research expertise is in sociolinguistics, pragmatics and discourse analysis. She has published on language and identity as well as teamwork and leadership in medical settings. Jo is currently working on a multidisciplinary project on migration and access to the labour market.

Kristin Bührig has been full professor for Linguistics of German Language at the University of Hamburg, Germany since 2007. She specialises in Linguistics of German as a second and a foreign language. Her main interests are communication in institutions, multilingual communication, community interpreting and functional grammar. She is head of the Hamburg Centre of Language Corpora (Hamburger Zentrum für Sprachkorpora HZSK).

Seongsook Choi is a lecturer in the Moray House School of Education, University of Edinburgh, UK. Her current research focuses on interdisciplinary talk and the development of analytical tools for mapping interactional patterns and representing these dynamically in visual formats. Her most recent publications appear in *Applied Linguistics* and *Discourse Studies*. She is currently writing *Interdisciplinary Discourse: Communicating across Disciplines*, to be published by Palgrave Macmillan.

Anne H. Fabricius teaches sociolinguistics at Roskilde University, Denmark where she is Associate Professor of English Language. She was a founding member of the CALPIU network and project (2009–13). Her research interests include internationalisation, language attitudes and language ideology in stable and transient lingua-franca communities, the sociolinguistic status of English in Denmark, and phonological variation and change in British elite sociolects.

Laurent Fillietaz is Professor of Adult and Vocational Education at the University of Geneva, Switzerland. He received his PhD in linguistics in 2000 and has developed an expertise in discourse analysis and multimodal approaches to interaction. He has conducted much research over the years on topics like language use in professional contexts, and social interaction in vocational education and training.

Anne Franziskus completed her PhD thesis on the language practices, norms and ideologies of cross-border workers in Luxembourg at the University of Luxembourg. Since 2014, she has been working as a research associate for Luxembourg's Institute of Statistics and Economic Studies (STATEC). Her current research interests cover the areas of multilingualism, social exclusion and poverty.

Janet Holmes is Emeritus Professor in Linguistics at Victoria University of Wellington in New Zealand and a Fellow of the Royal Society of New Zealand. She is Associate Director of the Wellington Language in the Workplace project, an ongoing study of communication in the workplace. Janet has also published in the areas of gender and language and New Zealand English. The team is currently researching the hospitality industry.

Marta Kirilova is a research associate at the Center for Internationalization and Parallel Language Use and the Department of Nordic Studies and Linguistics at the University of Copenhagen, Denmark. Her research interests include language, culture and ideology in workplace settings, Danish as a second language and migrant identities. She has published in a number of Nordic journals and has contributed to international co-edited volumes and handbook chapters on multilingualism, workplace language policy and the processes of performing identities and fitting in at work.

Julie Kerekes is an Associate Professor in Language and Literacies Education at the Ontario Institute for Studies in Education, University of Toronto, Canada. Her research and teaching focus on language and power in conversational and institutional settings, particularly workplace ESL, as well as on the professional development of second language teachers. Her current projects examine the employment trajectories of internationally educated professionals, interlanguage pragmatics in email communications, and provincial policies affecting second language teacher education.

Ewa Kuśmierczyk-O'Connor holds a PhD in Applied Linguistics from Victoria University, New Zealand. Her main area of work lies within the discourse of employability, with her PhD thesis exploring the multimodal aspects of job interview discourse. In her research, Ewa has drawn on a wide range of existing research within social psychology, business communication, HR, linguistics and pedagogy to explore the different aspects of employability. She currently works with Careers and Employment at Victoria University of Wellington as a researcher and employability programmes coordinator.

Stefano A. Losa holds a PhD in Sociology from the University of Geneva, Switzerland. Within the Faculty of Psychology and Educational Sciences of the University of Geneva, his teaching and research interests lie in multilingual practices and identity construction in institutional contexts. In particular, his investigations relate to the interactional dynamics of learning in workplace and vocational training contexts.

Meredith Marra is Director of the Wellington Language in the Workplace Project and has been involved in collecting and analysing naturally occurring data in New Zealand organisations since 1998. Her primary research interest is the language of business meetings, and she has published in the areas of humour, gender and ethnicity in workplace interactions.

Dorien Van De Mieroop is Associate Professor in the Linguistics department of KU Leuven, Belgium. Her main research interest is in the discursive analysis of identity, which she studies in institutional contexts and in research interviews. On this topic, she has (co-)authored more than twenty articles in international peer-reviewed journals as well as a book (*Master Narratives, Identities, and the Stories of Former Slaves*, with Jonathan Clifton, John Benjamins, 2016). She is associate editor of *Narrative Inquiry* (John Benjamins).

Jochen Rehbein studied medicine, Germanic philology, general linguistics and philosophy at various universities (including Berlin and Paris). He started teaching in 1971; in 1978 was appointed professor of sociology of language and foreign language acquisition in Bochum; and from 1983 until 2006 was professor of German as a foreign language in Hamburg. He was co-founder of the Graduate College on Multilingualism and Language Contact (1991–94) and of the Research Centre on Multingualism (1999–2011) at the University of Hamburg, Germany. He has published and conducted projects on functional pragmatics, discourse analysis, grammar and mental processes, various aspects of multilingualism, intercultural communication, Turkish linguistics, politeness and the methodology of linguistic analysis.

Sophie Reissner-Roubicek joined the University of Warwick's Centre for Applied Linguistics, UK, after completing her doctoral study at the University of Auckland, New Zealand. Her work on graduate job interviews and the critical nature of teamwork and leadership questions prompted her interest in the way teamwork and leadership are interactionally achieved. This has led variously to designing and delivering interdisciplinary training and degree level courses in professional communication, research on gender in STEM contexts and a focus on intercultural skills for employability.

Stephanie Schnurr is Associate Professor at the Centre for Applied Linguistics at the University of Warwick, UK. Her main research interests are professional and medical communication with a particular focus on leadership discourse, identity construction, gender, (im)politeness and the strategic uses of humour. She has published widely on these aspects and is also the author of *Language and Culture at Work* (with Olga Zayts, Routledge, 2017), *Exploring Professional Communication* (Routledge, 2013) and *Leadership Discourse at Work: Interactions of Humour, Gender and Workplace Culture* (Palgrave, 2009).

Minna Suni is a specialist in Finnish as a second language. She works as a professor at the Department of Languages, University of Jyväskylä, Finland. Her recent research projects and publications have focused on migrants learning and using a second language in working life, and she is one of the convenors of an AILA research network focusing on this theme. Currently she also chairs the Finnish Association for Applied Linguistics.

Introduction: Negotiating Boundaries at Work

Jo Angouri, Meredith Marra and Janet Holmes

1. Theorising *transitions*

This edited collection focuses on transition talk and boundary-crossing discourse in the modern workplace context.[1] Transitions form a normal part of life and the term typically denotes mobility and change. This includes movement across physical/spatiotemporal borders, life stages, intellectual or social boundaries. Transitions are particularly visible in the modern globalised workplace; the concept of a 'job for life' is outdated, and employees move between jobs, countries and even professions or industries during their working lives. Workforce mobility is particularly intense within and between national and international urban workplaces (Eriksson and Lindgren 2009) and career journeys involve increasingly complex paths, for both white and blue collar workers. The changing employment market also means frequent boundary crossing into new linguistic environments and new ways of doing work. This affects the ways in which professional identities are constructed, in a fast-paced, fluid and dynamic context. A range of disciplinary areas, theoretical stances, and methodological traditions have addressed the dynamic nature of transitions. Transitions involving crossing and operating at the interface of one or more geographical borders have been studied by management studies and organisational behaviour scholars, most notably the implications of boundary-crossing activities for role performance and team dynamics. International business studies have also analysed the significance of the use of multiple languages in the workplace (e.g. Piekkari and Westney 2017) while work in sociology and education has probed the complexity of the phenomenon (e.g. Duchscher 2009; Pickles and Smith 2005; Avelino and Rotmans 2009). Despite this, transitions remain an under-researched area in sociolinguistics in general and workplace discourse in particular. This publication addresses this gap.

In sociolinguistics, transitions have long been conceptualised as linear and sequential or as moving between a place/language X to a place/language Y. This, however, does not capture the dynamics of mobility in modern society. Vertovec (2007) writing on the 'diversification of diversity' or 'superdiversity', a term that has become widely cited and popular, foregrounds the pace of mobility, the fluidity of transitions, and the multiple spatiotemporal journeys that more accurately represent population flows quantitatively and qualitatively. Transitions have become common, unpredictable, multiple and diverse. Migration out of choice, opportunity or necessity (e.g. fleeing from war zones or for better career prospects) is affecting and will continue to affect large numbers of people from all parts of the world. This is not only debated in academic circles; the dynamics and challenges associated with migration, in the broadest sense, are prominent in public discourses and, at the time of writing, Europe is a case in point. Discourses of economic migration, integration and pressures on the 'receiving' societies proliferate. While one narrative associates migration and mobility with growth and wealth, superdiversity is not always portrayed in a positive light (see for example Wodak 2015 on the rise of far right); fear-based narratives associate migration with pressures on the welfare system, loss of employment for the host society, crime and erosion of values that threaten the imagined homogeneity and perceived social cohesion. In the context of these contrasting narratives, the workplace becomes a contested area, split between those who are 'in' and those who are attempting to gain access and are often commodified as a resource, brain power, knowledge worker, manual labour and/or a burden. These discourses feed into ideologies at a societal level and are in their turn reiterated or resisted in workplace interaction.

The modern workplace is and will continue to be transient and diverse and this requires new ways of thinking about the labour market, professional trajectories and also the multiple languages that form the everyday linguistic landscape in most workplace settings. Linguistic diversity and language change constitute traditional foci in (socio)linguistic enquiry. Second Language Acquisition (SLA) has foregrounded the dynamics of language choice, code-switching (e.g. Auer 2013) and the relationship between multilingual practice and identity, while variationist studies (Eckert 2012) have provided valuable insights on language use, language change and the associated social evaluations (e.g. Lippi-Green 1997). At the same time, postmodern approaches on (multilingual) language use move from focusing on 'language' or languages to the speaker and their multiple styles or repertoires (Rampton 2014, 2011). The concept of 'languaging' used by Swain (1985) aims to capture the dynamic process of 'using language to make meaning' (Swain 2006: 96), and terms such as 'code meshing' (Canagarajah 2007) similarly attempt to capture multilingual practice beyond code-switching or code-mixing which typically see languages as distinct entities.

The dynamics of globalisation and the complexity of transitions have important implications for negotiating professional identity and teamwork in the modern workplace. In our volume, we pay special attention to the strategies that individuals adopt for navigating multiple physical or ideological boundaries (language, workplace, country), and we suggest that this process is not linear but is rather in constant negotiation. In particular, the volume problematises the enactment of identities, the deconstruction of 'culture', the negotiation of norms, and the process of moving from the periphery to integrating into new groups.

These transitions are enacted linguistically in the situated 'here and now' of workplace discourse. Institutions as well as the broader sociopolitical and economic environment are 'talked into being' (Heritage 1984: 290) in situated interaction. In various professional events, from job interviews to business meetings, the interactants negotiate belonging and index group membership (or the opposite). This has serious implications for being accepted as 'one of us', that is, choosing whether or not to partake in the group's shared norms. Beyond the micro enactment of transitions, the negotiation between the individual and the group is visible at community level. Here, group norms are brought into scrutiny in terms of organisational shared meanings. In this first dedicated volume on transitions, our interest is the process of socialising into a new group and how individuals reflect on their own understanding of how things work, simultaneously negotiating their place and (re)creating group norms. This process is multilayered and includes the ongoing redefinition of personal, social and professional identities (Blommaert 2007; Eckert 2008; and a model encapsulating these constraints proposed in Holmes et al. 2011).

2. Structure and content

The contributors in the volume represent the range of work currently being undertaken and highlight the dynamic nature of traversing boundaries while drawing on diverse methodologies and theoretical traditions (e.g. Communities of Practices, Interactional Sociolinguistics, Ecolinguistics, Multimodality and Conversation Analysis) and datasets including interviews, interaction and narratives. The volume is structured in two parts: Part I focuses on crossing *into* a work environment or profession and negotiating gatekeeping events, while Part II puts the magnifying glass on crossings *within* a profession.

In the first part, Kerekes, Kirilova, Kuśmierczyk-O'Connor, Reissner-Roubicek, Van De Mieroop and Schnurr, and Losa and Filliettaz draw on the relationship between macro-level social structures or constraints and micro-level dynamic, fluid interaction in specific workplaces or communities of practice. Macro-level constraints range from the pressures of conflicting ideologies in multilingual contexts to the influence of established institutional practices and globally recognised leadership characteristics on highly structured discursive frameworks such as employment and appraisal interviews.

Macro-level constraints that are reflected in gatekeeping events can be identified in the form of societal norms and stereotypes. Kirilova and Kerekes both point to the negative outcomes of such stereotypes for potential employees from non-Western cultural and linguistic backgrounds. Often realised in the form of widespread negative public discourse, these stereotypes put great pressure on job candidates to challenge gatekeeping behaviours, which implicitly draw on such discourses. Negotiating a credible identity as a potentially valuable employee within a negative societal framework is a major issue for those attempting to access the labour market. Focusing on the Canadian context, Kerekes shows how important it is for job-seeking internationally educated professionals to demonstrate their ability to make such transitions into existing communities. Examining how individual attitudes, circumstances and adaptation to Canadian life have influenced their varied employment trajectories, she suggests that reasons for failure are frequently ideologically based rather than attributable to lack of English fluency as is often claimed. The link between macro-level stereotypes and lack of success in micro-level job interview contexts is evident. Kirilova and Kerekes, like others in the volume, question the relevance of cultural, national or ethnic differences in accounting for communication problems or misunderstandings, noting that 'culture' is often appropriated as a convenient shorthand for explaining away complex issues.

Examining this issue from a different perspective and using Multimodal Interaction Analysis, Kuśmierczyk-O'Connor focuses on micro-level features within the gatekeeping job interview, which facilitate a transition to the workplace. Her analysis demonstrates the intersection of macro-level workplace ideologies with micro-level professional and social identity construction. The ability to synthesise relevant workplace discourses must be demonstrated in dynamic face-to-face interaction drawing on a range of meaning-making resources, including speech, gesture and gaze, as well as written text.

Reissner-Roubicek also problematises the ways in which university graduates negotiate expectations of articulating teamwork experiences in job interviews. She shows that graduates often fail to properly read the cues and demonstrate understanding of the expected norms. She focuses on the analysis of naturally occurring interaction and like others in the volume she argues for a more dynamic understanding of gate-keeping discourses.

Consistent with a model that examines how interaction at the micro-level enacts, modifies, complexifies and contests such constraints, Van De Mieroop and Schnurr analyse how a leader constructs her role differently in response to diverse contextual features within apparently similarly structured appraisal interviews. The joint micro-level discursive negotiation of roles and identities has important macro-level outcomes, including the fact that it determines what will remain on the institutional record (macro-level constraint) of the organisation.

Finally, Losa and Filliettaz take a different approach and focus on the process of transition from being the apprentice to full membership in a community of practice. Detailed analysis of negotiated positionings in one-to-one interactions suggests the extent to which newcomers must acquire shared meanings in the process of moving from the periphery in order to integrate into and become legitimate members of a new workplace community. Losa and Filliettaz's chapter turns the focus to crossings within professions; this is further elaborated in the second part of the collection. To sum up, the chapters in the first part argue against a narrow and static conceptualisation of gatekeeping discourse and show the complex relationship between macro-level dis-courses and micro-level interaction.

In the second part, Bührig and Rehbein, Fabricius, Franziskus, Suni and Choi take a closer look at the complexities of the process of the transition. The chapters focus on the move from potential, peripheral or marginal membership in a workplace or community to fully legitimised core membership, with the challenge of acquiring some understanding of the predominantly implicit social values and taken-for-granted practices entailed in that integration process.

Bührig and Rehbein draw on biographical narratives of employees of an international enterprise to explore the perceived value of multilingualism for commercial enterprises and the experiences of the employees. The link between the international global and the local or individual level is again apparent. Introducing the concept of 'patiency', Bührig and Rehbein demonstrate the importance of opportunities to respond to the experience of being an individual employee in an international enterprise. They identify three different types of discourse that employees used to reflect on their workplace experiences, indicating how at the micro-level of face-to-face interaction, workplace narratives, in particular, function to provide distraction and relief from the pressures of the international globalised workplace.

Continuing the focus on the global multilingual space, Fabricius problematises the tensions faced by a Danish academic in the effort to reconcile the pressures of the global-national vs. the local-workplace norms. She explores the tension by focusing on the struggle and conflict created by the demand to perform in English in international professional contexts. Fabricius shows how commitment to the enactment of a local Danish identity generates a constant negotiation between the two levels and proposes the concept of a 'space between'. This is consistent with the notion of a multilayered analytical model (see Holmes et al. 2011), which accounts for how micro-level interaction, negotiating aspects of personal, social and professional identities, provides one means of resolving the tensions between the demands of the local academic workplace and the global international (academic or other) community.

Language ideologies are also evident at the micro-level of workplace interaction, as illustrated in Franziskus's research on Luxembourg cross-border workers. In line with the examination of the relationship between macro-level constraints and micro-level interaction, this chapter illustrates the ways in which employees manage the conflicting constraints of the multilingual workplace to negotiate their own positioning, drawing on congenial language ideologies to protect and promote their own place within the multilingual workplace environment.

Also illustrating the tensions between international or global pressures and local level workplace practices, Suni explores the interactions between the Finnish social system, the continuous changes in the employment environment, and the micro-level options and opportunities available for the individual. As she notes, the globalising work market is an obvious environmental factor influencing the general dynamics of immigration, but it is at the local work level of communities of practice that individual immigrants negotiate their positions in daily life. For instance, workplace language policies at the macro-level within organisations can either support or restrict the use of different languages at work and thus the quality of workplace experience for individuals. Both Suni's research and Franziskus's study illustrate the negotiation of workplace transitions and the relationship with language choice. Suni notes the dangers of 'a spiral of peripheral participation' for those who lack sufficient or socially relevant language skills. Developing competence in the dominant workplace language or lingua franca is a crucial step in facilitating the transition from peripheral to core workplace membership and in the construction of a convincing and credible professional identity. And Franziskus's detailed analysis of discussions of language practices among cross-border workers illustrates how in practice they linguistically negotiate their positions within new workplaces. She identifies a range of strategies for managing this transition, sometimes conforming to and sometimes contesting local norms in order to carve out a legitimate and acceptable membership position for themselves.

Addressing membership as a contested concept, Choi focuses on the emergence of a new and inherently interdisciplinary field, namely systems biology. As the field develops, so too do the norms about how to demonstrate membership and how to enact an identity, which is in line with shared understandings of the field. Rather than using multiple languages, this enactment relies on discourses which reflect particular sets of expertise, that is, alignment with 'wet' and 'dry' sciences. To belong means recognising and respecting differences. Against a backdrop of a field in flux, the norms for achieving a relevant identity also mean exhibiting the flexibility required to manage the transition from separate fields to a combined approach, while still anchoring yourself in a specific tradition.

To conclude, the chapters in the second part unpack multilingualism at work as well as the multilayered manifestations of social and cultural norms and show the ways in which they are negotiated in different events in the workplace. All chapters demonstrate rich and varied understandings of how complex social and cultural identities are discursively enacted and negotiated in the multicultural urban setting and abundantly illustrate some of the many ways in which workplace participants discursively manage complex transitions through their engagement in workplace talk.

3. Moving forward: bringing transitions to the fore

As the workplace is changing, unpacking the dynamics and implications of the multiple crossings and transitions becomes more and more relevant to the core of the work of workplace discourse analysts. The term 'transitions' has been used as a metaphor or umbrella for capturing transience and fluidity in the workplace. As the chapters in this volume indicate, however, this does not do justice to the complexity of transitions, nor does it contribute to work that is taking place in other disciplinary areas in social sciences. A multi-method sociolinguistic analysis can shed light on the perceived realities of transitions with(in) the multilingual workplace and the subtle ways in which they are linguistically enacted in different corporate, medical or educational contexts. It offers a way to analyse negotiations of power (im)balance and hierarchy in professional contexts without, a priori, negative evaluations superimposed by the researcher. This volume also shows the relevance of unpacking transitions for understanding social and professional identities at work and the process of negotiating membership into multiple communities in professional settings.

Identity and coterminous notions such as role and self in everyday workplace practice have attracted the interest of workplace analysts. As the field of workplace discourse is coming of age, established theoretical approaches and methodological traditions have built a rich body of empirical and evidence based studies. These different approaches focus on different layers of meaning and have provided the tools and metalanguage for tackling abstract concepts and phenomena. This is undoubtedly an achievement for the young field of workplace discourse, and the contributors in this volume showcase the existent diversity of views. At the same time, these multiple views often remain insulated within specific areas of enquiry. In this volume, we aim to create space for dialogue and for bringing different approaches together. Instead of taking one single view for the study of transitions, we seek to pave the way for plurality of voices and cross-fertilisation of ideas. Further work is necessary to address the complex realities of the modern workplace, and challenging established orthodoxies is a condition for theoretical innovation. This can only be achieved through collaboration and multi-method enquiry and this volume aims to raise issues of common concern future studies can address.

Note

1. The original concept for this book grew out of the work of a panel organised by the editors in the Sociolinguistic Symposium in Berlin (2014). Several of the panellists have contributed to this volume and others have supported us by providing generous feedback. We thank them on behalf of the authors. We also thank Kate Burian, the anonymous reviewers and Edinburgh University Press for their support throughout the process.

References

Auer, P. (ed.) (2013), *Code-switching in conversation: language, interaction and identity*, London: Routledge.

Avelino, F. and J. Rotmans (2009), 'Power in transition: an interdisciplinary framework to study power in relation to structural change', *European Journal of Social Theory*, 12: 4, pp. 543–69.

Blommaert, J. (2007), 'Sociolinguistic scales', *Intercultural Pragmatics*, 4: 1, pp. 1–19.

Canagarajah, S. (2007), 'Lingua franca English, multilingual communities, and language acquisition', *The Modern Language Journal*, 9: 1, pp. 923–39.

Duchscher, J. E. B. (2009), 'Transition shock: the initial stage of role adaptation for newly graduated Registered Nurses', *Journal of Advanced Nursing*, 6: 5, pp. 1103–13.

Eckert, P. (2008), 'Variation and the indexical field', *Journal of Sociolinguistics*, 12, pp. 453–76.

Eckert, P. (2012), 'Three waves of variation study: the emergence of meaning in the study of sociolinguistic variation', *Annual Review of Anthropology*, 41, pp. 87–100.

Eriksson, R. and U. Lindgren (2009), 'Localized mobility clusters: impacts of labour market externalities on firm performance', *Journal of Economic Geography*, 9: 1, pp. 33–53.

Heritage, J. (1984), *Garfinkel and ethnomethodology*, Cambridge: John Wiley & Sons.

Holmes, J., M. Marra and B. Vine (2011), *Leadership, discourse, and ethnicity*, Oxford: Oxford University Press.

Lippi-Green, R. (1997), *English with an accent: language, ideology, and discrimination in the United States*, New York: Psychology Press.

Pickles, J. and A. Smith (eds) (2005), *Theorizing transition: the political economy of post-communist transformations*, London: Routledge.

Piekkari, R. and D. E. Westney (2017), 'Language as meeting ground for research on the MNC and organization theory', in C. Dörrenbächer and M. Geppert (eds), *Multinational corporations and organization theory*, Bingley: Emerald.

Rampton, B. (2011), 'Style contrasts, migration and social class', *Journal of Pragmatics*, 43: 5, pp. 1236–50.

Rampton, B. (2014), 'Superdiversity and social class: an interactional perspective', in C. Stroud and M. Prinsloo (eds), *Language, literacy and diversity: moving words*, London: Routledge, pp. 149–65.

Swain, M. (1985), 'Communicative competence: some roles of comprehensible input and comprehensible output in its development', in S. Gass and C. Madden (eds), *Input in second language acquisition*, Rowley, MA: Newbury House, pp. 235–53.

Swain, M. (2006), 'Languaging, agency and collaboration in advanced language proficiency', in H. Byrnes (ed.), *Advanced language learning: the contribution of Halliday and Vygotsky*, London: Continuum, pp. 95–108.

Vertovec, S. (2007), 'Super-diversity and its implications', *Ethnic and Racial Studies*, 30: 6, pp. 1024–54.

Wodak, R. (2015), *The politics of fear: what right-wing populist discourses mean*, London: Sage.

Part 1 Transitions *to* a Profession

1

Language Mentoring and Employment Ideologies: Internationally Educated Professionals in Search of Work

Julie Kerekes

1. Introduction

This chapter considers the roles of language ability and professional background in job seekers' experiences; it investigates how internationally educated professionals' (IEPs') individual attitudes, circumstances and their adaptation to Canadian life have influenced their varied employment trajectories and transitions from seeking work to becoming employed – or not.[1] I first consider the economic and demographic context in which this study, set in the Greater Toronto Area of Ontario, Canada, takes place. Then, I briefly describe the Internationally Educated Professionals Project (IEPro), which is theoretically grounded in sociolinguistic literature on language and identity (Buckingham 2008; Gee 1996), gatekeeping encounters and co-membership (Johnston 2008; Kerekes 2006), and the role of trust in becoming gainfully employed (Kerekes 2003; Kerekes et al. 2013; Tsai et al. 2011; Uslaner 2010). From here, I present the cases of two employment-seeking engineers, and consider their implications for both pedagogy and employment practices.

2. Canadian employment context

The unemployment rate of IEPs is almost twice that of Canadian-educated professionals in the same fields (Zietsma 2010: 14), and the gap between their average earnings is growing (Abbott and Beach 2011). In 2006, only 24 per cent of IEPs were employed in their professions, as opposed to 62 per cent of their Canadian counterparts (Zietsma 2010). Professional challenges faced by IEPs who come to Canada include obtaining recognition of foreign education and credentials, a lack of Canadian work experience, and language (English or French) proficiency (Boyd and Schellenberg 2007; Engineers Canada and Canadian Council of Technicians and Technologists 2009; Frenette and Morisette 2003; Walters et al. 2006; Zong 2004). Professionally trained immigrants from English-speaking countries have been shown to have the highest likelihood of obtaining appropriate employment within their fields of training in Canada (Zietsma 2010: 18), lending credence to the perception that fluency in English and familiarity with its cultural milieu are key elements of employability. IEPs, many of whom are racialised minorities,[2] must also navigate discrimination and negative employer perceptions. Even among traditionally high-income professions (Novak and Chen 2013), Grant and Nadin (2007: 143) found that 'racialized Canadians with foreign training in these fields of study were the ones who tended to be most underpaid relative to White, native-born Canadians'.

Between 1986 and 1997, the number of internationally trained engineers (ITEs)[3] coming to Canada increased almost tenfold, a proportion that was higher than most other professions, including medical doctors (Zhao 2000). Today, over half of the IEPs who immigrate to Canada are ITEs (Zietsma 2010); they have more education (in terms of graduate degrees) and more management/supervisory experience than their Canadian-educated counterparts. Approximately one-third of Ontario's more than 73,000 licensed engineers were educated outside Canada (PEO 2011); the majority of them emigrated from India, China, Iran, Pakistan, Bangladesh, Romania and Iraq. In comparison with their Canadian-educated engineering counterparts, of whom fewer than 3 per cent are racialised minorities (Boyd and Schellenberg 2007), over half of the ITEs in Canada are racialised minorities, and two-thirds of them speak a language other than English or French in their homes.

Before qualifying for employment in their professions, ITEs face numerous gatekeeping situations and encounters they must successfully negotiate.[4] One of the greatest is the engineer licensing process, which involves multiple complex qualifications including: submission of documentation of (overseas) degrees, academic credentials and relevant course descriptions; a technical examination (unless the applicant has more than five years' professional experience and can demonstrate the adequacy of his or her experience to a committee of professional engineers in an Experience Requirement Committee Interview); the Professional Practice Examination (PPE); a minimum of four years' work experience in the field of engineering, of which at least one year must have been in Canada; and references from supervisors who can testify to the value of the applicant's Canadian work experience as well as experience abroad. Only after all of these steps have been assessed as acceptable may a candidate be granted the designation of Professional Engineer (PEng).

To add to their challenges, ITEs' 'ability to communicate in English' (or French in Quebec) has been identified as a key determinant in their employability (FC2I 2003: 49), but no official, standardised measurements of English ability are currently used. A 2014 survey commissioned by the Ontario Society of Professional Engineers reported that

> virtually all employers base their assessment of language proficiency on the (1) writing style of the cover letter that accompanies an application, (2) initial telephone interview, and (3) in-person interviews. Based on interviews with employers, it appears that most employers rely on the telephone interview as the primary screen for English language proficiency. A candidate with perceived weakness in English language skills is unlikely to pass the telephone screen. (Ontario Society of Professional Engineers 2014: 20)

Why and how English language skills are perceived as weak is based on subjective and inconsistent ways of measuring them (Lippi-Green 1997); informal assessments are not immune to ideological, cultural and racial biases (Fairbairn and Fox 2009; Laurier and Baker 2015). Attitudes and ideologies can play as great a role in comprehension and effective communication as do actual linguistic abilities (Lippi-Green 1997; Rubin and Smith 1990). On the one hand, Professional Engineers Ontario (PEO) reported in 2011 that 'instances of rejection due to English language deficiency are extremely rare and are not considered a significant barrier to entry-to-practice for the professional engineering profession' (PEO 2011: 26). FC2I, on the other hand, quotes employers who strongly disagree, such as one who stated, '[communication] is where the international engineering graduates really fall down. Communication is very difficult for them. This is primarily for the Asian trained engineers. Language and culture are the problem' (FC2I 2003: 51). Other participants in the report identified a 'more abrupt' communication style of some ITEs; difficulty participating in a new workplace culture; and challenges explaining technical issues to non-technical staff as common obstacles to finding suitable employment.

The validity of these contrasting perspectives must be considered in the context of the potentially detrimental effect of categorising migrants as 'second language speaker' or 'second language learner'. Such labels often presuppose certain normalised behaviours within the dominant (workplace) culture(s), as well as expectations that certain 'categories' of people do not naturally conform to these behaviours, thus serving as barriers to migrants in their employment pursuits: 'categorization processes reproduce particular structures of meaning and ideology that work to confirm unequal power relations and exclusionary practices' (Tranekjær 2015: 2). Thus, while the discrepancy between internationally educated and Canadian-educated professionals' employment rates has been attributed, in small part, to the fact that some IEPs have weak English language skills, the failure of many others, who speak fluent English, may have more to do with miscommunication based on subtle, ideological and socio-linguistic nuances in communicative styles, as well as a normalised positioning of immigrants/second language speakers as relatively powerless in the context of the dominant culture (Fleming 2010; Tranekjær 2015). It is within this context that this chapter presents a comparison of two key participants in the Internationally Educated Professionals Research Project (IEPro).

3. IEPro

From 2008 to 2012, the Social Science and Humanities Research Council of Canada funded my work on the Internationally Educated Professionals Project (IEPro) at the University of Toronto, which investigated the employment trajectories of internationally educated professionals – specifically, engineers and teachers – who had come to Canada. The research took place in the Greater Toronto Area, one of the most sociolinguistically diverse urban centres in the world. Sixty-three employment seekers and employees – forty engineers and twenty-three teachers – participated in this study; they were interviewed about their sociolinguistic and professional backgrounds, their transitions from their previous countries of employment to Canada, and the challenges they (had) faced in seeking suitable employment. IEPro used an interactional socio-linguistic and discourse analytical approach to describe their employment-seeking trajectories, and to understand their sources of difficulties and successes.

Of the sixty-three participants, seven became language mentees: they were matched with volunteer language mentors who were part of the IEPro research team. The mentors and mentees met for weekly sessions during which the mentees practised their spoken English, prepared for job interviews, and refined their résumés. Each mentor–mentee relationship lasted approximately four months. This chapter analyses the mentoring sessions involving two engineering language mentees and their mentors. Based on similar professional and educational backgrounds, these two mentees' employment-seeking experiences had many similarities, yet resulted in strikingly different trajectories. The data highlight the relationships between job seekers' experiences, attitudes, perceptions and outcomes.

4. Gatekeeping encounters, identity and trust

Existing sociolinguistic research on intercultural gatekeeping encounters attributes second language speakers' difficulties to cultural disparities (resulting in intercultural miscommunication) and inequitable power distribution in decision-making (Kerekes 2005). Empirical research clearly supports theories linking linguistic background, language use, perception of language use, and resultant variable rates of success in social and institutional interactions (Akinnaso and Ajirotutu 1982; Gumperz 1992). Interlocutors rely on their socially generated values and beliefs about their worlds to produce and interpret discourse (Fairclough 1989; Maryns and Blommaert 2002). While Gumperz's (1992) seminal work on intercultural gatekeeping encounters emphasises the importance of the actual verbal interactions and situations in which they occur, other scholars (as noted above) address the role played by the greater context – or 'pretext' – which includes structural parameters such as power dynamics, inequality and prejudice (Meeuwis 1994; Shea 1994). In Tranekjær's (2015) study of Danish internship interviews as gatekeeping encounters, the topic of the nationalities of the participants comes up as a way of differentiating the non-native-speaking interviewees from (native-speaking) Danes, that is, disaffiliating them from the category of 'Danish' national (Tranekjær 2015: 127), and casting doubt regarding the qualifications of the interviewees. Tranekjær points this out as a phenomenon by no means unique to her study, and, in fact, it mirrors the ideological settings in which Javier and Yelena, the participants in this study, find themselves as well.

Gee's (1996) concept of capital 'D' Discourse identifies many aspects of one's identity that contribute to the ways a message is conveyed and interpreted, beyond the language used. They include appearance, status and values, many of which are inseparable from cultural background. Social class, race and accent are, similarly, core elements of one's Discourse which, if not representative of the majority or dominant Discourse, can work against a person in workplace communication and gatekeeping encounters in general. While sharing such characteristics can be beneficial for establishing positive rapport through co-membership (Erickson 2001; Johnston 2008; Kerekes 2006), other compensatory characteristics have also been shown to have equally positive effects (Kerekes 2004).[5] Kerekes (2006) demonstrated that, in job interviews, differences in the sociolinguistic backgrounds of interviewers and interviewees (job seekers) do not necessarily cause negative or positive effects, but that establishing co-membership through positive rapport-building is associated with higher success. Kerekes (2003, 2006) identified and analysed the emically derived concept of 'trust', which proved to be critical in determining the success of job candidates. Contrary to indications from literature viewing non-nativeness as an often inappropriate handicap, speakers of English as a second language (ESL) in this context proved equally likely to gain their interviewer's trust and to achieve a successful interview (i.e. qualifying for job placement) as their English-dominant counterparts. Evidence points at critical inequities, however, both in minority members achieving or obtaining institutional trust, and in minorities trusting North American institutions (Campbell and Roberts 2007; Kerekes et al. 2013; Kuśmierczyk-O'Connor this volume; Tsai et al. 2011; Uslaner 2010). A sense of betrayal from institutions such as the Canadian government is experienced by many IEPs who immigrated to Canada with an understanding that their professional skills were very much in demand, yet subsequently found themselves unemployed and unable to qualify for work in their fields (Kerekes et al. 2013). It is in this context that I now examine the cases of internationally educated engineers in search of work in Canada.

5. Comparative case study

Two internationally trained engineers (ITEs) of the seven original IEPro language mentees participated in twenty-four language mentoring sessions. These sessions consisted of sociolinguistic interviews, English language tutoring, lessons in employment-seeking strategies, and guidance in creating effective résumés, practising job interview skills and professional networking. Using data collected during these sessions, this chapter seeks answers to the following research questions:

1. What are the roles of language and English language ability in ITEs' employment trajectories?
2. Have ITEs' employment-seeking experiences effected a change in their attitudes about employment and life in Canada? If so, what are these changes?

5.1 Methodology

5.1.1 Participants

Javier and Yelena (both pseudonyms) were selected for this comparative study due to their similar backgrounds and professional objectives, yet markedly different approaches to finding work, and eventual outcomes. Yelena was mentored by a Research Assistant on the project, Colette Peters, and I mentored Javier. They are described in the data analysis section.

5.1.2 Procedure

The mentees met regularly with their respective mentors over a four-month period, resulting in a total of ten mentoring sessions for Javier and fourteen for Yelena. All mentoring sessions were audio-recorded. During the first week of mentoring, semi-structured interviews were conducted in an attempt to discern how, in having sought Canadian jobs related to their professional training, the mentees perceived their employment opportunities and/or barriers, as well as to understand the role of their language use and ability in their experiences. The participants provided biographical information, much of which they elaborated upon as the weeks passed and the mentors and mentees became more familiar with one another.

Subsequent mentoring sessions were divided into two parts: during the first half of each session, the mentee chose a topic of concern or interest, and discussed it with the mentor. These discussions often centred on preparation for employment, including finding opportunities to meet prospective employers, networking, applying for a job, refining a résumé and carrying out mock job interviews. Sometimes the conversations were more casual and less directed, covering local events, anecdotes about being a newcomer (in my case, my mentee and I shared experiences of having both moved to Canada from other countries) and ways to become integrated in Canadian life. During the second half of each mentoring session, the mentors focused on discrete non-target-like language features they had observed during the first half, which they felt could be improved through consciousness-raising and practice. The mentors also met with each other weekly, between mentoring sessions, to share their field notes, discuss themes they had observed during the most recent mentoring sessions, and agree on strategies/approaches for the next week's mentoring sessions. They compared the topics and linguistic features they had addressed during the mentoring sessions.

An interactional sociolinguistic analysis of the transcriptions of the twenty-four audio-recorded mentoring sessions enabled me to examine not only the content of the mentoring interactions, but also the discursive construction of the mentees' expressed beliefs and attitudes, as well as the development of their linguistic abilities. Interactional sociolinguistics focuses on how meanings are made and interpreted by participants in verbal interactions, and acknowledges the role context plays in the creation of meaning (Schiffrin 1994). My analysis examined the sentiments and experiences of the mentees, in their own words, in combination with knowledge about them and about the sociocultural contexts in which they found themselves in need of employment. The analysis highlights insights into the participants' identities, and identifies ideologies that played a role in their (immigrant) employment experiences in Canada.

5.2 Findings, or, coming to Canada: the stories of two engineers

Yelena and Javier had both learned English as a foreign language in their home countries and immigrated to Toronto to seek better professional opportunities. Their outlooks and outcomes differed, however, once they were living in Canada, across the following emergent themes: their developing theories about Canadians and Canadian culture; their perceptions and reports of others' perceptions regarding their work prospects; and the relationship between their language learning, language use and their employment trajectories. These are addressed below, after first examining the contexts of their individual stories.

5.2.1 Javier

Professional identity and dreams
Javier, an outgoing and cheerful young man in his mid-thirties, obtained his Bachelor's degree in Civil Engineering and a Master's in Business Administration in El Salvador, his country of origin. He had already gained five years of experience in construction and four years in sales, within the aluminium industry, before moving to Canada. His Salvadorean employment required Javier to travel frequently among seven Central American countries, a fact which he saw as an asset in his applications for jobs in Canada.

At the time when Javier had applied to the Canadian government to immigrate to Canada, two years previously, he was not fully satisfied with his employment in El Salvador. Over the next two years, however, he managed to improve his employment situation such that, when he was notified by the Canadian government that he had ninety days to decide whether or not he wanted to immigrate to Canada, his decision to leave his enhanced Salvadorean life behind was difficult. It was made easier by his relatively carefree feeling of independence: He had

> some privileges [in El Salvador] and it was nice. But then, but then I just decided to come and I left all my things. I'm single I don't have any family, I mean, I'm not, not a wife no children and I decided to come to Canada.

Javier immigrated to Canada in order to work as a civil engineer – 'That's who I am' – and not in sales. He found civil engineering opportunities in El Salvador to be limited:

> Civil engineering in my country is construction – there's no way more . . . When I arrived to Canada and I start thinking wow, civil engineering is . . . it's different, there's so many opportunities, there are so many fields that I can fit into, and then I think well, I, I really like, want to, to became what I couldn't do in my former country. So that's why I decided.

Javier knew no one in Canada, but managed to live temporarily with a friend of a friend in Toronto. He eventually moved into a house shared by 'six housemates and two cats', all of whom were from Canada, a situation which suited Javier's desire to integrate into Canadian society: 'It is very interesting for me because I say, well it's going to be better if I get into the culture of the environment as soon as possible.'

Experiences learning English as a foreign language
Javier started to learn English in El Salvador at the age of twelve in a Saturday language programme. He lacked motivation, however, and found the class boring. He made a

second aborted attempt at learning English in high school. After completing his civil engineering degree, when Javier found only limited employment opportunities in El Salvador, he considered leaving his country. At this point he thought, 'Well, maybe I need some extra tools to, to, to know the world.' He made a third attempt at learning English, but his work consumed his time, so he stopped. When he was offered a job with a company in the aluminium industry, however, he was told that English knowledge would be necessary. His English proficiency was never tested, but when he attended business meetings in English at his new place of employment, he found he could understand very little, and that he could not speak English at all. Despite this experience, Javier did not pursue English studies further until after he immigrated to Canada.

PEO has a programme that assesses foreign credentials and qualifications in order to give the designation of 'engineer in training' to immigrant engineers. PEO waives the programme's $300–400 fee for ITEs within their first six months of residence in Ontario. As engineers in training, ITEs can obtain Canadian work experience and subsequently apply to be a Professional Engineer (PEng). At the time of data collection, Javier had already submitted his academic record for assessment, but not his experience report, due to his lack of confidence in his ability to prepare the document in English. During the course of the mentoring sessions, Javier continually took ESL courses, and subsequently completed and submitted his full application to the PEO.

Javier's approach to seeking work in Canada

Immediately upon arriving in Canada, Javier 'made research'. His two-pronged approach focused both on improving his language and on utilising institutional resources to navigate his professional and personal transitions in Toronto. Javier prioritised improving his English ability:

> My first goal was to prevent that the language was a barrier to, to get the job. I just decided okay, what do I need? I need first of all language . . . So immediately I get enrolled in the ELT [Enhanced Language Training] programme.

True to his approach, Javier stated, 'there's no been a day since I arrived that I am not in class'. To improve his listening, which he described as his weakest skill, Javier also listened to the radio, watched television and conversed in English with his housemates.

Meanwhile, Javier demonstrated expertise in finding resources such as ESL workshops, the YMCA (where he learned about Toronto's public transportation system, how to open a bank account and the application for Canadian permanent residency) and a four-week course on finding employment. This 'was very helpful because at the end of . . . my first month in Canada, I had the right tools . . . to make my résumé to, to start making some research for the labor market information and everything'. In fact, at the end of the course, he got an interview for a job as a sales representative for a metal distributor company, but was then told he was overqualified for the position.

Javier's arrival in Canada coincided with an economic downturn. During his first few months, he succeeded in getting two interviews with employers in the aluminium industry, but he faced the barrier of lacking Canadian experience. Javier reported that his interviewer had told him:

> Maybe you're very qualified because you have all this experience – four years experience in your area – but maybe we need some- someone with Canadian experience to know the markets. You know the product, but you don't know the market . . . But for, for the rest you seem really qualified for it.

Javier was thankful to this interviewer, however, for referring him to other professionals in the industry; when he followed up with them, he reported being told, 'Hey, this is not the right moment, it seems like things are cooling down.' Such experiences have been known to elicit a distrust among migrant job seekers (Kerekes et al. 2013); despite the frustrations and difficulties Javier encountered, however, he maintained a consistently optimistic attitude and appreciation of the positive sides of his interactions with prospective employers. Javier would have been happy to find a volunteer opportunity, wanting simply to 'put my feet on the door'. Javier demonstrated resourcefulness and savvy in networking and applying for jobs, but recognised his biggest flaw: he had no Canadian work experience.

In his first four months in Canada, Javier sent out fourteen résumés, a number he deemed to be quite low: 'I'm not trying to, to send résumés like crazy because I think that's not a very wise thing to do because I'm going to become more frustrated than the way I am at this moment.' He summed up his frustration thus: 'To me, in four months I have . . . I have been doing all my homework . . . but nothing is happening.'

5.2.2 Yelena

Childhood, professional training and immigration
A thoughtful and introspective woman in her early forties, Yelena was raised in Kazakhstan and spoke Russian at home with her parents. She never knew her grandparents, all of whom perished during the Second World War, but she heard about them in tales told by her Ukrainian-speaking great-grandmother, who often cared for her when her parents were too busy. Even as a child, Yelena was gifted in mathematics and curious about how things worked; she enjoyed taking things apart and putting them back together. She completed a Bachelor's degree in Mechanical Engineering in Moscow during the mid-1980s, and then worked as an engineer in Navoi, Uzbekistan (in the former Soviet Union) from 1990 to 2001. The company she worked for had been created to repair machinery for a uranium- and gold-mining company, but the government subsequently decided to use it as a pilot project to assemble machinery designed and produced elsewhere. After the fall of the former Soviet Union, many of the republics lacked basic consumer goods, and soon the company started designing and producing some products, such as washing machines. Yelena proudly recalled a product she designed herself: a type of grocery cart that could easily climb stairs, due to its three-wheeled design. Yelena seemed to be well regarded at her workplace, having been recommended for promotion to a supervisory position just before emigrating.

Yelena and her husband applied to immigrate to Canada in 2000. Between then and 2004, when they arrived in Canada, Yelena's marriage ended, so she raised her two sons in Canada as a single mother. At the time of data collection, the elder son was about to graduate from an aviation programme at a local college, and the younger was in middle school. Yelena was in the midst of seeking a new school for him, as she was not satisfied with his current school environment. Her ex-husband's inability to get a suitable job in Canada (he had previously been a high-profile IT executive) led to his return to Russia, where he was living with his second wife at the time of data collection.

Learning English in Uzbekistan and Canada
Before emigrating, Yelena studied English for one year with a private tutor in Uzbekistan. Her English language proficiency was assessed as a Canadian Language Benchmark (CLB) 3 when she arrived in Canada. She enrolled in LINC classes (Language Instruction for Newcomers to Canada, a federally funded programme that provides English language instruction to Canadian landed immigrants) and, three months later, tested as a CLB 5, which was a significant improvement.[6] Yelena was critical of LINC, however, for not being demanding enough and for not supporting the needs of newcomers who urgently needed to join the job market. In retrospect, she regretted taking LINC classes instead of full-time English at a local college, where she felt her English proficiency would have improved more.

Yelena's work and life adjustments in Canada
Six months after arriving in Canada, Yelena obtained a survival job through a friend as a cleaner. A key factor in her taking the job was its convenient location near her younger son's school. After two years, though, she could no longer bear to do survival work, which she described as a kind of 'live burial' to which many immigrants, unable to find employment in their trained professions, were subjecting themselves.

The tension between the demands of settling in a new country as a single mother, learning English and caring for her sons while seeking work for herself was a repeated theme in discussions with Yelena. Her sons' needs, whether an illness, a passport issue or the elder son's requirement to get licensed as a flight instructor, often eclipsed her own and left her little time to pursue work in her field. She appreciated that her boys benefited from activities in Canada, and she wanted to provide them with the best education possible. Particularly based on her concern for her younger son's progress in school, she decided not to apply for an engineering-related volunteer position, which would have required mainly evening and weekend work. Yelena was still seeking employment at the time of data collection, and was seeking support from the job developer attached to the Enhanced Language Training (ELT) course she had recently completed.

5.2.3 Javier's and Yelena's observations of Canadian life, people and work

At the time of data collection, during which Javier and Yelena were enrolled in the same ELT for Engineers course in order to improve their employment chances, neither of them was employed. While their employment disappointments were clearly reflected in their impressions of Canada and Canadians, they embraced different aspects of Canadian culture, and to varying degrees. Yelena had already been in Canada for six years when she joined the research project, while Javier was, in Yelena's words, a 'fresh arrival' (having been in Canada only two months when this study commenced). Yelena felt her outlook on work prospects in Canada was more realistic than that of recent arrivals. She explained that the discovery that finding a job in one's field is difficult or near impossible 'is upsetting especially when you are new here'.

Yelena and Javier faced the need to adjust their expectations not only in terms of employment possibilities, but also on a more personal, social level. They both articulated a keen awareness of the cultural differences they faced, and were quick to generalise about Canadians on the basis of what they had experienced. Javier exhibited an acceptance of the cultural differences he observed, explaining that he knew, for example, that he must become accustomed to the habits of his Canadian roommates, whom he found to be somewhat 'cold':

> They're different from my culture I mean, that's the whole point. I had to fit in; that's one thing that I really tried to, to prevent because I knew about [their being] cold. A lot of examples of people coming from their, to their own community and they don't go away from their community and they just get stuck. So my first thing was I have to go and face.

Indeed, the image of 'facing' could easily describe Javier's overall approach to settling in Canada; he showed an eagerness to face the challenges of settlement head on, trying to identify his own weaknesses in his new environment so that he could improve them. He demonstrated a level of comfort with the notion of 'becoming Canadian' (Fleming 2010) that Yelena, in contrast, resisted.

While Javier found his new Canadian acquaintances somewhat 'cold', Yelena saw hers as 'aggressive'. Her Kazakh upbringing had been rife with 'communist ideals', including the desire to be a team player who did not bring attention to herself: 'It was a team . . . you never have to stand out of team. You have to be like as a grass, when you cut the grass nobody has to stick up.' Sticking up was dangerous, and 'many people got hurt by that'. This ideal, similar to the Australasian tall poppy syndrome (Holmes et al. 2011: 26–41; 2012), contrasted starkly with the 'sell yourself' culture of the Canadian job market:

> Here it's everything about sales . . . You have to sell yourself and in Soviet Union it was restricted about selling. We didn't have own businesses, we didn't have, and people who were selling something like reselling something . . . they were – it was against the law.

Having been socialised to be the blade of grass in the former Soviet Union made it particularly difficult and painful for Yelena to promote herself in order to get a job: 'No, I understand I have to step over my, my- not habits my personality because sometimes when, it's like tears in your eyes.' As the mentoring sessions progressed, Yelena showed an increasing acceptance of the necessity to change her approach: 'I need to take some aggressive steps . . . to start to be more aggressive because you know it's like

Canada is about aggression.' Thus, for her, what here is considered self-promotion, 'selling yourself' or networking effectively, she sees through her own cultural lens as 'aggression', while still recognising the necessity of it. In contrast to the participants in Fleming's (2010) study of new Canadians who had felt discriminated against in their country of origin (India) and subsequently changed their national allegiance to Canada rather uncritically, Yelena was highly critical of the Canadian culture to which she had to adjust.

Despite coming from opposite sides of the globe, Yelena's and Javier's perspectives on the Canadian job market resembled each other in their views of Canadian specialists versus generalists in their home countries. Compared with the work she had done in Uzbekistan, involving many aspects of mechanical engineering and design work, Yelena exclaimed that 'here in Canada it's really, really narrow', meaning that she had to be able to identify with one particular specialisation within mechanical engineering. Javier also saw having a specialisation as being advantageous: 'I have seen here in Canada if you're good at something, in a very specific field, you have more chances.'

Javier's and Yelena's outlooks contrasted, however, in terms of their degrees of optimism about Canadian job prospects. Javier saw the significant differences between Salvadorean and Canadian civil engineering jobs as an opportunity to shift his own career and to embrace Canada's broad range of opportunities. While he acknowledged the marginalisation of foreign-born job candidates and 'the dominant culture's "othering" of their identity' (Campbell and Roberts 2007: 243), he came to terms with being 'normalized . . . into a dominant culture' (Fleming 2010: 589). Yelena, on the other hand, having worked in a survival job for too long, commented poignantly on what she saw happening to her qualifications and to those of other skilled immigrants who could not find work in their fields: 'I understand that's really nice to have educated cleaners and everybody, but then this is, you know, me I am losing- I'm losing my experience.' She was also losing her identity: that of a competent, accomplished, respected professional and a Soviet.

The fundamental qualification both Yelena and Javier lacked was Canadian work experience. They shared their perspectives on this familiar predicament faced by newcomers: to get Canadian experience, they needed to already have Canadian experience. As Yelena concisely stated, 'nobody wants to give a job without Canadian experience'. No amount of education upgrades, including a business administration course at a local college and extensive training in three computer-assisted design programs, could replace the Canadian work experience every prospective employer wanted to see. Lacking that requisite, both Javier and Yelena talked about breaking into the job market by 'getting a foot in the door'. For Javier, who acknowledged being able to dedicate himself fully to his job search because he was single, volunteer work was a possible point of entry. His perspective was, 'Just if you get a volunteering just say yes I am really interested because that could put my feet on the door and I want to.' Yelena, in contrast, could not consider volunteer placements. Even though one such volunteer opportunity offered the possibility of leading to her obtaining her engineering licence, Yelena's perspective was 'I can't afford this one', referring to both the financial cost of long-term volunteer work and also the cost to her family.

Yelena's Discourse exhibited characteristics both attractive and unattractive to prospective employers. She related an experience visiting a local factory with her ELT class, in which they had an opportunity to meet the owner. Rather than words of encouragement for the newcomer engineers, however, the owner emphasised that he would not hire overqualified immigrants for positions in the factory, because he predicted they would leave after a few years to pursue their chosen profession. In other words, her Discourse, which encompassed her identity as a professional engineer with proven expertise in her country of origin, was judged negatively in comparison with the less qualified members of the dominant culture who sought the same job. Reflecting on this particular factory owner's willingness to hire immigrants less qualified than she was, she observed, 'Like everybody here . . . who get your foot in the door . . . But, who knows what's behind the door.' Yelena's scepticism reflected her lengthy residence in Toronto without successfully finding suitable work; her challenges of caring for two sons as a single mother while seeking work as an engineer; and her awareness of a mismatch between her Soviet-era socialisation and the expectations she felt Canadians held for newcomer job-seekers.

Javier, in contrast, saw the differences in Canadian culture and employment practices from what he was accustomed to as opportunities to expand and adapt to his new life, in which he intended to succeed professionally and personally. He demonstrated a willingness and ability to 'become Canadian' by bridging the gap between his Salvadorean, university-educated, professional engineer English Language Learner Discourse with that of the Canadian employee he aspired to become.

6. Conclusion and implications

Yelena's and Javier's language abilities are inextricable from their many other individual characteristics as well as characteristics of the people and cultures of their new surroundings, in determining their professional opportunities as newcomers in Canada. Yelena made explicit her consciousness of the challenges she faced in finding suitable work, including her age, her single parenthood and her challenge to overcome what she called the 'methodology' of her (Soviet) socialisation so that she could adopt the 'sales orientation' of the culture in which she now found herself. Javier recognised that his independence as a single man in his thirties allowed him to make the most of his opportunities to learn and to enhance his flexibility in terms of possible employment options, whether it meant relocating for a job or taking a job that would provide a foot in the door, even if it was not in his preferred area (e.g. sales rather than manufacturing). Yelena's and Javier's characteristics and personal circumstances played into their unique Discourses (Gee 1996), how they were perceived and received, and how they perceived others.

The roles of gender, age and personal circumstances in understanding or explaining IEPs' employment trajectories cannot be underestimated. While unemployment rates are significantly higher for IEPs than their Canadian-educated counterparts, research also indicates that female IEPs, particularly those who were successfully employed in their home countries before immigrating to Canada, are even more negatively impacted than male IEPs, due to inadequate child care and language training options (Kenny and Cap 2003; Man 2004). Another study suggests that female IEPs experience a higher 'intensity of their feelings of loss, pain, and uprootedness' (Khan and Watson 2005: 316).

While the recent creation of Enhanced Language Training and other career-focused classes for newcomers has demonstrated recognition for the need for better support for highly skilled immigrants seeking employment, societal and systemic practices and perceptions continue to produce obstacles of inequitable reception and treatment of many ITEs. It is no wonder that, while they are greeted with a high degree of institutional distrust in terms of the lengths to which they must go to prove their qualifications for employment, many of them also develop a distrust of the Canadian systems of which they have become a part (Kerekes et al. 2013).

Training in language programmes can certainly be improved by addressing areas of pragmatics and intercultural communication at a high level, appropriate for those who are already proficient speakers of English as an additional language but who are new to the Canadian employment context. This will never be enough to combat issues of power imbalances between English-dominant (prospective) employers (and their respective English-dominant institutions) and their diverse clientele of prospective employees, whose ways of communicating represent the cultural richness of varied backgrounds and experiences that could and should be used to enhance the Canadian workforce.

While one recognised approach to teaching 'culture' involves 'helping students become more tolerant of ambiguity rather than instruction in specific aspects of culture' (Thomson and Derwing 2004: 20), it is our job as applied linguists who prepare the teachers of such courses to examine other angles of the problem as well: how much are Canadian teachers, employers and prospective employers encouraged to tolerate these same kinds of ambiguity? We, as language educators and service providers, are tasked not only with assisting IEPs in their quests for jobs in Canada, but also with a responsibility of informing and educating those in power to understand the merits of embracing diversity. By helping employers develop a new culture of support, newcomer Canadian jobseekers may make a smoother employment transition.

7. Epilogue

A few months after the completion of this study, Javier happily accepted a job in sales; while it utilised his engineering background, he remained hopeful that this position would serve as a stepping stone to his eventually finding a job working as an engineer. Yelena remained unemployed and in search of a job for which her expertise could be used.

Notes

1. I am grateful to Colette Peters for her assistance and insights during data collection, and to Jeanne Sinclair for providing critically constructive comments on an earlier draft of this chapter. I am also indebted to the two Internationally Trained Engineers (ITEs) who agreed to participate in this study, Yelena and Javier; I wish them every success with their professional goals in Canada, and thank them for

contributing to the improvement of prospects for those who will follow in their footsteps.

2. The term 'racialised' or 'racialised group' is used to draw attention to racialisation as a process, and in conscious opposition to the term 'visible minority'.
3. In some older literature, ITEs may be referred to as 'IEEs', or Internationally Educated Engineers.
4. Gatekeeping encounters or situations are understood here as exchanges between two or more individuals, one (or more) of whom has institutional authority to make a decision affecting the other person's future, as in licensing examinations and job interviews, among others.
5. Kerekes's (2004) study of intercultural gatekeeping encounters (job interviews) identified three features present in the interviews that made a positive impression on the job interviewers (the gatekeepers): presenting oneself in a positive light, including offering self-praise and self-promotion; building rapport with the interviewer through informal chit-chat ('small talk'); and demonstrating flexibility in the types of assignments and conditions of work one is willing to accept.
6. Canadian Language Benchmark Level 3 is associated with basic language ability in everyday, non-demanding contexts of personal relevance. At this level, effective communication relies on a slow rate of speech/reading, simple sentences and limited vocabulary, contextual non-verbal clues and requests for clarification. CLB 5 is the initial stage of 'intermediate language ability'. Fewer contextual clues are necessary for effective communication within moderately demanding contexts. Main ideas, important details and implied meanings are understood. A faster rate of communication, an increased vocabulary and emerging complexity of sentence structures occur at this level, although some clarification may still be necessary (Pawlikowska-Smith 2012).

References

Abbott, M. G. and C. M. Beach (2011), *Do admission criteria and economic recessions affect immigrant earnings?*, Montreal: Institute for Research on Public Policy.

Akinnaso, F. and C. Ajirotutu (1982), 'Performance and ethnic style in job interviews', in J. J. Gumperz (ed.), *Language and social identity*, New York: Cambridge University Press, pp. 119–44.

Boyd, M. and G. Schellenberg (2007), 'Re-accreditation and the occupations of immigrant doctors and engineers', *Canadian Social Trends*, Ottawa: Statistics Canada, <http://www.statcan.gc.ca/pub/11-008-x/2007004/10312-eng.htm> (last accessed 10 November 2016).

Buckingham, D. (2008), 'Introducing identity', in D. Buckingham (ed.), *Youth, identity, and digital media*, Cambridge, MA: MIT Press, pp. 1–24.

Campbell, S. and C. Roberts (2007), 'Migration, ethnicity and competing discourses in the job interview: synthesizing the institutional and personal', *Discourse & Society*, 18: 3, pp. 243–71.

Engineers Canada and Canadian Council of Technicians and Technologists (2009), *Engineering and Technology Labour Market Study: Final Report*, <http://www.devita.

com/PEO/Engineering%20And%20Technology%20Labour%20Market%20
Study%20-%20Final%20Report-pdv.pdf> (last accessed 10 November 2016).

Erickson, F. (2001), 'Co-membership and wiggle room: some implications of the study of talk for the development of social theory', in N. Coupland, S. Sarangi and C. N. Candlin (eds), *Sociolinguistics and social theory*, London: Longman, pp. 152–81.

Fairbairn, S. and J. Fox (2009), 'Inclusive achievement testing for linguistically and culturally diverse test takers: essential considerations for test developers and decision makers', *Educational Measurement: Issues and Practice*, Spring, pp. 10–24.

Fairclough, N. (1989), *Language and power*, London: Longman.

Fleming, D. (2010), 'Becoming citizens: racialized conceptions of ESL learners and the Canadian language benchmarks', *Canadian Journal of Education*, 33: 3, pp. 588–616.

Frenette, M. and R. Morisette (2003), 'Will they ever converge? Earnings of immigrant and Canadian-born workers over the last two decades', *Analytical Studies Branch Research Paper Series*, catalogue no. 11F0019MIE – No.215, Ottawa: Statistics Canada.

From Consideration to Integration (FC2I) Steering Committee (2003), *From consideration to integration: an environmental scan of the international engineering graduate experience before immigration and once in Canada. Final report from phase I*, Ottawa: Canadian Council of Professional Engineers.

Gee, J. P. (1996), *Social linguistics and literacies: ideology in discourses*, 2nd edn, London: Falmer Press.

Grant, P. R. and S. Nadin (2007), 'The credentialing problems of foreign trained personnel from Asia and Africa intending to make their home in Canada: a social psychological perspective', *International Migration & Integration*, 8, pp. 141–62.

Gumperz, J. (1992), 'Interviewing in intercultural situations', in P. Drew and J. Heritage (eds), *Talk at work: interaction in institutional settings*, Cambridge: Cambridge University Press, pp. 302–27.

Holmes, J. (2015), 'Joining a new community of workplace practice: inferring attitudes from discourse', in Elke Stracke (ed.), *Intersections: applied linguistics as a meeting place*, Newcastle-upon-Tyne: Cambridge Scholars Publishing, pp. 2–21.

Holmes, J., M. Marra and B. Vine (2011), *Leadership, discourse and ethnicity*, Oxford: Oxford University Press.

Holmes, J., M. Marra and B. Vine (2012), 'Politeness and impoliteness in ethnic varieties of New Zealand English', *Journal of Pragmatics*, 44: 9, pp. 1063–76.

Johnston, A. M. (2008), 'Co-membership in immigration gatekeeping interviews: construction, ratification and refutation', *Discourse & Society*, 19: 1, pp. 21–41.

Kenny, M. and I. Cap (2003), 'Community-based language training for immigrant women and seniors in Manitoba', ERIC Reproduction Document ED 476 120, Winnipeg: Manitoba Advanced Education and Training.

Kerekes, J. A. (2003), 'Distrust: a determining factor in the outcomes of gatekeeping encounters', in J. House, G. Kasper and S. Ross (eds), *Misunderstanding in social life: discourse approaches to problematic talk*, London: Longman Pearson, pp. 227–57.

Kerekes, J. A. (2004), 'Preparing ESL learners for self-presentation outside the classroom', *Prospect*, 19: 1, pp. 22–46.

Kerekes, J. A. (2005), 'Before, during, and after the event: getting the job (or not) in an employment interview', in K. Bardovi-Harlig and B. Hartford (eds), *Interlanguage pragmatics: exploring institutional talk*, Mahwah, NJ: Lawrence Erlbaum, pp. 99–131.

Kerekes, J. A. (2006), 'Winning an interviewer's trust in a gatekeeping encounter', *Language in Society*, 35: 1, pp. 27–57.

Kerekes, J., J. Chow, A. Lemak and Z. Perhan (2013), 'Trust or betrayal: immigrant engineers' employment-seeking experiences in Canada', in C. N. Candlin and J. Crichton (eds), *Discourses of trust*, New York: Palgrave Macmillan, pp. 269–84.

Khan, S. and J. C. Watson (2005), 'The Canadian immigration experiences of Pakistani women: dreams confront reality', *Counselling Psychology Quarterly*, 18: 4, pp. 307–17.

Laurier, M. and B. Baker (2015), 'The certification of teachers' language competence in Quebec in French and English: two different perspectives?', *Language Assessment Quarterly*, 12: 1, pp. 10–28.

Lippi-Green, R. (1997), *English with an accent: language, ideology, and discrimination in the United States*, New York: Routledge.

Man, G. (2004), 'Gender, work and migration: deskilling Chinese immigrant women in Canada', *Women's Studies International Forum*, 27: 2, pp. 135–48.

Maryns, K. and J. Blommaert (2002), 'Pretextuality and pretextual gaps: on de/refining linguistic inequality', *Pragmatics*, 12: 1, pp. 11–30.

Meeuwis, M. (1994), 'Leniency and testiness in intercultural communication: remarks on ideology and context in interactional sociolinguistics', *Pragmatics*, 4: 3, pp. 391–408.

Novak, L. and C. P. Chen (2013), 'Career development of foreign trained immigrants from regulated professions', *International Journal for Educational and Vocational Guidance*, 13: 1, pp. 5–24.

Ontario Society of Professional Engineers (2014), 'From the world to the workforce: hiring and recruitment perceptions of engineering employers and internationally trained engineers in Ontario', Toronto: Prism Economic and Analysis, <https://c.ymcdn.com/sites/ospe.site-ym.com/resource/collection/E88C7AF3-7300-4B51-B591-48F87116255B/OSPE-Research-Report-From-the-World-to-the-Workforce-Aug19.pdf> (last accessed 10 November 2016).

Pawlikowska-Smith, G. (2012), 'Canadian language benchmarks: English as a second language for adults', Ottawa: Centre for Canadian Language Benchmarks, <http://www.cic.gc.ca/english/pdf/pub/language-benchmarks.pdf> (last accessed 10 November 2016).

Professional Engineers Ontario (PEO) (2011), *PEO Entry-to-Practice Review*, Toronto: Professional Engineers Ontario, <http://docplayer.net/6481793-Peo-entry-to-practice-review.html> (last accessed 5 December 2016).

Rubin, D. L. and K. A. Smith (1990), 'Effects of accent, ethnicity, and lecture topic on undergraduates' perceptions of non-native English speaking teaching assistants', *International Journal of Intercultural Relations*, 14, pp. 337–53.

Schiffrin, D. (1994), *Approaches to discourse*, Oxford: Blackwell.

Shea, D. (1994), 'Perspective and production: structuring conversational participation across cultural borders', *Pragmatics*, 4: 3, pp. 357–89.

Thomson, R. I. and T. M. Derwing (2004), 'Presenting Canadian values in LINC: the roles of textbooks and teachers', *TESL Canada Journal*, 21: 2, pp. 17–33.

Tranekjær, L. (2015), *Interactional categorization and gatekeeping: institutional encounters with otherness*, Bristol: Multilingual Matters.

Tsai, M. C., L. Laczko and C. Bjørnskov (2011), 'Social diversity, institutions and trust: a cross-national analysis', *Social Indicators Research*, 101: 3, pp. 305–22.

Uslaner, E. M. (2010), 'Segregation, mistrust and minorities', *Ethnicities*, 10: 4, pp. 415–34.

Walters, D., K. Phythian and P. Anisef (2006), 'Understanding the economic integration of immigrants: a wage decomposition of the earnings disparities between native-born Canadians and immigrants of recent cohorts', *CERIS Working Paper Series*, 42, Toronto: Joint Centre of Excellence for Research on Immigration and Settlement.

Zhao, J. (2000), 'Brain drain and brain gain: the migration of knowledge workers from and to Canada', *Education Quarterly Review*, 6: 3, pp. 8–35.

Zietsma, D. (2010), 'Immigrants working in regulated occupations', *Perspectives*, 11: 2, pp. 13–28.

Zong, L. (2004), 'International transference of human capital and occupational attainment of recent Chinese professional immigrants in Canada', *PCERII Working Paper Series*, WP03-04, Edmonton: Prairie Centre of Excellence for Research on Immigration and Integration.

2

'Oh It's a DANISH Boyfriend You've Got': Co-membership and Cultural Fluency in Job Interviews with Minority Background Applicants in Denmark

Marta Kirilova

1. Job interviews across borders

Moving between geographic and linguistic boundaries in order to find opportunities for personal and professional self-fulfilment is a common experience in the age of globalisation. Whether motivated by a personal choice, as is often the case with students and free movers, or by a political agenda, as is the case with asylum seekers and migrants from less developed countries, workforce mobility increasingly shapes our lives. The 'job for life' paradigm has become obsolete, since lifetime employment no longer suits the dynamics of globalisation and mobility. To keep pace, contemporary employees must muster not only practical skills of sustenance but also adequate linguistic competences, flexibility in a variety of contexts, and adaptiveness to challenges in space and time. These efforts are aggravated by employers who rely on employment strategies that do not account for candidates' full range of potentials. One of the widely known methods for selection in professional contexts is the job interview. Employers use job interviews to determine whether a given person is suitable for a given job or not. Although candidates are required to have a solid set of qualifications to be selected for a job, it is usually what happens in the interactional moment that matters. In this sense the job interview is a ritual of power with rules often obscure to candidates.

To find out how candidates are selected for a job and to shed light on the intricacies of such a selection process, this chapter discusses and analyses data from two authentic job interviews conducted in Denmark. It focuses on the following two questions: first, what discourses develop in the communication between applicants and interviewers, especially when the interlocutors do not share a common first language; second, how do these discourses influence the interviewers' assessments of applicants?

By answering these questions, the chapter provides insight into shortfalls in institutional selection processes within the field of migration studies and institutional communication in the age of globalisation. Through the concept of cultural fluency it also offers a more nuanced understanding of the ideology of intercultural communication in professional contexts. The study suggests that, while crossing linguistic boundaries has become a common practice as people move around the world, crossing cultural boundaries and shifting between cultural identities is much less common. Thus, the study contributes to the body of literature within the field of language and discrimination, exemplifying how non-Western cultural identities are seen as problematic because they are equated with inability to fit in.

2. Selecting candidates for integration

In 2005, the Danish government implemented an integration initiative aimed at providing a starter kit to immigrants and descendants of immigrants with limited Danish language skills and little experience within the Danish labour market. The initiative was called Integration and Training Job Positions, or 'IO-stillinger' in Danish. It was meant as a one-year contract. During the first year, IO employees should receive 80 per cent of their salary while 20 per cent was used for individual mentoring, Danish language classes and culture courses. After the introductory year, the IO positions were converted to permanent positions with 100 per cent pay. Any person with a non-Danish background and a primary, secondary or tertiary education from either Denmark or their home country could be considered for an IO position. In terms of salary (apart from the first year), promotions and health care insurance, the IO positions did not differ from ordinary jobs. To apply for an IO position, however, all applicants were required to submit a cover letter in Danish, and those selected were requested to speak Danish at the interview. Clearly, the main objective of the IO positions was to provide a more direct gateway to the Danish labour market through taking possible linguistic barriers into consideration. In practice, however, the IO selection process contained an inbuilt paradox: although the initiative was intended for minority background citizens with perceived linguistic and cultural challenges, the applicants had to speak Danish and go through a Danish selection ritual in order to obtain mentoring and language classes. Yet another paradox was the lack of clarity over how much Danish the applicants should be able to speak at the job interview. I shall return to the IO context but first let us look at the theoretical backdrop of the study.

3. Language and culture in institutional communication

According to Erickson and Schultz (1982), institutional interaction is both socially and culturally organised. It is socially organised, because it takes place in and is constituted by the succession of moments in real time; it is culturally organised, because the participants in an interaction interpret the communicative actions of each other on the basis of shared knowledge of, for example, styles, norms or cultural conventions learned outside the communicative occasion. Many practices in institutional interaction are unwritten and conveyed through subtle moves and signals, which Gumperz (1982) describes as contextualisation cues. According to Gumperz, culturally specific communicative styles hinder successful communication, as the gatekeepers from the majority community use the cultural and linguistic differences against the minority community members to create an environment of disadvantage (Auer and Kern 2001). In a number of studies, Gumperz and his students and colleagues demonstrate the linguistic dimensions of social discrimination and argue that language and sociocultural knowledge interact to produce and reproduce inequality (see also Akinnaso and Ajirotutu 1982; Jupp et al. 1982; Roberts et al. 1992). In addition, several extensive studies of job interviews in Great Britain (Roberts and Campbell 2006; Roberts et al. 2008) point out that first generation ethnic minority candidates fail the job interview because of the interview's cultural and linguistic demands. Such candidates face 'a linguistic penalty' which, according to Roberts and Campbell, arises not from a lack of fluency in English, but from the hidden demands on applicants to talk in 'institutionally credible ways' as well as 'from a mismatch of implicit cultural expectations, evidenced by mutual misunderstandings, protracted attempts to resolve them and negative judgements by interviewers' (Roberts and Campbell 2006: 1). Thus, job candidates are judged by the interviewers to be poorer users of English, but the term 'poor English' becomes ideological as it sweeps together the applicants' different communicative styles and interactional difficulties as well as the interviewers' language attitudes and personal preferences.

At the same time, applicants who present themselves as quick learners, willing to do anything to get the job and who try to convince the interviewers that they have no problems whatsoever are perceived as problematic. Roberts and Campbell (2006: 137) call this willing-to-do-anything discourse 'the immigrant story' and propose that interviewers look for statements of resilience rather than favourable presentations as diligent, working under any conditions, and denying negative work experience from the past.

In another iconic interactional study of student counselling sessions, Erickson and Shultz (1982) suggest that moments of 'interactional arrhythmia' correlate with the students' background and ethnicity: if students and counsellor share the same ethnicity or panethnicity (e.g. White Catholics), the students who share ethnic background with the counsellors tend to receive more interactional help than students with a different ethnic background. Erickson and Shultz (1982) argue that social identities and communicative style are crucial to the character and the outcome of the gatekeeping interview. They introduce the term 'co-membership' to describe the interactionally produced connections between interlocutors. As co-members of an interactional micro speech community (Gumperz [1968] 2009), the interlocutors project acts and stances that index group membership through a co-constructed ideology. A crucial point in the ideology of co-membership is how group membership shifts thematically and situationally. A shared identity may accidentally occur to create a common point of interest, but it may also disappear or transform into a non-membership. The lack of a common point of interest may then lead to turning away a job applicant, simply stating that he or she does not fit in. Thus, co-membership goes together with interpersonal solidarity, providing an explanatory framework for how social categories are co-constructed and used both exclusively and inclusively (see also Adelswärd 1988; Scheuer 2001; Kerekes 2006; Lipovsky 2006).

One way of signalling co-membership is through confirming statements that function as moments of acceptance of one's responses. Roberts and Campbell (2006) show that co-membership through confirming statements is characteristic of the context of successful interviews. It is often used to appraise the candidates' responses positively and make them relevant for the institutional discourse (Roberts and Campbell 2006). Co-membership is then created in favour of those applicants whose communication style is most similar to that of the interviewer (Erickson and Shultz 1982). In Kirilova (2013), I found that co-membership was important for how applicants develop fluency. When interviewers credit applicants for 'good' Danish, it is not necessarily tied to grammatical or phonological standardness. Rather, it is a discursive dialogical practice through which interlocutors negotiate mutual understanding and approve of each other's interactional choices. This conception of fluency is emic and related to Hymes's (1972) communicative competence and Thomas's (1983) socio-pragmatic competence. It has an important cultural dimension for which I propose the term 'cultural fluency' (Kirilova 2013, 2014).

Yet another important concept that sheds light on the interactional dynamics and the ideology of spoken discourse is positioning. Building on the Foucauldian notion of subjective positioning, Davies and Harré (1990) develop a theory of discursive positioning. While to Foucault (1972) interlocutors are both producers and recipients of social discourse, Davies and Harré suggest that interlocutors take up positions and position themselves in relation to discourse whenever they produce utterances in a conversation. Their conceptualisation of positioning is parallel to Bakhtin's (1986) theory of dialogism. Bakhtin proposes that every time we establish a discursive position for ourselves in making an utterance, we also offer the other person(s) we are addressing a position (or a choice of positions) from which to respond (see also Billig 1996; Winslade 2005; Liebscher and Dailey O'Cain 2009).

Mutual positioning and the process of construction and co-construction of social meaning is particularly important in gatekeeping events such as job interviews. The way applicants present themselves (their 'persona') through the interaction order (Goffman 1959) and the way they do 'being them' in a situation where 'being them' is evaluated, adds an important dimension to the understanding of the selection process.

Before I examine and apply these theoretical notions in the data, I briefly outline the main methodology and present the data samples.

4. Interactional Sociolinguistics and the devil in the detail

Interactional Sociolinguistics (IS) is a theory and a method for systematic micro discourse analysis drawing on a number of disciplines such as ethnography, sociology, linguistic anthropology and studies of discourse. IS combines the theoretical interest of sociolinguistics in linguistic and cultural diversity with a number of practical tools originally developed by Gumperz in the late 1970s. It is also influenced by Goffman's (1983) notion of interaction as a separate order of analysis through which we can study how interlocutors display shared perceptions and identity to maintain involvement with each other. In terms of method, IS includes conventions from micro sociology and Conversation Analysis (CA; see Sacks et al. 1974), but, unlike CA, it draws attention to the fact that shared conditions for understanding should not be taken for granted in linguistically and culturally diverse societies. According to Gumperz (1982, 1999), different groups may use culturally and situationally specific styles of communication, which may differ from local standards or shared assumptions of standards. Of course, we would not necessarily have to expect differences: it is exactly our task as analysts to discover the extent to which speakers in any interaction share communicative resources or not. Roberts and Campbell (2006: 19) argue that IS allows us to search for evidence in interviewers' claims about candidates; they suggest that IS's concern with interactional detail is consistent with the practices of the interview itself, where 'the devil is in the detail'. As a lot of information can be hidden in even the tiniest bits (e.g. words, prosody, register shifts, overlaps), the micro analysis allows us to look closer into categories such as nationality, gender and religious affiliation to gain a broader discursive understanding of what is going on and why. Since Gumperz, IS and its microanalytical variants has been broadly used in sociolinguistics for analysis of both institutional and private encounters, for example classroom interaction (Rampton 2006), leisure time conversations (Ochs and Schieffelin 1994; Tannen 2005) and workplace encounters (Roberts 2000; Roberts et al. 1992; Angouri and Marra 2011; Holmes 2006).

5. Data collection

In 2009, I started ethnographic fieldwork at nine offices in the municipality of Copenhagen and audio-recorded forty-one job interviews for nine different IO positions. I recorded interviews with municipal staff, members of job panels and applicants immediately after the job interview. I also collected observation logs in which I listed different details, rich points (Agar 2006) and possible questions that I later asked staff and applicants. During my observations and recordings, which consisted of approximately fifty hours of data, I noticed a number of interesting practices in the selection of applicants with a minority background. For example, although there were no formally described guidelines about the ethnic background of the IO applicants, employers seemed to agree that applicants from non-Western countries were better served in an IO position than applicants from Western Europe. Staff members explained in an interview that non-Westerners were considered to have greater difficulties in integrating into the Danish society, so an IO position should be given to them. However, there had been a single case in which an applicant from Western Europe was appointed an IO job. This appointment was seen as ambiguous by many staff members and prompted discussions about appropriate selection criteria.

To give an idea of how language and culture are constructed in the data, I have chosen two applicants whom I call Hannah and Arabella. Both of them applied for a front desk secretary position. Hannah, aged thirty-eight, was born in Western Europe. She moved to Denmark to live with her Danish boyfriend in Copenhagen a year before the recordings; she took Danish classes and had a part-time job as a newspaper carrier. Arabella, aged forty-one, was born in Central Africa. She married a Dane and moved to Denmark, where she spent nine years with her husband and their two children. She attended a business college in Copenhagen and worked as a tourist agent for several years. Arabella was the first candidate to be interviewed for the job. The second candidate was a Thai woman who refused to be recorded and asked me to leave the room during the job interview. Hannah was the third and last candidate in the session.

I selected Arabella and Hannah for an analysis because they were approximately the same age, applied for the same position and were assessed by the same job panel. However, they had different cultural backgrounds and, according to the interviewers, spoke Danish at a different level. Arabella's Danish was assessed as 'fine' and 'understandable', while Hannah was considered 'the worst at Danish in the group but still understandable'. As previously mentioned, candidates like Hannah confuse the interviewers as interviewers cannot decide whether or not she is in the IO target group for integration: on the one hand, Hannah barely speaks Danish and needs a lot of linguistic support, but on the other hand, she has a Western background which the interviewers interpret as her having cultural similarities and therefore less need for (cultural) integration in the workplace. I shall come back to that in the analysis.

In the following analysis, I compare the discursive positionings of the two applicants to explore to what extent these positionings contribute to the interviewers' evaluations of the applicants. I present two parallel sequences and three related examples in which Hannah and Arabella are introduced to similar topics and asked similar questions. I provide an English translation for each example.[1]

5.1 Sequence 1: The network for integration

In sequence 1, the employee (EMP) tells Arabella (example 1.1) and Hannah (example 1.2) about a network for social activities and cultural integration through which they can learn about Danish culture. Apart from EMP, the interviewing panel consists of three other members: a female manager (MAN), and two male employees – ROB and EMX.

Example 1.1 Arabella (05:43–07:05)

English translation		Danish	
1	EMP: so erm there'll be some	1	EMP: så øhm der vil være nogle
2	network meetings	2	netværksmøder
3	(.) you'll get a mentor erm	3	(.) du vil få en mentor øh
4	<ARA: mmh mmh> who	4	<ARA: mmh mmh> som
5	who'll take care of you	5	som tager sig af dig
6	and can answer all	6	og kan svare på alle
7	your questions (.)	7	dine spørgsmål (.)
8	we others would like	8	alle vi andre vil også
9	to answer them as well	9	meget gerne svare
10	<MAN: mmh> but we	10	<MAN: mmh> men vi
11	are all here altogether	11	er her jo allesammen
12	but there will be one	12	men der er en bestemt
13	in particular who who who	13	som som som
14	will act as a go-between	14	du øh har
15	<ARA: mmh> in erm in	15	<ARA: mmh> fast
16	connection to those erm	16	tilknytning til øhm i
17	networks erm	17	de her netværks øh
18	you'll also be able to	18	sammenhænge vil du
19	learn something more	19	også lære noget mere
20	about Danish culture	20	om dansk kultur

21		erm why we do as		21		øhm hvorfor vi gør som
22		we do		22		vi gør og
23		<ARA: mhm mhm >		23		<ARA: mmh mmh>
24		laugh when we laugh and		24		griner når vi griner og
25		<ARA: yes> [laugher]		25		<ARA: ja> [latter]
26	EMP:	say what we say		26	EMP:	siger som vi siger
27		[laughter]		27		[latter]
28	ARA:	I have learned a bit about		28	ARA:	det har jeg lært lidt om det
29		that <EMP: yes>		29		<EMP: ja>
30	ARA:	I have also a erm		30		jeg har også en øh
31		Danish husband		31		danske mand
32	EMP:	yes <ARA: he is>		32	EMP:	ja <ARA: han er>
33		but it can be		33		men det kan være
34		difficult		34		svært
35	ARA:	yes that's right		35	ARA:	ja det er jo det
36		<EMP: erm yes> [laughs]		36		<EMP: øh ja> [griner]
37	ARA:	yes		37	ARA:	ja
38	EMP:	so erm if it's		38	EMP:	så øh så så hvis det
39		gonna be you we'll also		39		bliver dig skal vi også
40		talk about well what		40		tale om jamen hvad
41		what do you		41		hvad er det du
42		need to learn		42		har behov for at lære
43		more <ARA: yeah>		43		mere <ARA: ja>
44		how can we help		44		hvordan kan vi hjælpe
45		you as good as possible		45		dig bedst muligt
45	ARA:	mmh it sounds		46	ARA:	mmh det lyder
47		exciting mmh mmh		47		spændende mmh mmh

Example 1.2 Hannah (06:15–06:56)

	English translation				Danish	
1	EMP:	erm there're will be		1	EMP:	øh der bliver også lavet
2		some sort of network for		2		sådan et netværk for alle
3		everyone employed in		3		dem der bliver ansat
4		an IO position at the		4		i integrationsstillinger i
5		municipality		5		kommunen
6	HAN:	okay		6	HAN:	okay
7	EMP:	so so you meet once in a		7	EMP:	så så man mødes engang
8		while and exchange		8		imellem og kan udveksle
9		<HAN: okay> experience		9		<HAN: okay> erfaringer
10		about how erm to		10		om hvordan øh
11		handle this and that or		11		håndterer du det eller
12		what do you		12		hvad synes det
13		think I think that's difficult		13		synes jeg er svært

14		do you think so	14		synes du det
15		<HAN: okay> or	15		<HAN: okay> eller
16		<HAN: that's good>	16		<HAN: det var da godt>
17		can you give some good	17		har du et godt råd eller
18		advice or <HAN: yeah> erm	18		<HAN: ja> øh og der
19		and there'll be some	19		vil blive noget
20		teaching in Danish culture	20		undervisning i dansk kultur
21	HAN:	yes xxx [laughs]	21	HAN:	ja xxx [griner]
22	EMP:	erm so one can learn a bit	22	EMP:	øh så man kan lære lidt
23		about why we are	23		om hvorfor vi er
24		as we are and	24		som vi er og
25		laugh when we laugh and	25		griner når vi griner og
26	HAN:	okay haha	26	HAN:	okay haha
27	EMP:	erm how one avoids	27	EMP:	øh hvordan man undgår
28		offending us and	28		at fornærme os og
29		things like that I think	29		alt sådan noget tror jeg
30	HAN:	okay [laughs]	30	HAN:	okay [griner]
31		<ROB mmh>	31		<ROB: mmh>
32	EMP:	erm not that I think	32	EMP:	øh ikke fordi jeg tror
33		we get easily	33		vi er så nemme
34		offended	34		at fornærme
35	HAN:	well <ROB: mmh>	35	HAN:	nå <ROB: mmh>
36		<EMP: erm>	36		<EMP: øhm>
37	EMP:	but altogether a little bit	37	EMP:	men alt sådan lidt
38		about the culture	38		om kulturen
39		why we are like this	39		hvorfor er vi sådan
40	HAN:	yes	40	HAN:	ja
41	EMP:	so this is basically	41	EMP:	så det er egentlig
42		what it's about	42		primært det men
43		but it's a permanent position	43		det er jo en fast stilling
44		which which hopefully	44		som som man gerne
45		one can keep	45		skulle kunne beholde
46		for many years	46		i mange år
47	HAN:	okay yes that sounds good	47	HAN:	okay ja det lyder godt

In both interviews, the network of integration is presented as a resource for learning about Danes and Danish practices on the assumption that new IO employees possess no knowledge of Danish culture. The employee (EMP) draws on differences between Danes and non-Danes to establish an antithesis relation between Danish employers and IO applicants. The two examples contain various contrastive positionings, and at first glance, there are quite a number of similarities. However, a closer look reveals that the narrative about the IO position as a gateway to mentorship and learning about 'the culture', as EMP utters it, is presented to the two applicants in different ways.

In example 1.1 Arabella is addressed with the personal pronoun 'you' (e.g. 'you'll get a mentor . . . who'll take care of you and can answer all your questions'). The interviewer tells Arabella that she will be able to learn about Danish culture. Then, after listening to EMP's account, Arabella suddenly interrupts her objecting that she is already familiar with Danish culture because she has been married to a Dane. The interviewer, however, takes little notice of that claim, insisting that 'it can be difficult'. Accordingly, the interviewer suggests that Arabella's Danish family is not a resource for cultural integration. Despite the nine years Arabella has spent in Denmark, EMP positions her as 'foreign'. Arabella accepts the positioning ('yes, that's right', 'it sounds exciting') and she also laughs in an approving manner perhaps to signal politeness or to close the topic.

In example 1.2 Hannah is addressed indirectly through the indefinite pronoun 'one' ('so one can learn a bit about why we are as we are', 'how one avoids offending us'). With Hannah, the interviewer uses a more nuanced discourse and less personal utterances to describe the IO network: she talks about exchanging experience to tackle possible difficulties and instead of 'help' and 'mentoring', she mentions a possibility for being provided with 'advice' and 'some instructions' in regards to Danish culture. EMP mentions also that the position is permanent and could be kept for many years. This indicates that foreignness is not made relevant to Hannah in the same way as it was made relevant to Arabella. To demonstrate further the different forms of address, let us consider sequence 2.

5.2 Sequence 2: Job experience from Denmark

The manager (MAN) interviews the applicants about previous jobs to find out more about their areas of expertise. Questions on earlier experience are common in job interviews as they are linked to an assumption that the way candidates performed in earlier jobs stands for the way they will perform in the next job. The interview as a proxy for the job is taken for granted by the interviewers, but it is not made clear to candidates (Roberts and Campbell 2006).

Example 2.1 Arabella (09:29–10:38)

English translation			Danish		
1	MAN:	what s-what did you see was	1	MAN:	hvad s-hvad så du så var
2		was or what what do you think	2		eller hvad hvad synes du
3		was the most difficult thing	3		var det sværeste
4		about working in Denmark	4		ved at arbejde i Danmark
5		what was the most	5		hvad var det der
6		difficult thing for you	6		var sværest for dig
7	ARA:	yes the first time it was a bit	7	ARA:	ja første gang det var lidt
8		difficult because they they	8		svært fordi de de skulle
9		should get to know me	9		lære mig at kende
10	MAN:	yes	10	MAN:	ja
11	ARA:	yes and then sometimes	11	ARA:	ja og så nogle gange
12		people are afraid of those	12		folk er bange for dem
13		coming outside	13		der kommer og uden

		English			Danish
14		countries or something like	14		fra lande eller sådan
15		that but it wasn't	15		noget men det var ikke
16		so ss-the firs-the	16		så ss-det førs-det
17		first week it was I	17		første uge det var jeg
18		could see that	18		kunne sige det det
19		it was like what's it called	19		var lidt hvad hedder det
20		they didn't want to talk so	20		de ville ikke snakke så
21		much with me	21		meget med mig eller
22		or sort of	22		sådan noget
23	MAN:	mmh	23	MAN:	mmh
24	ARA:	but it doesn't last	24	ARA:	men de bliver ikke
25		long cos erm I	25		længe fordi øh jeg jeg
26		could {easily} laugh with	26		kunne godt grine med
27		them and hear what	27		dem og høre hvad
28		they say and make	28		de siger og lave
29		one little comment and	29		et lidt kommentar og
30		what they then they also	30		hvad de så de kunne
31		could say and I I very much	31		sige også jeg jeg ville
32		want to be part of of their	32		gerne gå ind i i deres
33		erm group	33		øh gruppe
34	MAN:	yes	34	MAN:	ja
35	ARA:	so but afterwards a week	35	ARA:	så men bagefter en uge
36		after they were all	36		efter det var allesammen
37		my friends and	37		mine venner og
38	MAN:	okay <ARA: xxx> okay	38	MAN:	okay <ARA: xxx> okay
39	ARA:	mmh mmh I don't have	39	ARA:	mmh mmh jeg har ikke
40		problems today	40		problemer i dag
41	MAN:	no	41	MAN:	nej
42	ARA:	mmh and I like	42	ARA:	mmh og jeg kan godt
43		smile and xxx	43		lide smile og dri-øh
44		erm laugh and talk with	44		grine også snakke med
45		people and	45		folk og
46	MAN:	yes	46	MAN:	ja
47	ARA:	be [part of] conversation eh	47	ARA:	være en konversation eh

Example 2.2 Hannah (10:00–10:43)

		English translation			Danish
1	MAN:	mmh okay do you have what	1	MAN:	mmh okay har du hvad
2		jobs have you had	2		for nogen job har du haft
3		in Denmark	3		i Danmark
4	HAN:	oh now i work at	4	HAN:	åh jeg arbejder nu hos
5		erm the post office	5		øh posten
6	MAN:	okay yes that's true that's	6	MAN:	nå ja det er rigtigt det

7		what you did <HAN: yeah>	7		gjorde du <HAN: ja>
8	HAN:	but only on Saturdays	8	HAN:	men kun om lørdagen
9		<MAN: or what was it>	9		<MAN: eller hvad var det>
10		yes yes only Saturdays	10		ja ja kun om lørdage
11		<MAN: yeah> I I drive a car	11		<MAN: ja> jeg jeg kører
12		and erm I erm I	12		rundt i bil og øh jeg
13		drive around with erm	13		øh jeg kører rundt med øh
14		advertising circulars and with	14		reklame og med
15		recommended lat-letters	15		anbefalede brav-breve
16	MAN:	mmh mmh	16	MAN:	mmh mmh
17	HAN:	so I don't have	17	HAN:	så øh jeg har ikke så
18		much contact with	18		meget kontakt med
19		the citizens	19		de indbyggere
20	MAN:	no	20	MAN:	nej
21	HAN:	xxx not so many	21	HAN:	xxx ikke ja ikke så mange
22		but erm	22		men øh
23		<MAN: no> only with the	23		<MAN: nej> kun med de
24		recommended letters but	24		anbefalede breve men
25		it's okay	25		det er ok
26		<MAN: yeah mmh mmh>	26		<MAN: ja mmh mmh>
27		so but	27		så men øh der er sådan øh
28		erm that's it erm July so	28		juli så det er ikke så
29		it's not so long yet but erm	29		langt endnu men øh
30	MAN:	ah you've been there	30	MAN:	nå du har været der
31		since July	31		siden juli
32	HAN:	yes since July <MAN: okay>	32	HAN:	ja siden juli <MAN: okay>
33	MAN:	so <HAN: ja> it's	33	MAN:	så <HAN: ja> det er
34		quite new yes	34		ret nyt ja
35	HAN:	yes it's a bit new yeah [laughs]	35	HAN:	ja det er lidt nyt ja [griner]
36		<MAN: yeah> but erm it's	36		<MAN: ja> men øh det er
37		okay	37		okay
38	MAN:	yeah	38	MAN:	ja
39	HAN:	it's fine <MAN: okay>	39	HAN:	det går fint <MAN: okay>
40	MAN:	oh that's good	40	MAN:	nå det er godt

In 2.1, Arabella is asked to tell about 'the most difficult thing' during her work experience. The attention is drawn to a presupposition that Arabella has had hard times working in Denmark. Arabella starts explaining that every beginning is difficult before people get to know each other. She tells the interviewer that some people are afraid of 'those coming outside countries' but 'afterwards a week they were all my friends'. The discourse of foreignness we saw in the previous sequence is maintained and co-constructed by Arabella. However, while she positions herself as a foreigner, she also struggles to demonstrate that being a foreigner is not equal to being a problematic individual. She seeks to establish herself as an indulgent, positive and easy-going colleague.

Throughout Arabella's turn, the manager's feedback is remarkably scarce. She provides only backchannelling and does not comment on any of Arabella's accounts. Only in the end, she sums up: 'so you don't think in reality it's difficult'. This utterance resembles EMP's remark in example 1.1 about the difficulty of acting as a Dane and is further evidence of the discourse of problems and difficulties created by the interviewers, regardless of whether Arabella positions herself as an outsider or an insider.

In example 2.2, instead of addressing difficulties, the manager asks Hannah what jobs she has had in Denmark. When Hannah explains that she has been working at the post office, the manager immediately reacts: 'okay yes that's true that's what you did' (lines 6–7). In contrast to example 2.1, the manager provides evaluative statements and supportive comments ('okay yes that's true', 'it's quite new yes', 'that's good'). This interactional feedback indicates a higher level of personal engagement. The manager not only follows Hannah's utterances but also immerses herself into the conversation. Let us consider one further example to illustrate not only the manager's but also the other interviewers' level of engagement with Hannah.

In example 3, Hannah accounts for what she usually does when she is not at work. She has just mentioned that she likes biking, and as a response to that, the manager asks her where she lives.

Example 3 It's a big city, Hannah (15:27–15:41)

English translation			Danish		
1	MAN:	where do you live	1	MAN:	hvor er det du bor henne
2	HAN:	in [area]	2	HAN:	i [område]
3	MAN:	well you ↑do live in	3	MAN:	nå:h du ↑bor i
4		↓Copenhagen	4		↓København jo
5	HAN:	yes yes	5	HAN:	ja ja
6	MAN:	yes yes yes <EMP: yes> yes	6	MAN:	ja ja ja <MED: ja> ja
7	EMP:	oh well it's a big city	7	MED:	arhmen det ER en stor by
8		<MAN: [coughs]>	8		<MAN: [hoster]>
9	MAN:	yes <HAN: yes>	9	MAN:	ja <HAN: ja>
10	HAN:	it is	10	HAN:	det er det
11	MAN:	it's a big city	11	MAN:	det er en stor by
12		<ROB: yes>	12		<ROB: ja>
13	HAN:	yes it is	13	HAN:	ja det er det
14	EMP:	I can still lose myself	14	MED:	jeg kan ↑stadig↓væk blive
15		in <HAN: oh>	15		væk i <HAN: åh>
16		it <HAN: okay> yeah	16		i den <HAN: okay> ja
17	HAN:	[laughs]<ROB: yes> yes it is	17	HAN:	[griner] <ROB: ja> ja det er

Hannah answers that she lives in one of the suburbs of Copenhagen, and all members of the panel immediately provide turns. When Hannah says that she finds Copenhagen a big city, the manager agrees and the employee adds that she can still lose herself in the city of Copenhagen (lines 14–16). The other employee, ROB, who has been quiet until that moment, also responds ('yes', line 12). This manifold interactional feedback creates positive dynamics in Hannah's interview. Through questions, comments and positive evaluations, the interlocutors develop a highly personalised interaction and gradually co-construct an environment of shared views and common values (co-membership). As the next example reveals, the interviewers become more lenient with Hannah after they have established a co-membership.

In example 4, Hannah explains that her boyfriend's family lives in Jutland, part of Denmark.

Example 4 'oh it's a DANISH boyfriend', Hannah (13:37–13.47)

English translation			Danish		
1	HAN:	they live in [city] in Jutland	1	HAN:	de bor i [by] i Jylland
2		so it's not so	2		så det er ikke så
3	MAN:	oh it is a ↑DANISH	3	MAN:	nå det er ↑DANSK
4		<HAN: so close>	4		<HAN: så tæt>
5		↓boyfriend you've got	5		↓kæreste du har
6		<HAN: yes yes yes> okay	6		<HAN: ja ja ja> okay
7		<HAN: yes> ↑m-mmh↓	7		<HAN: ja> ↑m-↓mmh
8		so ↑that's how	8		så det er ↑sådan
9		you came ↓here	9		du er kommet ↓herop
10	HAN:	yes <MAN: yes yes> [laughs]	10	HAN:	ja <MAN: ja ja> [griner]
11	MAN:	yes okay <HAN: yes>	11	MAN:	ja okay <HAN: ja>
12		that sounds nice	12		det lyder da ↑fint
13		<HAN: yes> I really think you	13		<HAN: ja> jeg synes da
14		very are ↑very ↓good at	14		du er ↑meget↓god
15		↑Danish	15		til at tale ↑dansk

Hannah has just told the panel that her boyfriend's family lives in Jutland. When the manager hears that, she interrupts Hannah with the exclamation: 'oh it's a ↑DANISH ↓boyfriend you've got'. She pronounces the adjective 'Danish' with a notable stress and rising intonation, while 'boyfriend' is pronounced with falling intonation. The same rising and falling pattern is repeated in lines 8–9: '↑that's how you came ↓here', followed by the evaluative statement 'that sounds nice'. Then in lines 13–15, the manager concludes: 'I really think you are ↑very ↓good at ↑Danish'. Now she compliments Hannah for her Danish language skills, although in a talk after the job interview she describes Hannah as 'the worst at Danish in the group'. Thus, her appraisal is not a linguistic assessment but an act of acknowledgement that constructs Hannah as 'Danish' after several strongly expressed signs of co-membership. This is a fundamental event in Hannah's job interview showing exactly how co-membership emerges in the interaction. Remember that Arabella also has a Danish partner, to whom she has been married for nine years, but the interviewers never address it as a shared value. To illustrate the stark contrast between Hannah's and Arabella's assessment, I provide one last example from Arabella's interview, in which her ethnic background is mentioned indirectly by the manager in an attempt to demonstrate a tolerant attitude towards migrants. However, it comes to serve the opposite purpose as it highlights ethnic differences.

In example 5, the manager describes the IO workplace as multilingual and multicultural. She is particularly cautious about using the controversial term 'New Danes' (line 12) which, together with the expression 'other ethnic background', has become common in the public debate to address non-Western minority background citizens.

Example 5 'nobody's scared of another religion or another skin colour', Arabella (11:20–11:50)

English translation			Danish		
1	MAN:	we have also many employees	1	MAN:	vi har også mange medarbejdere
2		here in the house <ARA: yes>	2		her i huset <ARA: ja>
3		who have different	3		som har forskellige
4		backgrounds	4		baggrunde
5	ARA:	yes	5	ARA:	ja
6	MAN:	I think mmh what	6	MAN:	jeg tror mmh hvad
7		↑ one third	7		↑ en tredjedel
8	EMP:	mmh	8	MED:	mmh
9	MAN:	I think so <EMP: there are	9	MAN:	tror jeg <MED: der er
10		quite a lot>	10		mange i hvert fald>
11		yeah in the ho-the house here	11		ja i hu- har i huset her
12		who are New Danes	12		som er nydanskere
13		<ARA: yes> or what the heck	13		<ARA: ja> eller hvad pokker
14		<ARA: yes> one should call	14		<ARA: ja> man skulle kalde
15		<ARA: yes> it	15		<ARA: ja> det for
16	ARA:	mmh mmh	16	ARA:	mmh mmh
17	MAN:	it doesn't seem right	17	MAN:	det virker efterhånden
18		to call them	18		forkert at kalde dem
19		other ethnic [background]	19		anden etnisk
20		<ARA: yes [laughs] any longer	20		<ARA: ja [griner]> altså
21	EMP:	yes	21	MED:	ja
22	MAN:	yes <ARA: yes>	22	MAN:	ja <ARA: ja>
23	ARA:	mmh	23	ARA:	mmh
24	MAN:	so it's not	24	MAN:	så så det det er heller ikke
25		a problem either	25		et problem
26	ARA:	no <MAN: in any way>	26	ARA:	nej <MAN: på nogen måde>
27		mmh	27		mmh
28	MAN:	nobody's	28	MAN:	der er ikke nogen der er
29		scared of	29		forskrækket over
30		<ARA: no> another	30		<ARA: nej> en anden
31		religion or another	31		religion eller en anden
32		skin colour or	32		hudfarve eller
33	ARA:	mmh mmh	33	ARA:	mmh mmh
34	MAN:	or anything else	34	MAN:	eller noget som helst
35		no it's not	35		det er der ikke
36	ARA:	yes it <MAN: mmh>	36	ARA:	ja det <MAN: mmh>
37		I think so too	37		tror jeg også

In lines 17–19, MAN admits that 'it doesn't seem right to call [the employees] other ethnic background'. On the one hand, she says that employees are used to meeting people from different ethnic backgrounds at that particular workplace; on the other hand, however, she brings religion and skin colour into a discourse of fear ('nobody's scared of another religion or another skin colour', lines 30–2). By discursively constructing 'another' religion and 'another' skin colour as non-Danish, the manager once again positions Arabella as an outsider to Danish cultural practices (see also Tranekjær 2015 on similar ethnic categorisations). I shall return to that.

5.3 Who got the job?

After the job interviews were conducted, I spoke to the members of the panel to find out which of the three candidates has been selected for the front desk secretary position. The manager told me that the job was offered to Hannah. She explained the decision as follows:

Example 6 Manager about Hannah (post-interview conversation; my translation)
We did it because culturally we imagined that she could match the job and the existing job description better. We were all a bit concerned about the other two who were too eager to get a job. And their cultural background contributes to the fact that since they will be cooperating with me, for instance, they will become too submissive in relation to the job and to me. Whereas she is educated and socialised in another system and she has had fifteen years of experience. This was very important as well. In this kind of job she will be able to start as an equal. Also the fact that she will become our peer, also when it comes to working relations, that is, she will be able to make demands on equal terms with other colleagues and give them the necessary sparring.

Example 7 Manager about Arabella (post-interview conversation; my translation)
The first one was – I think we all agree – too fragile. Her manner was fragile. Very sweet, extremely competent also, experienced also, not so many years, but clearly experienced. She was SO eager for getting that job and looked extremely fragile. I could be really concerned (. . .) that she was simply too fragile to manage it with that manner of hers. Because she was also extremely eager to provide service (. . .) [she] is someone you would actually like to take by her hand and invite home and then do something for her, right? Because she really needs someone to take care of her, otherwise I don't think she will get started. But you can't do that at a workplace.

According to examples 6 and 7, the manager constructs Hannah as the applicant who fits the job 'culturally', because she would be able to participate on 'equal terms' with her new colleagues. She stresses the fact that Hannah has been 'educated and socialised in another system', indicating at the same time that 'the system' Arabella comes from is different from the Danish one. While Hannah is portrayed as an independent and equal individual, Arabella is perceived as dependent and fragile. The two positionings are linked to two different types of education and upbringing: one is 'culturally' close to the Danish system, while the other conflicts with it. Because of these differences, applicants like Arabella are considered difficult to integrate into Danish workplaces. The attribute 'eager to provide service' is also a negative evaluation linked to a stereotype of a subservient foreigner, which stands as a paradox in relation to the job description where front desk secretary actually requires service skills. The clear division between 'us' and 'them' creates an in group 'us'. While 'us' is associated with a certain set of (positive) characteristics, it also requires applicants to create the right 'persona' for themselves (Angouri and Wodak 2014). Such positionings reveal a discursive discrimination coined in the literature 'new racism' (Van Dijk 2000; Reisigl and Wodak 2000). In new racism, people do not want to appear extremists or rightists. They distance themselves from the idea of minorities as biologically inferior but instead they talk about 'difficulties' and 'problems' with 'foreign' language or culture.

6. Co-membership and cultural fluency

Generally, the practice of selecting applicants for an IO position contains a number of contradictions: on the one hand, interviewers try to make a fair selection of the most qualified and 'strong' candidate; on the other hand, they address the IO applicants as 'vulnerable', which many interviewers interpret as a need for special treatment towards the interviewees. One interviewer explained to me that she was 'differently obliged', because she knew that an IO position was many applicants' 'only chance' to obtain a work permit in Denmark.

There is also some controversy over how much Danish the applicants should be able to speak at the job interview in order to be considered for a job and at the same time qualify for Danish classes. In an e-mail from the head office, I was told that IO applicants should be 'relatively fluent' in Danish yet 'neither too good nor too bad at Danish'. Besides, 'it is not unimportant what ethnic background they had'. Such ambiguous statements are highly characteristic of the IO context and crucial for how candidates and panels understand the interactional environment.

My analysis of Hannah's and Arabella's interviews has shown differences in the positioning and the co-construction of the two applicants. Hannah succeeds in establishing an interactional co-membership around living and working in Copenhagen, which invites the interviewers to perceive her as 'Danish'. Through the category 'Danish', the interviewers create a number of positive connections and position Hannah as an independent individual with values related to their own. Unlike Hannah, Arabella and the interviewers fail to establish an interactional co-membership. She is constructed as 'foreign' and at the same time evaluated as dependent and 'fragile'. However, the assessment of Arabella as 'fragile', as someone who requires being handled with care as the manager in example 7 phrased it, is difficult to explain. During the job interview Arabella seems calm, maintains good eye contact and does not speak or act cautiously. On the contrary, she takes a number of turn initiatives, for example when she interrupts the interviewer to resist being positioned as foreign after nine years of marriage to a Dane (example 1.1). The interviewer's perception that Arabella needs extra care may be explained by a stereotype linked to 'New Danes' (example 5). With 'another religion' and 'another skin colour', 'New Danes' are a burden on the workplace as they cannot sustain an egalitarian relationship with their colleagues and bosses. Although such labelling might seem relatively neutral and innocent, it has huge implications for who is allowed 'in' and who stays out.

How much such stereotyping is brought about and how much is brought along in the conversation it is difficult to say, but there is evidence in the data that Arabella struggles with the negative stereotype of a culturally inadequate foreigner. Paradoxically, from the perspective of the IO project, Arabella is exactly the kind of applicant the IO wants to target: to provide less experienced minority background employees with knowledge and understanding of Danish workplace practices, including linguistic and cultural skills. However, Arabella is not offered the job precisely because of the 'foreign' positioning. Contrary to IO policy, Hannah is the preferred candidate, since she can navigate a 'system' that resembles the Danish one. Although she speaks Danish at a beginner's level, she is constructed as a culturally fluent member of the Danish workplace. Cultural fluency encapsulates the main result of the analysis of IO job interviews, that is, applicants offered a position are not necessarily linguistically fluent in Danish but they can navigate culturally specific institutional conventions, norms and rules to meet the expectations of the interviewers.

One key element of cultural fluency is co-membership. Throughout the IO job interview, the interviewers look for connections and shared (cultural) values. If they cannot find them in the interaction, they fail to establish a co-membership with the applicant. As a result, interviewers disapprove of applicants, and evaluate them on the basis of brought along ethnic stereotypes. Ideally, cultural fluency is a dialogic process, but in bureaucratic institutional communication, it is rather seen as a monologic skill to which minority background applicants are expected to adapt. Applicants socialised in hierarchically oriented societies are often deselected either because they cannot position themselves as equal colleagues or because the interviewers maintain the unequal positioning.

7. Conclusion

Job interviews are complex cultural events which oblige applicants to address the interview as a set of standard, institutional rules, on the one hand, and on the other as an authentic and personal communicative event. For minority background applicants the tension between the standardised and the individual is further increased by culturally specific local norms. The ambiguous IO context adds another challenge to the selection process. On paper, the applicants are 'allowed' to have difficulties with speaking and writing in Danish, as the improvement of Danish is a priority during in-service training. In reality, however, those applicants who already are integrated into Danish cultural practices are the preferred ones. As a consequence, the credibility of integration projects such as the Danish IO is undermined. Clearly, the IO project is designed to integrate those individuals who could not be integrated in other ways. It is supposed to encourage integration, yet it generates marginalisation. However much the panels try to make the interview different (e.g. by giving applicants special consideration), they evaluate the applicants by resorting to common-sense norms. When the panels interview applicants whom they consider too far removed from Danish cultural standards, there is a risk of basing the evaluation on stereotypes. Thus, many IO-like projects are characterised by an inherent paradox: by categorising groups as separate from the host culture in order to assist them, they inevitably become marginalised. This paradox inconveniences both applicants and interviewers. The applicants need to meet a number of cultural expectations without exactly knowing what they are, while the interviewers have to conduct a bureaucratic selection in a fair manner and consider how to give special treatment to the most vulnerable applicants.

The idea of shared culture is the eye of the needle through which applicants need to pass through. When applicants and interviewers assume they share cultural values through interaction, it is likely that interviewers will help applicants develop cultural fluency. This finding is not new in the literature of job interviews, where shared personal interests and likeability in general are seen as pivotal in determining who gets the job (e.g. Rand and Wexley 1975). However, in the context of the IO integration project, my study exemplifies a new form of discrimination (see also Van Dijk 2000; Reisigl and Wodak 2000 on new racism). Although dynamics and development of social and cultural identities have been a recurrent theme in various studies (e.g. Friedman 1994; Peirce 1995; Hall 1996), there seems to be a widely held view that a language can be learned but a culture cannot. In other words, although crossing geographic, national and linguistic boundaries has become popular and widely accepted, crossing cultural boundaries is still problematic for many non-Western immigrants. The focus on culture as an insurmountable barrier reveals an alarming view on identity as stable and unchangeable, which directly undermines workforce immigrants' chances for integration and creates a discourse of social exclusion.

Transcription conventions

(.)	untimed brief pause
<hello>	overlap
HELLO	emphasis
hello	quiet voice
he:llo	sounds stretch
hello↑	rising intonation
hello↓	falling intonation
hh	ex- or inhalation
[laughs]	non-verbal communication
xxx	incomprehensible word or phrase
(. . .)	omission

Note

1. Translating non-standard Danish into non-standard English has been a serious challenge to this research. Although Danish and English are both Germanic languages and thus related in many ways, when it comes to translating non-standardness, it is impossible to preserve the same level of indexicality. For entirely practical reasons,

all utterances are translated into colloquial English closest to the Danish original. However, the applicants' contributions sound slightly more standard in the English translation than they are in the Danish version (see more on translation choices in Kirilova 2013).

References

Adelswärd, V. (1988), *Styles of succes: on impression management as collaborative action in job interviews*, Linköping: Linköping University.

Agar, M. (2006), 'Culture: can you take it anywhere? Invited lecture presented at the Gevirtz Graduate School of Education, University of California at Santa Barbara', *International Journal of Qualitative Methods*, 5: 2, pp. 1–16.

Akinnaso, F. N. and C. S. Ajirotutu (1982), 'Performance and ethnic style in job interviews', in J. J. Gumperz (ed.), *Language and social identity*, Cambridge: Cambridge University Press, pp. 119–44.

Angouri, J. and M. Marra (eds) (2011), *Constructing identities at work*, Basingstoke: Palgrave Macmillan.

Angouri, J. and R. Wodak (2014), '"They became big in the shadow of the crisis": the Greek success story and the rise of the far right', *Discourse & Society*, 25: 4, pp. 540–65.

Auer, P. and F. Kern (2001), 'Three ways of analysing communication between East and West Germans as intercultural communication', in A. Di Luzio, S. Günthner and F. Orletti (eds), *Culture in communication: analyses of intercultural situations*, Amsterdam and Philadelphia: John Benjamins, pp. 89–114.

Bakhtin, M. (1986), *Speech genres and other late essays, V*, trans. V. W. MacGee, Austin, TX: University of Texas Press.

Billig, M. (1996), *Arguing and thinking: a rhetorical approach to social psychology*, Cambridge: Cambridge University Press.

Davies, B. and R. Harré (1990), 'Positioning: the discursive production of selves', *Journal for the Theory of Social Behavior*, 20: 1, pp. 43–63.

Erickson, F. and J. Shultz (1982), *The counselor as gatekeeper: social interaction in interviews*, New York: Academic Press.

Foucault, M. (1972), *The archeology of knowledge and the discourse on language*, New York: Pantheon.

Friedman, J. (1994), *Cultural identity and global process*, London: Sage.

Goffman, E. (1959), *The presentation of self in everyday life*, New York: Doubleday Anchor.

Goffman, E. (1983), 'The interaction order: American Sociological Association, 1982 presidential address', *American Sociological Review*, 48: 1, pp. 1–17.

Gumperz, J. J. (1982), *Discourse strategies*, Cambridge: Cambridge University Press.

Gumperz, J. J. (1999), 'On interactional sociolinguistic method', in C. Roberts and S. Sarangi (eds), *Talk, work and institutional order: discourse in medical, mediation and management settings*, Berlin: Mouton de Gruyter, pp. 453–71.

Gumperz, J. J. [1968] (2009), 'The speech community', in A. Duranti (ed.), *Linguistic anthropology: a reader*, 2nd edn, Malden, MA: Blackwell, pp. 66–73.

Hall, S. (1996), 'Who needs identity?', *Questions of Cultural Identity*, 16: 2, pp. 1–17.

Holmes, J. (2006), *Gendered talk at work*, Malden, MA: Blackwell.

Hymes, D. H. (1972), 'On communicative competence', in J. B. Pride and J. Holmes (eds), *Sociolinguistics: selected readings*, Harmondsworth: Penguin, pp. 269–93.

Jupp, T. C., C. Roberts and J. Cook-Gumperz (1982), 'Language and disadvantage: the hidden process', in J. J. Gumperz (ed.), *Language and social identity*, Cambridge: Cambridge University Press, pp. 232–56.

Kerekes, J. (2006), 'Winning an interviewer's trust in a gatekeeping encounter', *Language in Society*, 35: 1, pp. 27–57.

Kirilova, M. (2013), 'All dressed up and nowhere to go: linguistic, cultural and ideological aspects of job interviews with second language speakers of Danish', PhD dissertation, University of Copenhagen.

Kirilova, M. (2014), '"Det kan være svært" – om sprog og kultur i andetsprogsdanske ansættelsessamtaler', *Nordand: Nordisk tidsskrift for andrespråksforskning*, 19: 1, pp. 9–36.

Liebscher, G. and J. Dailey O'Cain (2009), 'Language attitudes in interaction', *Journal of Sociolinguistics*, 13: 2, pp. 195–222.

Lipovsky, C. (2006), 'Candidates' negotiation of their expertise in job interviews', *Journal of Pragmatics*, 38, pp. 1147–74.

Ochs, E. and B. Schieffelin (1994), 'Language acquisition and socialization: three developmental stories and their implications', in Benjamin G. Blount (ed.), *Language, culture, and society: a book of readings*, Prospect Heights, IL: Waveland Press, pp. 470–512.

Peirce, B. N. (1995), 'Social identity, investment, and language learning', *TESOL Quarterly*, 29: 1, pp. 9–31.

Rampton, B. (2006), *Language in late modernity: interaction in an urban school*, Studies in Interactional Sociolinguistics, 22, Cambridge: Cambridge University Press.

Rand, T. M. and Wexley, K. N. (1975), 'Demonstration of the effect, "similar to me", in simulated employment interviews', *Psychological Reports*, 36: 2, pp. 535–44.

Reisigl, M. and R. Wodak (2000), *Discourse and discrimination: rhetorics of racism and antisemitism*, London: Routledge.

Roberts, C. (2000), 'Professional gatekeeping in intercultural encounters', in S. Sarangi and M. Coulthard (eds), *Discourse and social life*, London: Longman, pp. 102–20.

Roberts, C. and S. Campbell (2006), *Talk on trial: job interviews, language and ethnicity*, Department for Work and Pensions Research Report no. 344, Leeds: Corporate Document Services, <http://webarchive.nationalarchives.gov.uk/20130314010347/http://research.dwp.gov.uk/asd/asd5/rports2005-2006/rrep344.pdf> (last acces sed 8 November 2016).

Roberts, C., E. Davies and T. Jupp (1992), *Language and discrimination: a study of communication in multi-ethnic workplaces*, London: Longman.

Roberts, C., S. Campbell and Y. Robinson (2008), *Talking like a manager: promotion interviews, language and ethnicity*, Department for Work and Pensions Research Report no. 510, Norwich: Her Majesty's Stationery Office, <https://www.resear

chonline.org.uk/sds/search/download.do?ref=B9845> (last accessed 8 November 2016).

Sacks, H., E. Schegloff and G. Jefferson (1974), 'A simplest systematics for the organization of turn-taking for conversation', *Language*, 50: 4, pp. 696–735.

Scheuer, J. (2001), 'Recontextualisation and communicative styles in job interviews', *Discourse Studies*, 3, pp. 223–48.

Tannen, D. (2005), *Conversational style: analyzing talk among friends*, New York: Oxford University Press.

Thomas, J. (1983), 'Cross-cultural pragmatic failure', *Applied Linguistics*, 4, pp. 91–112.

Tranekjær, L. (2015), *The power of categories: gatekeeping nationality, language and religion*, Clevedon: Multilingual Matters.

Van Dijk, T. A. (2000), 'New(s) racism: a discourse analytical approach', in S. Cottle (ed.), *Ethnic minorities and the media: changing cultural boundaries*, Buckingham and Philadelphia: Open University Press, pp. 33–49.

Winslade, J. M. (2005), 'Utilising discursive positioning in counselling', *British Journal of Guidance and Counselling*, 33: 3, pp. 351–64.

3

Constructing a 'Mission Statement': A Multimodal Perspective on Believable Identity Construction in a Job Interview

Ewa Kuśmierczyk-O'Connor

1. Introduction

The job interview forms an integral part of workplace discourse, and is a crucial stage in an individual's transition into new employment. As a gatekeeping encounter, it operates within the discursive boundaries of existing workplace ideologies and is a site of professional and social identity construction. Research on job interviews has shown that constructing a 'believable identity' is a key element in promoting positive outcomes (Kerekes 2006; Roberts and Campbell 2006). In order to achieve this, prospective employees are expected to demonstrate situational competency characterised by their ability to combine various discourses – personal, professional and institutional (Iedema 2003; Roberts and Campbell 2006).

The gatekeeper's analysis of this competency centres on the candidates' background presentations – their first opportunity to establish a believable identity. This process typically takes place in a face-to-face setting in which speech is only one of many communicative means available to the participants. It is thus inherently multimodal, as modes such as gesture, gaze, body orientation and written text intersect with speech in the creation of meaning. This chapter extends the existing research on gatekeeping by applying a multimodal approach that considers interaction as an 'ensemble' in which individuals utilise different communicative means in co-constructing meaning (Jewitt 2009) and ultimately negotiating their identities. To this end, multimodal interaction analysis (Norris 2004a) is applied to observe the different discourses in action.

2. The job interview: a transition gate

The transition into employment typically revolves around the evaluation of an individual's discourse expected to evoke organisation-specific values and competencies (Erickson and Shultz 1982; Roberts 2000). This requirement often takes the form of a criteria list not revealed to the applicant but embedded in the interview questions (Adelswärd 1988; Iedema 2003; Roberts 1985; Roberts and Campbell 2006). It is a conversation but, at the same time, so much more than just a conversation. It is where the candidate's identity is evaluated against an institutionally predetermined list; this identity, created in the here-and-now of the job interview, is then used as a predictor of more or less desired workplace behaviours and, ultimately, the candidate's fit with the organisation and their suitability for the job.

The interviewer's perception of the applicant as trustworthy has been identified as a fundamental element of the gatekeeping process. In a series of reports on employment and promotion interviews in the UK, Celia Roberts and colleagues (Campbell and Roberts 2007; Roberts and Campbell 2006; Roberts et al. 2008) point to the candidate's ability to seamlessly blend various discourses – institutional, occupational and personal – as the central elements driving the interviewer's perception of the individual's self-presentation as that of a 'real self':

> It is crucial that candidates are seen to be credible since it is assumed that their real selves will be revealed through the interview process. They need to design their turns in such a way that they are seen as coherent, consistent and authentic and, therefore, are deemed credible, persuasive and trustworthy. (Roberts and Campbell 2006: 26)

They aptly demonstrate that the candidates who are able to move along a continuum from analytic-objective to personal-subjective in their talk tend to be judged as believable and trustworthy individuals (Roberts et al. 2008). These findings highlight the performative nature of the job interview interaction, focused around a discursive enactment of one's skills, competencies and values (see Scheuer 2001). It can thus be said that the interview is also based around the transition from a disembodied state – the candidate's résumé or CV – into a narrative performance of self. This is an embodied process, in which meaning emerges from a variety of communicative means – such as speech, gesture, gaze, body orientation and written text.

The evaluation process takes place throughout the interview and comes into play very early in the interaction. Within discourse analysis, strong links have been made between early establishment of rapport and trust, characterised by the interviewer's belief that the candidate's values match the organisation's values, and that they will perform well in the job (Kerekes 2005, 2006, 2007; Kuśmierczyk 2013a). Wider literature on social encounters shows that the initial judgements individuals make upon meeting others tend to influence ways in which they interpret their interlocutors' responses (Ambady and Skowronski 2008; Demarais and White 2005). This is particularly relevant to situations in which some sort of evaluation takes place (see Barrick et al. 2012). The importance of making a positive first impression has perhaps been most noticeably highlighted in popular literature on job interviews. Claims that the decision whether to hire an individual or not is often made within the first minutes of the procedure are often followed by tips on how to make a good first impression (e.g. Corfield 2009; Dorio 2009; McLachlan 1999: 199). Often, great emphasis is placed on the way in which individuals look and behave as they 'walk in the door' (e.g. Eggert 2007; McDermott 2006); however, evidence presented to support these claims is less than straightforward. Studies on first-time encounters, for example, report various amounts of time it takes individuals to form impressions (e.g. Bar et al. 2006; Barrick et al. 2012; Curhan and Pentland 2007). The general consensus is that applicants have only two to five minutes (Bar et al. 2006; Judge et al. 2000). The accuracy of judgements made regarding individuals' character and future work performance is also mixed (see Barrick et al. 2012; Viswesvaran et al. 2001).

Furthermore, embodied conduct such as eye contact and facial expression, as well as paralinguistic features, have been found to play a role in creating first impressions (DeGroot and Kluemper 2007; Pollak Levine and Feldman 2002). Interestingly, in a study of 'real-life' job interviews, Dougherty et al. (1994) found that if an interviewer forms a positive first impression of an applicant, it is likely that the interviewer will display more positive regard for the applicant throughout the interview. The mixed evidence suggests that initial judgements made by the interviewers are more complex than just an impression gauged from the first few moments of the encounter, or based only on what the candidates say. What makes it even more complex is the fact that the process is inextricably connected to associations between an individual's behaviours and various personal, social, professional and institutional characteristics (Lievens and Peeters 2008; Roberts 2011). One way of viewing these attributions is as emerging through social interaction while individuals act and react to each other's actions as well as objects around them. The process relies on actions taken before (i.e. the candidate's CV, a phone conversation with the interviewer) and during the interview. As excerpts presented in this chapter will show, all of these actions come into play in the candidate's background presentation and thus constitute an important part of their transition into employment.

3. Multimodal approach to identity construction

In their self-presentation, candidates can draw on multiple identity elements – professional, organisational, individual, ethnic, national, and so on. Importantly, however, it is the way in which they combine these elements that forms the basis of the interviewer's perception of the individual as more or less believable and thus suitable for the job. It is an inherently multimodal process. Within a wider body of research on job interviews, however, the various communicative means have typically been studied in isolation. While the study of interview interactions within discourse analysis tends to be qualitative in character and focus on linguistic features, research on other aspects such as gesture and body movement or vocal characteristics has traditionally relied on quantitative methods, often in controlled experimental settings. Each of these approaches offers an opportunity for a detailed analysis and has contributed valuable knowledge regarding interaction in the job interview context. Real-life interactions, however, rely on the combination of these diverse communicative means. The goal here is, therefore, to examine how they intersect with each other in meaning-making and identity construction.

Multimodal Interaction Analysis (MIA) is particularly suitable for this type of analysis as it takes into account the orientations and interpretations realised by the individuals using a variety of semiotic means (i.e. modes) (Jewitt 2009; Norris 2004b). MIA grew out of Goffman's (1969, 1974) work in interactional sociology, and studies within interactional sociolinguistics (Gumperz 1999; Schiffrin 1995), and builds on

Scollon's (2001) Multimodal Discourse Analysis. These frameworks place a strong focus on self-presentation as a social process, the interpretations made by the individuals in interaction, and the role of context as a vital part of meaning-making. MIA is also predominantly interested in naturally occurring interaction in 'authentic' situations. Such an approach provides tools for observing the diverse communicative means candidates and interviewers employ in the encounter. Importantly, these tools facilitate the observation of the complex interrelations and impacts that the various means have in what is essentially a significant life encounter for the candidate and a multifaceted decision-making process for the interviewer.

Within MIA, the analysis is focused around 'action', seen as the basic unit of social interaction (Norris 2004a). It is construed of various modes including audio-visual representation (e.g. speech, sound, text, images, appearance, colour), bodily movement (e.g. gesture, gaze, body shifts) and spatial arrangements (e.g. layout, proxemics). Actions can be arranged in a continuum of lower- to higher-level actions, with the former typically emerging through the use of a single mode (e.g. a gesture, a posture shift). Lower-level actions are fluidly performed and build upon each other in multiple modes, constituting higher-level actions (e.g. a conversation). Higher-level actions can thus be imagined as chains of lower-level actions, within each mode and across the modes which are in constant interplay (Norris 2004a, 2011). Some higher-level actions can be embedded in other higher-level actions (e.g. a conversation is embedded in the higher-level action of the job interview) (see Norris 2009). The higher the level of the action is, the more complex it becomes. Importantly, each action is seen within MIA as potentially linking to identity elements (Norris 2011).

Higher-level actions are typically bracketed by social openings and closings that are at least partially ritualised (Norris 2004a). For example, in the job interview context, the higher-level action of 'interviewing and being interviewed' is constituted by multiple lower-level actions carried out by the candidate and the interviewer with the use of various modes (e.g. spoken units, gestures, body shifts, gaze). Additionally, this higher-level action is influenced by the wider context in which the interview takes place – the ideologies and norms that shape the procedures to be followed, the expectations present and made apparent throughout the interview, as well as the space and time within which the interview takes place.

Norris (2004a) distinguishes between actions performed through embodied (e.g. speech, gesture, body movement) and disembodied modes. Disembodied modes, such as print (e.g. the candidate's CV), can play as important a role in constructing higher-level actions as embodied modes. The disembodied modes are incorporated into the unit as frozen action. Frozen actions are typically higher-level actions performed with/upon an object or the environment at an earlier time than the time of the particular interaction under analysis (Norris 2004a). They become relevant as social actors incorporate them into the interaction (e.g. candidate or interviewer referring to the CV). In this study, the lower, higher-level and frozen actions comprise a set of analytic tools that are applied in the observation of the interaction between the candidate and the interviewer. At the lower level, the social actors' speech, gestures, body movement as well as gaze are observed as they combine with each other to form more complex, higher-level actions. As a result, the analysis is led not only by what is being said, but also by what is being done through various communicative means.

4. Identity construction in background presentations

The excerpts discussed in this chapter come from a data set collected as part of a study on job interviews in New Zealand. The excerpts presented here come from job interviews collected at an international recruitment agency in a large city. The design of the study aimed to reflect an approach that calls for naturalistic interaction data (Holmes and Stubbe 2003; Roberts and Sarangi 2003). The candidates included males and females from a range of cultural, ethnic and linguistic backgrounds, reflecting the local employment market. All interviews were video recorded in order to capture actions across various modes. They were recorded during a period of recruitment for a large organisation and included candidates applying for positions ranging from advisory to management roles. This was the second stage in the process (following phone screening), with consultants making a decision to recommend (or not) candidates for a final interview directly with the employer. The interviews were followed by recall sessions with the interviewers.[1] The interviewers were asked to judge to what extent each candidate was considered successful and to provide reasons for such judgement.

The discourse addressed in the current analysis comes from the initial stages of the job interview during which candidates were asked to introduce themselves or provide reasons for applying for the position. I refer to this stage as the background presentation. One of the reasons for focusing on the background presentation in the analysis was the fact that this is the candidate's first opportunity to demonstrate their suitability for the job during the interview. What is crucial at this stage is the shift from the informative to the performative mode of interaction (Scheuer 2001). This is apparent in the fact that the interviewers, although already familiar with the information provided in the application (having read it while shortlisting candidates for the interview), invite the candidate to provide a spoken account of what they already know. Essentially, this 'invitation to perform' (Scheuer 2001: 229) prompts the candidate to transform the identity presented in the document into a spoken, face-to-face real-time performance, co-constructed with the interviewer. Such a move also highlights the discursive demands of the interview as the candidates are largely judged on the way they deliver the information in addition to the information itself (Roberts and Campbell 2006). Parallel to the evidence showing that early achievement of mutual understanding facilitates the establishment of a positive interactional environment (Kuśmierczyk 2013a, 2014), the argument here is that the candidate's response to this first interview question is a crucial site of identity construction that can drive the interviewer's judgements throughout the encounter.

5. The first question: an invitation to perform

The shift from the informative to the performative highlighted above provides the initial interpretative challenge for the candidate. Figure 3.1 illustrates the tension between different identity elements that come into play at this point in the encounter.

Figure 3.1 An invitation to perform

The excerpt comes from an interview between Elizabeth (the interviewer, right) and Tanya (the candidate, left)[2] who is applying for a senior advisory role at an organisation providing services to youth.

Several observations can be made with regard to the excerpt above. The interviewer's prompt illustrated in Figures 3.1a–c initially appears to be simply a 'warm-up' question that comes in just over one minute into the interview. At first glance, the invitation for Tanya to describe a role she is interested in (Figure 3.1c: 'what kind of role you're interested in') gives an impression that the question is of a consultative nature – finding out about Tanya's professional preferences so that she can be matched with the right job. Simultaneously, however, this seemingly general question requires the candidate to provide a list of criteria that match the position she is applying for. Elizabeth's actions that accompany speech – rearranging documents and preparing for note-taking – are clear signals that Tanya's answers will be subject to institutional processing. The performative character of the background presentation is highlighted by a metaphorical gesture that marks the required action for the candidate (Figure 3.1a: Elizabeth makes several small circles with her right hand on 'describe a little bit'). As noted above, what is important here is that this information has already been provided by the candidate both in her cover letter and during the initial phone screening and now is to be performed in such a way as to convince the interviewer about her suitability for the position.

6. Mission statement in action

So how does Tanya respond to this initial interpretative challenge? Figure 3.2 illustrates how she blends various identity elements to construct her professional 'mission statement' that aligns with the position she is applying for.

The element most noticeably foregrounded at the beginning of this short

(6 seconds taken out)

Figure 3.2 Mission statement in action

presentation is Tanya's professional stance. In speech, Tanya orients to past actions, that is, 'influencing' and 'supporting' a particular social group, that constitute her considerable 'work history'. Her closed body position and lack of movement below her neck (Figure 3.2a–d: chair pulled in, sitting straight, elbows resting on the table, hands clasped) contribute to creating this professional image. She words her answer carefully (Figure 3.2a–f: frequent minimal pauses, repetition), while monitoring the interviewer's actions (Figure 3.2c, f, h: gaze directed at Elizabeth as she is note-taking). She also brings in the institutional element apparent in her orientation to the contribution she could make in the job (Figure 3.2e–f: 'I want to be able to in some way influence . . .') (see Roberts and Campbell 2006). Simultaneously, however, Tanya also foregrounds a more personal identity element, by framing her work as 'service' and her professional goals as things she 'wants to be able' to do. Her presentation concludes with a summary in which Tanya brings her experience to the forefront, hence highlighting the professional identity element again. This is achieved in a series of small actions, such as the slight gestural punctuation that coincides with 'years of work', followed by a metaphoric gesture on 'I've served' that offers this experience for the interviewer's consideration (Figure 3.2h: both hands open up and towards the interviewer) (McNeill 1992). A gaze shift towards Elizabeth and rising intonation at the end of this statement also call for the interviewer's engagement, which Elizabeth reacts to by providing minimal responses (Figure 3.2h).

Altogether, these actions constitute Tanya's 'mission statement', establishing an image of a professional not only with considerable experience, but also personal commitment to the core tasks of the job – providing support to a particular social group. But how can one conclude that such a discursive blend results in a credible identity? The key to determining whether Tanya's self-presentation has the right elements is the interviewer's follow-up, illustrated in Figure 3.3a–c. Here, the interviewer contributes to Tanya's identity construction by way of summarising her background presentation.

It is noticeable that Elizabeth's summary is doing more than just repeating the information provided by Tanya. She is portrayed as someone with an ambition to be in an influential role and have impact, which, compared with Tanya's initial statement focused on support, seems to align more closely with the senior advisory role. It is apparent, however, that this reinterpretation of Tanya's professional identity is a shared effort. As the interviewer reformulates the initial question (see Figure 3.1a–c), she stops writing and shifts her gaze to Tanya (Figure 3.3b). A beat gesture (Figure 3.3b: right hand goes up then strokes down on 'influential') makes this professional element more prominent, and it is immediately followed by Tanya's backchannel that confirms

Figure 3.3 Contributing to identity construction

this interpretation (Figure 3.3c: head nod + 'yea:h yeah'). Importantly, this action mirrors Tanya's earlier action in Figure 3.2f (right hand makes a beat gesture with the pen on 'influence'), indicating an alignment in the meaning behind Tanya's actions and Elizabeth's interpretation of them (Kuśmierczyk 2013b). In other words, they are on the same wavelength when it comes to Tanya's identity in relation to implicit expectations pointed out above. Through this co-constructed summary, Tanya's background presentation is incorporated into the institutional format – a brief written note (Figure 3.3c) that states her professional focus (see Kuśmierczyk 2013a; Roberts and Campbell 2006). This seemingly minor action can have considerable consequences as the decision about the candidate's suitability for the job often relies on this written record.[3] Needless to say, Tanya was recommended for the final interview with the employer.

7. From 'mission' to 'missing out'

As illustrated above, the implicit requirement to transform the disembodied identity on paper into an appropriate and position-aligned 'mission statement' is at the centre of believable identity construction in the initial stages of the interview. It is realised by a personalised statement of one's professional motivations expressed by actions that originate within the individual (e.g. by the use of action verbs such as *support*, *influence*, *serve*). Perhaps the best way to demonstrate the importance of this 'mission statement' is by way of a contrasting excerpt from an unsuccessful interview. The excerpt below is an interesting comparison with Tanya's interview as it involves the same recruitment consultant, Elizabeth, who is this time interviewing Patricia (NZ Pākehā) for a similar type of role – a high-level advisory role. Elizabeth's question in Figure 3.4 follows directly from Patricia's comment on the status of the current local employment market, indicating that she would be interested in permanent opportunities.

The way in which Elizabeth structures the prompt suggests a need to be convinced about Patricia's genuine interest in the position. As in the first excerpt, on the surface it appears that Elizabeth is asking a more general question about taking up permanent work (Figure 3.4b: 'criteria for you to actually go into a permanent role'); however, a deictic gesture towards the document in Elizabeth's hands (Figure 3.4a: right hand outlines an arrow-like shape on the document) marks a reference to the particular role, thus indicating an implicit expectation that Patricia will demonstrate her alignment with the position.

Figure 3.4 From mission statement . . .

Figure 3.5 . . . to missing out

Figure 3.5 illustrates Patricia's response to the question.

The key to Patricia's lack of success seems to lie in the way she foregrounds the professional identity element in relation to her motivation. Several actions become relevant in this process. In speech, Patricia portrays her motivation as that of wanting to be a team member, but also to receive training (Figure 3.5a, b). Immediately after, however, there is a visible shift in her bodily stance as she orients to the identity of a contractor (Figure 3.5c: 'I have been a consultant contractor for over twenty years'; leans forward, arms spread to the side), and remains in this position as she talks about her experience (Figure 3.5c–e). While highlighting her professional experience, Patricia orients to the external aspects of her motivation (i.e. things that she could gain from permanent employment). She additionally portrays her professional experience of being a contractor in terms of 'missing out' on things and being treated differently

(Figure 3.5e). A more personal identity element comes to the foreground as Patricia summarises her presentation and returns to her original body position (Figure 3.5g); however, framing her decision to apply for a permanent position as originating in the fact that her children have reached adulthood (Figure 3.5g) further reinforces the external source of Patricia's motivation. Patricia's use of *you* and *you know* as she talks about her experiences here evokes an appeal to shared knowledge and encourages the interlocutor's participation (Jucker and Smith 1998). In contrast to her interview with Tanya, Elizabeth remains only minimally involved with a brief gaze directed to Patricia, a nod and minimal neutral backchannels, with no follow-up that would incorporate Patricia's self-presentation into the requirements of the role.

8. Believable identity production: embodied transition within boundaries

Tanya's and Patricia's interview performances illustrated in the excerpts above emphasise the importance of a candidate's ability to discursively transform their identity to fit into the requirements of the role and the organisation. Central to this process is the blending of personal, institutional and professional identity elements that build towards a 'mission statement' – a personalised declaration of one's professional goals and values. This feature has typically been related to the concept of the 'new work order' (Gee et al. 1996), characterised by the emphasis on employees' personal and attitudinal alignment to the institutional categories. Roberts (2011), for example, talks about the expectation that the individual will create an image of a person whose personal values and attitudes align with organisational priorities. She links it to the perception of being consistent and credible, which depends on the extent to which candidates can synthesise more personal discourse with institutional discourses. As the above excerpts show, the construction of believable identity relies at least to some extent on portraying one's motivation as an internal drive for more than just career progression or work-related benefits.

It is interesting to trace this requirement back to the interviewer's prompt. By initiating a more personal discourse (i.e. asking the candidate to talk about their motivation to apply for the job) at the beginning of the encounter, the interviewer marks a connection between the institutional and the personal. The background prompt contains important signposts regarding relevant identity elements expected in the candidate's performance. The tension between the elements relevant in the candidate's identity production is evident across different modes. While the personal identity elements materialise most prominently in speech (e.g. framing the candidate's response as 'talking' about one's background or 'describing' one's professional interests and preferences), the professional and institutional identity elements seem to metadiscursively hover above as the interviewers orient to the documents and actions that produce their institutional identities (e.g. pointing to the documents, preparing to process the candidate's answers on paper). This constitutes an interpretative challenge to the candidate – that of responding in such a way as to express the 'real self', while fitting in with the job and the organisation. These actions also index the power that the interviewers are invested with regarding interpretations being made (e.g. how a candidate's narrative is processed into notes that later support the interviewer's evaluation of the candidate's performance) (Briggs 2003; Cook-Gumperz and Gumperz 2002).

The embodied construction of a believable self also relies heavily on reciprocity. For instance, the interviewer's deictic reference to the document on the table in Figure 3.4 serves as a visual cue for the candidate with regard to the link to the role she is applying for. Pointing and gestural reference to the candidate's CV has been identified as a display of epistemic authority – signalling the existing knowledge or the right to know more (Glenn and LeBaron 2011; Heritage and Raymond 2005). In Figure 3.4a, however, the speech–gesture action seems to outline the boundary of the candidate's expected answer by indicating an expected alignment with the job she is being interviewed for.

Another embodied aspect of the construction of one's identity apparent in the analysis is speech–gesture mimicry. The mirroring of a beat gesture and a lexical item in Tanya's interview creates important links between the candidate's self-presentation and the interviewer's interpretation. The mimicked speech–gesture actions in the current data set can be seen as pragmatic means that tighten the link between the interlocutors' interpretations. As such, they mark a convergent orientation in shaping the candidate's narrative into a format that can be bureaucratically processed (Kuśmierczyk 2013a).

Finally, changes in body position and orientation have been shown to be some of the means with which individuals can express their attitudes and positioning (Goodwin 2007). While Tanya's body position and limited movement mark her professional stance, Patricia's shift in body position highlights her changing orientation between the professional and the personal. In the context of the job interview, they can be seen as performative means that contribute to presenting oneself as a candidate suitable for the job.

9. Conclusion

This chapter has analysed job candidates' self-presentation in the initial stages of the interview using believable identity as a concept that links their situated performance with the organisation-specific expectations. The discussion of the concept of believable identity presented at the beginning of this chapter highlighted the importance of not only what information is included but also how it is presented to the interviewer. The chapter has shown that the candidate's identity transpires through the way in which they explicate their motive to apply for the job. Bringing to the forefront one's intrinsic motivation and personal engagement evokes agency and contributes to the construction of a 'mission statement'. As a result, the performed identity is seen as believable.

The main contribution of this chapter lies in gaining a better understanding of the subtleties of identity construction in workplace discourse, and situations of transitions in particular. Observing how the candidate's identity is actioned and interpreted across different modes can shed more light on the process of evaluation, and assist in providing tools for enhancing practices on both sides of the gate. The analysis presented here shifts from conceptualising discourse as conveyed in speech to discourse as action composed of various communicative means. In order to show the multilayered nature of identity produced within the first minutes of the interview, several multimodal aspects were brought to attention – orientation to objects (i.e. documents), gesture, body movement and gaze. By demonstrating how interview participants bring into play various embodied actions as they negotiate the candidate's performance, this chapter extends the existing knowledge regarding interactional features of gatekeeping encounters.

In terms of practical applications, expanding one's awareness of these implicit expectations can assist the candidates in formulating their own 'mission statements' – a genuine expression of one's motivations and perceived fit with the job and the organisation. On the interviewers' side, the awareness of ways in which candidates construct their identities, at least in the initial stages of the job interview, can assist in making more informed interpretations and evaluations.

Notes

1. Recall sessions in this particular data set were carried out with the interviewers only as per the recruitment agency's conditions. In order to avoid any interference with the decision-making process, the sessions were scheduled after the candidates had been shortlisted. Such timing provided an additional benefit in that the interviewers were able to provide information regarding the candidate's overall success in applying for the job. Despite the time gap between the interview and the recall session, the interviewers were able to share their insights as they relied on detailed notes they took during the interviews.
2. The images in the excerpts are presented in split screen mode, with the candidate to the left, and the interviewer to the right.
3. The interviewers in this study commented on the decision-making process as reliant on a detailed report based on interview notes used to justify their recommendation.

References

Adelswärd, V. (1988), *Styles of success: on impression management as collaborative action in job interviews*, Linköping: University of Linköping.

Ambady, N. and J. J. Skowronski (2008), *First impressions*, New York: Guilford Press.

Bar, M., M. Neta and H. Linz (2006), 'Very first impressions', *Emotion*, 6: 2, pp. 269–78.

Barrick, M. R., S. L. Dustin, T. L. Giluk, G. L. Stewart, J. A. Shaffer and B. W. Swider (2012), 'Candidate characteristics driving initial impressions during rapport building: implications for employment interview validity', *Journal of Occupational and Organizational Psychology*, 85: 2, pp. 330–52.

Briggs, C. L. (2003), 'Interviewing, power/knowledge, and social inequality', in J. F. Gubrium and J. A. Holstein (eds), *Postmodern interviewing*, Thousand Oaks, CA: Sage, pp. 243–54.

Campbell, S. and C. Roberts (2007), 'Migration, ethnicity and competing discourses in the job interview: synthesizing the institutional and personal', *Discourse Society*, 18: 3, pp. 243–71.

Cook-Gumperz, J. and J. J. Gumperz (2002), 'Narrative accounts in gatekeeping interviews: intercultural differences or common misunderstandings?', *Language and Intercultural Communication*, 2: 1, pp. 25–36.

Corfield, R. (2009), *Successful interview skills: how to prepare, answer tough questions and get your ideal job*, London and Philadelphia: Kogan Page.

Curhan, J. R. and A. Pentland (2007), 'Thin slices of negotiation: predicting outcomes from conversational dynamics within the first 5 minutes', *Journal of Applied Psychology*, 92: 3, pp. 802–11.

DeGroot, T. and D. Kluemper (2007), 'Evidence of predictive and incremental validity of personality factors, vocal attractiveness and the situational interview', *International Journal of Selection and Assessment*, 15: 1, pp. 30–9.

Demarais, A. and V. White (2005), *First impressions: what you don't know about how others see you*, New York: Bantam Dell.

Dorio, M. A. (2009), *The complete idiot's guide to the perfect interview*, 2nd edn, Indianapolis: Alpha Books.

Dougherty, T. W., D. B. Turban and J. C. Callender (1994), 'Confirming first impressions in the employment interview: a field study of interviewer behavior', *Journal of Applied Psychology*, 79: 5, pp. 659–65.

Eggert, M. (2007), *Perfect interview*, London: Random House UK.

Erickson, F. and J. J. Shultz (1982), *The counselor as gatekeeper: social interaction in interviews*, New York: Academic Press.

Gee, J., C. Lankshear and G. A. Hull (1996), *The new work order: behind the language of the new capitalism*, St Leonards, NSW: Allen & Unwin.

Glenn, P. and C. D. LeBaron (2011), 'Epistemic authority in employment interviews: glancing, pointing, touching', *Discourse and Communication*, 5: 1, pp. 3–22.

Goffman, E. (1969), *The presentation of self in everyday life*, London: Allen Lane.

Goffman, E. (1974), *Frame analysis: an essay on the organization of experience*, Cambridge, MA: Harvard University Press.

Goodwin, C. (2007), 'Participation, stance and affect in the organization of activities', *Discourse & Society*, 18: 1, pp. 53–73.

Gumperz, J. J. (1999), 'On interactional sociolinguistic method', in S. Sarangi and C. Roberts (eds), *Talk, work and institutional order*, Berlin and New York: Mouton de Gruyter, pp. 453–71.

Heritage, J. and G. Raymond (2005), 'The terms of agreement: indexing epistemic authority and subordination in talk-in-interaction', *Social Psychology Quarterly*, 68: 1, pp. 15–38.

Holmes, J. and M. Stubbe (2003), *Power and politeness in the workplace: a sociolinguistic analysis of talk at work*, Harlow: Longman.

Iedema, R. (2003), *Discourses of post-bureaucratic organization*, Amsterdam and Philadelphia: John Benjamins.

Jewitt, C. (2009), 'An introduction to multimodality', in C. Jewitt (ed.), *The Routledge handbook of multimodal analysis*, London and New York: Routledge, pp. 14–27.

Jucker, A. H. and S. W. Smith (1998), 'And people just you know like "wow":

discourse markers as negotiating strategies', in A. H. Jucker and Y. Ziv (eds), *Discourse markers: descriptions and theory*, Amsterdam: John Benjamins, pp. 171–201.

Judge, T. A., D. M. Cable and C. A. Higgins (2000), 'The employment interview: a review of recent research and recommendations for future research', *Human Resource Management Review*, 10: 4, pp. 383–406.

Kerekes, J. (2005), 'Before, during, and after the event: getting the job (or not) in an employment interview', in K. Bardovi-Harlig and B. Hartford (eds), *Interlanguage pragmatics*, Mahwah, NJ: Lawrence Erlbaum Associates, pp. 99–132.

Kerekes, J. (2006), 'Winning an interviewer's trust in a gatekeeping encounter', *Language in Society*, 35: 1, pp. 27–57.

Kerekes, J. (2007), 'The co-construction of a gatekeeping encounter: an inventory of verbal actions', *Journal of Pragmatics*, 39: 11, pp. 1942–73.

Kuśmierczyk, E. (2013a), '"The only problem is finding a job" – multimodal analysis of job interviews in New Zealand', unpublished PhD thesis, Victoria University of Wellington.

Kuśmierczyk, E. (2013b), 'Critical points in the negotiation of understanding: multimodal approach to job interviews in NZ context', *TESOLANZ Journal: The Journal of the TESOL Association of Aotearoa New Zealand*, 21, pp. 57–77.

Kuśmierczyk, E. (2014), 'Trust in action: building trust through embodied negotiation of mutual understanding in job interviews', in K. Pelsmaekers, H. Jacobs and C. Rollo (eds), *Trust and discourse: organisational perspectives*, Amsterdam: John Benjamins, pp. 11–44.

Lievens, F. and H. Peeters (2008), 'Interviewers' sensitivity to impression management tactics in structured interviews', *European Journal of Psychological Assessment*, 24: 3, pp. 174–80.

McDermott, J. (2006), *Interview excellence: 12 step program to job interview success*, London: Anson Reed.

McLachlan, M. (1999), *Job winning in New Zealand: how to get the job you want today*, Auckland: Penguin Books.

McNeill, D. (1992), *Hand and mind: what gestures reveal about thought*, Chicago: University of Chicago Press.

Norris, S. (2004a), *Analyzing multimodal interaction: a methodological framework*, New York: Routledge.

Norris, S. (2004b), 'Multimodal discourse analysis: a conceptual framework', in P. LeVine and R. Scollon (eds), *Discourse and technology: multimodal discourse analysis*, Washington, DC: Georgetown University Press, pp. 101–15.

Norris, S. (2009), 'Modal density and modal configurations: multimodal actions', in C. Jewitt (ed.), *The Routledge handbook of multimodal analysis*, London and New York: Routledge, pp. 78–90.

Norris, S. (2011), *Identity in (inter)action: introducing multimodal (inter)action analysis*, Berlin and New York: Walter de Gruyter.

Pollak Levine, S. and R. S. Feldman (2002), 'Women and men's nonverbal behavior and self-monitoring in a job interview setting', *Applied H.R.M. Research*, 7: 1, pp. 1–14.

Roberts, C. (1985), *The interview game and how it's played*, London: British Broadcasting Corporation.

Roberts, C. (2000), 'Professional gatekeeping in intercultural encounters', in S. Sarangi and M. Coulthard (eds), *Discourse and social life*, Harlow: Longman, pp. 102–20.

Roberts, C. (2011), '"Taking ownership": language and ethnicity in the job interview', in K. Pelsmaekers, C. Rollo, T. Van Hout and P. Heynderickx (eds), *Displaying competence in organizations: discourse perspectives*, Houndmills and New York: Palgrave Macmillan, pp. 10–26.

Roberts, C. and S. Campbell (2006), *Talk on trial: job interviews, language and ethnicity*, Department for Work and Pensions Research Report no. 344, Leeds: Corporate Document Services, <http://webarchive.nationalarchives.gov.uk/20130314010347/http://research.dwp.gov.uk/asd/asd5/rports2005-2006/rrep344.pdf> (last accessed 8 November 2016).

Roberts, C., S. Campbell and Y. Robinson (2008), *Talking like a manager: promotion interviews, language and ethnicity*, Department for Work and Pensions Research Report no. 510, Norwich: Her Majesty's Stationery Office, <https://www.researchonline.org.uk/sds/search/download.do?ref=B9845> (last accessed 8 November 2016).

Roberts, C. and S. Sarangi (2003), 'Uptake of discourse research in interprofessional settings: reporting from medical consultancy', *Applied Linguistics*, 24: 3, pp. 338–59.

Scheuer, J. (2001), 'Recontextualization and communicative styles in job interviews', *Discourse Studies*, 3: 2, pp. 223–48.

Schiffrin, D. (1995), 'Interactional sociolinguistics', in S. McKay and N. H. Hornberger (eds), *Sociolinguistics and language teaching*, Cambridge: Cambridge University Press, pp. 307–28.

Scollon, R. (2001), *Mediated discourse: the nexus of practice*, New York: Routledge.

Visweswaran, C., D. S. Ones and L. M. Hough (2001), 'Do impression management scales in personality inventories predict managerial job performance ratings?', *International Journal of Selection and Assessment*, 9: 4, pp. 277–89.

4

Teamwork and the 'Global Graduate': Negotiating Core Skills and Competencies with Employers in Recruitment Interviews

Sophie Reissner-Roubicek

1. Introduction

Graduate job interviews are a pivotal event in the transition from university to the professions. Because studies of interaction are rare in this context, the influence of current organisational discourses on how participants (re)create norms and practices in these gatekeeping encounters remains largely unexplored. Efforts to render the recruitment process more transparent and accessible to students through clearer definitions of employment competency criteria have highlighted the increasing importance placed on soft skills in the global workplace and the high priority of teamwork on employers' wish lists. Teamwork is explicitly thematised as a skill and an associated discourse in graduate job interviews, but discursive norms for talking about teamwork experiences remain relatively opaque. This aspect of the employment competency framework has specific potential to obstruct candidates' progress in the transition to the professional workplace. A closer look at the activities of interviewers and interviewees in articulating the experience of teamwork in line with bureaucratic expectations and discursive norms will reveal why. For example:

> Last year we had the mock interviews and one of the students says 'I've got good communication skills and good teamwork' and this MTEC person – HR – he stood up onto the ta- he stood up straight on his chair, and he said 'It is up to me to decide whether you have got good communication skills and teamwork – let me decide. <u>You</u> do not tell <u>me</u>, you know, what skills–those kind of skills? Let me decide from your experience!' (Hari, post-interview)

The incident related by Hari is not only useful in highlighting and defining a particular challenge to candidates in graduate recruitment interviews, it also illustrates how extreme (or explicit) the strategies that professionals draw on to monitor expert/novice boundaries in a situated institutional practice can be. The story of a visiting HR manager who lost his cool when interviewing a student appears to have achieved somewhere between anecdotal and apocryphal status among Hari's peers, as it was also mentioned by other students who had been alarmed, as well as amused, by the force of this reaction to an unsubstantiated claim about skills.

The particular competencies referred to in the anecdote are not incidental. Over the last decade, employers' wish lists for graduate skills have continuously featured teamwork and communication among those they prize most highly (e.g. Vic Careers n.d.; Archer and Davison 2008; Lowden et al. 2011; Careers NZ 2012; Adams 2013, 2014; Gray and Koncz 2014; Yate 2015). In a ranking of 'global graduate' competencies by graduate employers, 'the ability to work collaboratively in teams of people from different backgrounds and countries' was the outright high scorer with communication skills some way behind in second place (Diamond et al. 2011: 8), reflecting 'the corporate world's increasing focus on teamwork' (Yate 2008: 214) and the conviction that 'in the vast majority of graduate roles, being able to work well with colleagues is crucial' (TARGETjobs n.d.). Teamwork questions should be expected in competency-based job interviews for graduate programmes. Even when companies have actual teamwork observed 'live' under the microscope of an assessment centre setting, the requirement to articulate teamwork skills in appropriate ways in a job interview remains a core feature of the graduate recruitment process.

Furthermore, the anecdote illustrates the salience of boundary monitoring by the more powerful interlocutor in these gatekeeping encounters. Sometimes, in practice or mock interview contexts such as this one, that boundary marking is made explicit. In other instances, when employers volunteer to act as expert mentors in giving interview practice, they may implicitly (re)produce discursive norms surrounding identities and hierarchies in order to provide a realistic apprenticeship (Reissner-Roubicek 2012). This is because in real interviews, boundary monitoring tends to be more implicit, as employers are under pressure to serve an institutional agenda of fairness and accountability, which typically entails following a set structure of prescribed questions, and quantitative scoring of answers in terms of the behavioural indicators previously identified for the competency. Implicitness is a characteristic feature of interviewers' attempts to withhold what would be 'natural' conversational responses, or feedback, in case it encourages or otherwise helps one applicant more or less equally than another (Roberts and Campbell 2005, 2006; Campbell and Roberts 2007), especially when an answer is dispreferred (cf. Button 1992).

As elaborated below, this chapter first adds to the literature by exploring how boundaries are monitored in the enactment of expert/novice roles and identities that are constructed in job interviews. Second, it fills a gap in the literature by focusing on a core discursive site in which this takes place: teamwork discourse is a crucial skill to succeed in the gatekeeping encounter of the job interview.

Through the analysis of mock interview data in which unsatisfactory responses occurred, this chapter explores how participants enact and negotiate power in identifying, constructing and monitoring boundaries in graduate job interviews, thereby co-constructing their expert/novice professional identities. In the process, they (re)create norms and practices in what proves to be a complex and important variant of an asymmetric workplace encounter.

2. Approaches to power and identity in interaction

The arguments made in this chapter start from the theoretical premise that power and identity are 'dynamically enacted and negotiated in interaction' rather than fixed attributes belonging to particular roles and positions (Schnurr 2013: 118). Power is understood as achieved through discourse, just as identities are thought of as 'talked into being' (Heritage 1984); various ways of exerting power in interaction include interruptions, questioning strategies and the highlighting of mistakes (Roberts et al. 2014). Despite what Roberts (1985) calls 'a pretence of equality' between interviewer and interviewee, the job interview is a traditional gatekeeping encounter where the asymmetric nature defines those interlocutors respectively as 'someone who has the right or privilege to know and the other in a less powerful position who is obliged to respond' (Akinnaso and Ajirotutu 1982: 120). The gatekeeping task of job interviews has traditionally been 'to demarcate and divide members and non-members of the organization' (Campbell and Roberts 2007: 266).[1] As the person 'who gets to define the purpose or significance of the interaction and who influences the direction in which it develops' (Holmes 2007: 1996), the interviewer is an inherently more powerful interlocutor. However, the ways in which power is manifested, when and by whom, are fluid; power is an integral part of the interactional patterns that define workplace practices (Sarangi 2005). One gatekeeper may 'do' power more overtly than another, and/or with another, or in monitoring one boundary more closely than another. This reflects Holmes's understanding of power as 'dynamically constructed and exercised, both implicitly and explicitly, in different aspects of a specific interaction' and, very importantly, that 'different participants manifest power in diverse ways as they construct their own identities and roles in response to the behaviour of others' (Holmes 2007: 1996). Everything is co-constructed in interaction, with 'all participants being actively involved in the production of action at all times' (Sarangi 2005: 161; see also Jacoby and Ochs 1995) and responsibility for the creation of identities being distributed among interlocutors. It is important to consider what is made relevant by participants, at what stage, on what terms and in what ways, and to note that 'members inhabiting an interpretive community of practice are guided by a vague set of norms which are partially open to adaptation in every situation of use' (Sarangi 2005: 162).

This approach has particular relevance to how interviewer identities are conceptualised in the mock interviews analysed here. Like real interviews, these expert/novice interactions serve both to reproduce the particular discursive practices involved in graduate recruitment and to (co)construct professional identities in ways that are institutionally relevant. Graduate interviews by their nature involve a gap in age and experience between the person in the position of power and the 'subordinate' or, rather, candidate, reinforcing further what is inherently unequal about selection interviews.

At the same time, interviewer identities are multi-faceted, bound up in 'displays of situated interactional expertise' (Sarangi 2010: 177) that characterise their different gatekeeping roles. One of these roles is what Holmes (2007) characterises as 'facilitative gatekeeping' in counterpart to the more traditional notion of gatekeeping (Schiffrin 1994; Campbell and Roberts 2007; Tranekjær 2015). As she explains, it 'stretches the concept of gatekeeping' away from repressive interaction and in the direction of facilitative interaction, where 'the person in the position of power takes initiatives to open gates, and even prods the subordinate in the direction of movement over hurdles' (Holmes 2007: 1995). In this respect, some employers who provide mock interviews see themselves as an expert voice to guide novices 'through the gate' into employment (Reissner-Roubicek 2010).

But even when gatekeeping is more facilitative than repressive in these encounters, the dynamic aspect of identity as 'an interactional problem' (He 1995) is particularly visible, inextricably entwined with power, in the mutual shaping of interlocutors' identities as novice/expert professionals. What interviewers are doing can be ana- lysed as scrutiny and ratification/non-ratification of identity claims. That teamwork is highly relevant to professional identity is evident in Campbell and Roberts's (2007: 249) definition of the job interview as 'a detailed and personalised disclosure of the self as a subject, which demands descriptions of the candidate's relationship to the self, the public, and other members of the team' (see also the literature on employable identities, e.g. Fugate et al. 2004; Hinchliffe and Jolly 2011; Holmes 2013; Cole and Tibby 2013). Candidates for graduate roles may need particular prodding to get them over the teamwork hurdle, namely to construct themselves appropriately as a member of a team.

The core of this challenge is framed by Gee et al.'s (1996) critical perspective on discourses surrounding the rationale for and function of teams. They identified a contradiction inherent in the new-capitalist rhetoric of teamwork that poses a particular ideological challenge in job interviews: the implicit requirement of the interview's competency framework, in line with values underpinning the new work order (Gee et al. 1996: 222), to promote oneself as an individual at the same time as fitting into 'broad, homogenising institutional categories' of which 'being a good team worker' is an example (Roberts and Campbell 2006: 38). Negotiating this particular contradic- tion is complex and, as Campbell and Roberts point out, demands a specific kind of 'discursive skill' (Iedema 2003), described by them as 'the synthesizing of personal and institutional discourses to produce an acceptable identity' (Campbell and Roberts 2007: 244). The challenge of personalising teamwork experiences while simultaneously aligning with corporate values is something HR practitioners recognise (implicitly or explicitly) as a barrier in graduate job interviews.

By way of illustrating this point, this chapter presents some examples of interac- tional sequences involving unsuccessful teamwork answers in gatekeeping encoun- ters between employers and students. Data from so-called mock interviews with employers have proved highly useful in the discussion of comparable 'real' inter- views, helping to capture the essence of asymmetries in variations of the gatekeeping encounter (Reissner-Roubicek 2010). Such interviews jointly characterise the transi- tion from higher education to the workplace in countries where the 'new spirit of capitalism' (Boltanski and Chiapello 2007) has imposed a common business culture. This discursive background is underpinned by common categories across occupational boundaries – teamwork being a particularly representative example.

The examples are drawn from a subset of twenty interviews collected during one recruitment season at the University of Auckland in New Zealand. The interviews are explored to reveal how professional gatekeepers monitor both particular boundaries and also links between micro-level discourses (talk in interviews) and macro-level discourses (norms and ideologies of self and group identities in the workplace) in relation to teamwork. Novice/expert construction of professional identities will be discussed with particular reference to the way power is enacted in displays of interactional expertise triggered by infelicitous responses to the teamwork question.

3. Context of the study

Preparing students to articulate their experiences to an employer in relevant institutional terms is a pressing concern for higher education stakeholders. Well-funded faculties such as business and engineering with dedicated employer liaison roles regularly attract corporate recruiters to the campus to provide help with interviews. The present study included seven employers (including engineering managers and company directors) from different companies who were all members of an international organisation, the Institute of Electrical and Electronic Engineers (IEEE).

Due to variations in the way mock interviews have been defined in the literature, before presenting the examples it will be useful to consider how this term has been applied and accordingly the extent to which an interview intended to prepare a student for a gatekeeping encounter may itself be a gatekeeping encounter. The terms 'simulated' and 'role-played' are sometimes used interchangeably with 'mock' as category of interview, and are legitimately warranted if the type of activity involves teachers or peers playing the role of interviewers. In Sniad's (2007) study, for example, the US work-training programme under investigation involved five- to ten-minute interviews conducted forum-style. Sniad set out to explore how 'the instructional method of role play' is used in preparing people for a real gatekeeping event.[2] In respect of her own research context, she explains that

> unlike job interviews, mock interviews (1) do not impact the students' access to the industry; (2) are situated in a learning environment, in front of an audience of learners; and (3) are preceded and followed up with metalinguistic discussion between the actors and the audience. (Sniad 2007: 1975)

In contrast, mock interviews in the present study were conducted one-to-one with professional experts, all of whom were potential employers for the student cohort. There was no peer audience,[3] and the feedback, perhaps more properly called metapragmatic or metacognitive than metalinguistic, was given to each interviewee in the concluding part of their half-hour interview. These employers asked only certain students at the end of their interview to send a CV to the company, which was evidence of not just an effective interview but also of the employers' recruitment agenda. This suggests that even in the absence of high stakes, certainly something important is at stake, and that what transpires will have an impact on the students' access to the industry, whether this is positive or negative.

The IEEE employers, who as volunteer interviewers might be expected to facilitate entry through the gate in some way for their novice counterparts, could be described as gatekeepers of a profession, as well as of a particular institution with the power to bestow a specific position in the company's graduate programme. The latter is in line with the traditional understanding of gatekeeping defined by Schiffrin (1994). In real interviews, the main constraint on gatekeepers' own actions is accountability, that is, for their decisions to be accountable in institutional terms (Reissner-Roubicek 2010). Other salient factors that potentially influence the way employers monitor the boundaries delineating the transition to professional employment are shared with mock interviews and will be explored and discussed in the light of intersections between power and professional identity.

4. Data and procedures

As mentioned above, this analysis is based on data drawn from an opportunistic sample of twenty mock interviews with employers, collected in one recruitment year at the University of Auckland. The majority of candidates were born abroad, representing different lengths of time living and studying in the national context. Some had joined the New Zealand educational system during secondary school, others prior to the final year of study or in time to start university, and many were international students.[4]

The interviews were recorded using digital voice recorders that the interviewers operated themselves, and were scheduled to run for twenty-five minutes each. Examples are presented from three interviews with multilingual born-abroad students (pseudonyms Hari, Neela and Thanh) and their monolingual interviewer counterparts (pseudonyms Bob, Mack and Phil). These interviews were chosen because they represented salient trends in interviewer responses to unsatisfactory interviewee answers.

5. Analytical approach

The analytical approach draws broadly on Sarangi's (2005, 2010) proposal for activity analysis, beginning with structural, interactional and thematic mapping of encounters in order to identify the conditions for talk and, in turn, any critical, or 'telling' moments (Roberts et al. 2014) for closer analysis. It is theoretically premised on Levinson's (1979) notion of activity type, of which the job interview is 'a paradigm example'. The interactional mapping of the encounters involves identifying patterns of difference and similarities in the way talk is organised in terms of turns (type, length, volume, etc.). Thematic mapping was followed by identification of analytic features that further constitute activity analysis, including alignment and framing. Particular attention was drawn to alignment as an analytical feature specifically relevant to elaborating the focal theme, inasmuch as alignment – a notion 'based on a view of interaction as jointly produced' (Sarangi 2005: 161) – is about doing power (Roberts et al. 2014). Alignment intersects with framing and other features that variously signal (dis)alignment as well as breaches of norms in a goal-oriented action framework. Inferences are closely tied up with 'constraints on what can or cannot be said' (Sarangi 2005: 166) in such frameworks for analysing institutional encounters.

Categories are drawn on selectively and integrated in the analysis to illustrate as organically as possible the interdependent and overlapping tensions that arise in articulating and evaluating teamwork skills in a graduate job interview.

6. Analysis

The analysis is organised in terms of where interviewers fall on a continuum of implicit to explicit discursive enactment of power in boundary monitoring. These examples reflect a range of interviewers' reactions to infelicitous responses to questions about teamwork. The first example from a mock interview shows a particular activity norm being made explicit by the employer concerned, although he attempts to do so indirectly at first.

In example 1, Thanh (Student 19) is explaining her final year team project to Mack (Employer 5), a senior manager in a large electronics firm. As in example 2 following, although the employer's question does not include the word 'teamwork' itself, both interviewer and interviewee have a shared understanding that a project is a group project. The mention of projects implicitly indexes teamwork, and teamwork is explicitly thematised in the 'telling moment' that unfolds.

Example 1 Mack (Employer 5) and Thanh (Student 19)

1	E5:	so tell me about your project
2	S19:	now my project is mobile sensors in robotic fish
		[39 lines omitted]
41	E5:	yep
42	S19:	and we're trying to implement google earth
43	E5:	m'hm,
44	S19:	to see exactly–
45	E5:	oh good! okay
46	S19:	it is! ((laughing)) that is to find the location of the fish
47	E5:	m'hm, m'hm, m'hm,
48	S19:	which is basically ah /electrode
49	E5:	m'hm,
50	S19:	simple [chloride electrode
51	E5:	[just looking for potential difference=
52	S19:	=exactly
53	E5:	yep
54	S19:	so at the moment we're all trying to get individual product work–
55		individual components working,
56	E5:	m'hm,
57	S19:	combine them together,
58	E5:	m'hm
59	S19:	collect information,
60	E5:	yep, m'hm
61	S19:	put it in the database, analyse it, xxx xxx xxx xxx. that is my project
62		I'm working on at the moment
63	E5:	okay
64	S19:	yes
65	E5:	and that is what *you're* doing /or what the team is doing
66	S19:	teamwork

67 E5:   the team
68 S19:   yes
69 E5:   and what in particular are *you* doing
70 S19:   I'm doing measuring-
71 E5:   you're trying to- just pause here for a moment /you're trying to sell
72   what *you* do /your skills /yes it was part of a team
73 S19:   yes
74 E5:   but I'm not thinking of employing the team /I'm thinking about
75   employing *you*
76 S19:   sure
77 E5:   so tell me what *you* did
78 S19:   sure /I'm measuring the application of the sensors so I'm working on
79   the g p s and the:: um temperature sensors . . .

Thanh and Mack's alignment as interlocutors in lines 42–62 – in a section featuring over-laps (e.g. lines 50–1), collaborative completions (e.g. latching in lines 51–2), laughter, and considerable interactional feedback from the employer – is affiliative. Response tokens are variously deployed in enacting listenership norms (Holmes et al. 2013; Norrick 2009, 2010, 2012; O'Keeffe and Adolphs 2008; Knight and Adolphs 2008). Four categories of response token, namely continuers, convergence tokens, engaged response tokens and information-receipt tokens (O'Keeffe and Adolphs 2008) are in evidence. Particularly of note are the trio of continuers 'm'hm, m'hm, m'hm' (line 47), and convergence tokens, or what McCarthy (2003) calls yes-plus tokens, such as 'yep' (lines 41, 53, 60), signalling increased alignment. The engaged response token 'oh good!' (line 45) is a marker of high engagement (O'Keeffe and Adolphs 2008: 84). The fact that an information receipt token 'okay', which is more reflective of the asymmetric nature of the encounter (O'Keeffe and Adolphs 2008: 84), is part of the same turn in no way undermines the analytical inference that can be made at this point – that the participants are constructing each other primarily as fellow engineers, as opposed to expert and novice.

However, in line 65, the first of three different ways of exerting power in interaction given by Roberts et al. (2014) can be seen in (a) the questioning strategy initiated by Mack. It is triggered by the pronoun use in Thanh's story. Aside from the self-references bracketing the story – the single instance of 'I' in the final turn of her answer (line 62), and 'my project' twice (lines 2, 61), the description of carrying out the project features only 'we' forms (fourteen occurrences in lines 3–62). This pattern of first-person plural vs. singular pronouns in her story constructs her as subsumed within the collective identity of the team.

Mack's first question is a hint in the form of an option 'And that is what *you're* doing, or what the team is doing?' (line 65). When his emphatic stress on 'you' fails to elicit the preferred response, he echoes her answer 'the team' (line 67). Repetition of a phrase is an implicit pedagogical correction strategy (Lyster and Ranta 1997); on the other hand, 'echoing' is a situated display of interactional expertise, designed to prompt elaboration by the client (Sarangi 2005). Mack's second question in line 69 again uses emphatic stress combined with the disambiguating 'in particular': 'And what in particular are *you* doing?' Although the preferred response is now forthcoming – 'I'm doing measuring-' (line 70) – it is met with (b) an interruption designed to (c) highlight a mistake. The interruption 'just pause here for a moment' (line 71) constitutes a frame-switch from the interviewing frame to the advising frame so as to provide some metacognitive explanation (Tannen and Wallat 1993; Ensink 2003; Cornelissen and Werner 2014).

The interplay of framing with alignment is significant. In the interview frame, there is a positive mutual alignment around engineering expertise, which may momentarily mask the nature of the 'I' in the recounted world of teamwork. In their consecutive turns 'teamwork', 'the team', 'yes' (lines 66–8), Thanh's understanding of 'one-with-the-team' as the 'right' answer is implicitly contested by Mack, signalling the boundary relating to normative expectations regarding teamwork.

The point of Mack's interruption in line 71 is to emphasise why it is important for Thanh to differentiate her individual contribution from that of the team. He makes his point increasingly explicit, reduplicating the contrastive stress on *you/your/you/you* in 'you're trying to sell what *you* do – *your* skills – yes, it was part of a team . . . but I'm not thinking of employing the team, I'm thinking about employing *you*, so tell me what *you* did' (lines 71–7). Thanh then completes what she started to do in the turn that was interrupted (line 70); in defining her unique contribution (lines 78–9) she shows her compliance. The strong evidence of affiliative and interactional alignment and mutual construction of what are first and foremost engineering identities during the description of the interviewee's project seems initially to signal a positive evaluation of her response, but this is belied by the interviewer's critical scrutiny of her discursive self-positioning vis-à-vis the respective contributions of the team members.

Example 2 highlights a critical moment in a mock interview between Bob (Employer 3), representing a prestigious engineering firm, and Hari (Student 13). As in example 1, although projects are the ostensible target, teamwork is explicitly thematised as a discourse and a skill; here, in contrast, it is instigated by the interviewee.

Example 2.1 Bob (Employer 3) and Hari (Student 13)

1	E3:	in managing projects/ have you got any experience there?
2	S13:	we only had one project so far, that was in university/a couple of
3		projects /we had /problems /sometimes the team members they're
4		not pulling their weight,
5	E3:	that's always the way
6	S13:	the same /yes /u:m-
7	E3:	even in my time
8	S13:	[(((laughing))
9	E3:	[(((laughing)) yes yes

Interactional aspects of alignment do not necessarily indicate ideological agreement between speakers (Roberts et al. 2014: 36), but Bob's turns additionally demonstrate key features of affiliative alignment that do, starting with an expression of overt understanding 'that's always the way' (line 5), which is a token for converging on 'shared common ground . . . between participants' (Knight and Adolphs 2008: 84). He also does self-deprecating humour, 'even in my time' (line 7), laughter and a double confirmation, 'yes yes' (line 9). These various features largely serve to construct Bob and his interlocutor as more equal than unequal, but the humour, which is based on indirectly referencing his own age and experience, also works on another level to implicitly do power by indexing a senior professional identity.

Significantly, these features remove any barrier to Hari's further revelations about the unsatisfactory behaviour of other team members 'not pulling their weight'. Looking ahead at the concluding lines (35–7) of his two-minute story (which are sufficient by way of reflecting the way he positions the underperforming team member – i.e. relatively neutrally – for the purposes of the analytical point about to be made), Bob's reaction (lines 38–9) appears consistent with his earlier response:

Example 2.1 (continued)
35	S13:	and I told him as well / you're really good but you didn't have time
36		I agree / but you should have managed your time somehow (.) and he
37		said *okay*
38	E3:	yeah, that's unfortunate about a bad project isn't it / there's always
39		someone in the team who doesn't pull their weight . . .

The alignment strategies in Bob's turn (lines 38–9) include agreement plus orientation to the other's concerns ('yeah, that's unfortunate'), another example of a convergence token to demonstrate common ground (O'Keeffe and Adolphs 2008) and the tag-question ('isn't it') that additionally signals engagement. Affiliative alignment is particularly evident in the way Bob reuses the same expression 'there's always someone in the team who doesn't pull their weight' that Hari himself used: 'sometimes the team members they're not pulling their weight' (lines 3–4).

During the feedback stage at the end of the interview, after commenting favourably on Hari's smart appearance, significant part-time industry experience, sought-after specialism and extra abilities (e.g., 'He can test! This guy's talented' as a projection of what he would be thinking about Hari in a 'real' interview), Bob sounds a more serious note in reinvoking the interviewing frame.

Example 2.2 Bob (Employer 3) and Hari (Student 13)
1	E3:	it's cool that you've done voluntary work / community work /
2		good call (.) and really important to me is how you fit into a team,
3	S13:	m'hm
4	E3:	I've got some little concerns about how you related to your team there
5	S13:	m'hm
6	E3:	cos I sensed you're a wee bit ready to blame other members of the team–
7		be careful how you present it / you might not be at all Hari / but be
8		careful how you present it / I picked that up ((sucks in air through his
9		teeth)) and I was thinking *I'm not too happy about that* you know, *not*
10		quite the right answer.

Bob's list of positive feedback ends with the informal endorsement 'good call' (line 2). A brief pause marks a shift to negative feedback, belied somewhat by the non-contrastive conjunction 'and', serving to frame (not) fitting into a team as another thing that's 'really important to me' (line 2). On the one hand, this fronting of himself as professional evaluator underlines Bob's expert power to judge the novice performance; on the other, the softeners 'little' (line 4) and 'a wee bit' (line 6) are typical of affiliative alignment (Roberts et al. 2014: 58), serving to mitigate the criticism of Hari's inclination to 'blame the other members of the team' (line 6). In the same way, Bob's aside, 'you might not be at all Hari' (line 7), serves to mitigate the repeated warning 'be careful how you present it' (lines 7–8) that simultaneously implies Hari's discursive skill has potential for improvement. Bob's use of the interviewee's name is both personalising and confrontational. His re-enactment of misaligned expectations is animated with self-quoted direct speech, 'I was thinking *I'm not too happy about that*' (line 9) following the 'non-linguistic sound' (Norrick 2009) of sucking air in sharply through his teeth (line 8). As a signal of negative emotion, and therefore an affective response, this paralinguistic feature may also – if counter-intuitively – be classified as a marker of high engagement (O'Keeffe and Adolphs 2008) with the interlocutor. If Bob's strategy for helping the novice Hari seems surprisingly like tough love, it is not an isolated example among the employers, as will be seen in the third example involving employer Phil, also presented in two parts. Bob also has strategies in common with Mack (above), most strikingly their co-construction of the novices as sometimes more equal than unequal through their marked expressions of affiliative alignment.

In the third example, Phil (Employer 6), a senior project leader at a well-known engineering manufacturer, asks Neela (Student 22) what is known as a 'strengths' question.

Example 3.1 Phil (Employer 6) and Neela (Student 22)
1   E6:   hey /if I employed you at P & K?
2   S22:   m'hm?
3   E6:   and you were part of my design team,
4   S22:   m'hm?
5   E6:   what strengths would you bring to my design team
6   S22:   okay I can-like as I've written in my personality thing, uh it said- I do
7   have an attitude of getting along with people
8   E6:   m'hm
9   S22:   I've not been so: /demanding and /so stubborn that I want my way to be
10   done? because when we worked /for all these projects /last semester /
11   it was a group of four /um /we never <u>really</u> ended up having any /
12   conflict on something? on anything? and <u>probably</u> I can /like /when it
13   comes to meeting the deadlines /I have the ability of working hard (.)
14   and putting in an extra effort (.) not feeling *okay this is the time to go*
15   *home* /that's it
16 E6:   yeah
17 S22:   so. I have those /like I can get along with the team?
18 E6:   yeap (.)

The highly informal marker 'hey' (line 1) Phil uses to signal the topic shift (Norrick 2012) has a deinstitutionalising effect on the formulaic approach 'if I employed you at P & K', which is a hypothetical frame for the enquiry about strengths so as to link it specifically to the employer's own context. This framing arguably teases the interviewee with a vision of success and reinforces the differences between them in terms of power and professional identity.

Evidence of interactional alignment in this example includes Neela's signalling with the discourse marker 'okay' (line 6) her understanding of Phil's question (lines 1, 3, 5) about strengths she could bring to his team. Neela infers this to relate to her teamwork skills. She characterises these primarily as interpersonal, 'getting along with people'/'the team' (lines 7, 17); she constructs them as strengths in terms of their opposite attributes, being 'demanding and stubborn' (line 9). Her evidence 'we never really ended up having any conflict' (line 11) to support this claim is hedged, as is her claim to working harder to meet deadlines, 'probably I can' (12). The rhetorical device of quoted direct speech '*okay this is the time to go home, that's it*' (lines 14–15) constructs her in terms of what she is not (cf. de Fina 2003), a team member who throws in the towel. Phil's turns, yes-plus (or convergence) tokens 'yeah' and 'yeap' (lines 16, 18) signal increased alignment, and accordingly appear to validate her answer. There are no cues given by the employer that the answer is inappropriate, although the lack of interactional feedback at either listening-response-relevant moment (Erickson and Schultz 1982), namely the two instances of high-rising terminal intonation in lines 10 and 12, may possibly be salient in this respect.

As in example 2.2, it is only made explicit at the feedback stage that the interviewer considered the answer inappropriate. The misalignment or mismatch in expectations lies in the interviewee's incorrect inference about the question.

Example 3.2 Phil (Employer 6) and Neela (Student 22)

1	E6:	I was /struggling to try and identify /what your strengths really were
2	S22:	m'hm
3	E6:	um /and then when I- I asked you that specifically /*what strengths would*
4		you bring to my team,
5	S22:	m'hm
6	E6:	it was sort of like /I'm a /I'm a good team player and I'm easy to get on
7		*with* /like like like /you spoke about your /your personality?
8	S22:	m'hm?
9	E6:	you didn't really talk about- I'm /I'm not first employing a personality
10		I'm employing a designer /I'm /I'm employing somebody who's
11		who's really into engineering
12	S22:	yes
13	E6:	and /you know somebody whose strength is /*I'm going to do good-*
14		like you know /like *design-led work or engineering* (.) THAT's really
15		what an employer's looking for
16	S22:	yes
17	E6:	is someone who can /can actually do that part of the job?

Framing mismatches are problematic for participants because they reveal differences in participants' goals as well as in their expectations (Ensink 2003). In picking up on and negatively evaluating Neela's response about team-related strengths, Phil uses the advising frame to provide insights into his goal 'to identify what your strengths really were' (line 1). With this advisory hat on (Goffman 1981), he highlights the association she made between being a good team player and (an easy-to-get-on-with) personality, which reinforces the notion of being a team player as a 'soft' or relational skill. Affiliative alignment is evident in the softening strategies 'sort of like' (line 6), 'like like like' (line 7), 'you know' (line 13) and 'like you know' (line 14) that serve to mitigate the criticisms made by the employer in this advisory frame. His false start (line 9) focusing on the deficit in her answer, or what she 'didn't really talk about' is corrected by a shift back to his own goals to make an implicit contrast with what she did in fact talk about (personality), and the way it signals a lack of technical skills incompatible with 'somebody who's really into engineering' (lines 10–12). This explicit contrast between technical and relational skills implicitly highlights the discrepancy between Neela and Phil in terms of professional identity as novice/expert in the wider community of practice that is engineering (Reissner-Roubicek 2012). It proves ultimately too complex for Neela to successfully negotiate multiple competing identities: the discourse identity or activity role of 'interviewee' juxtaposed with transportable identities of 'student', together with 'novice engineer' and 'girl' (see Reissner-Roubicek 2012), and it seems most problematically, 'team player'. Interdependently, Phil has to manage a whole rack of hats: mentor and advisor, interviewer, male employer in a male-dominated profession, professional engineer and the one he makes most relevant, team leader.

7. Discussion and conclusion

Boundary-monitoring by interviewers in graduate job interviews intensifies in respect of teamwork, whether the context is a typical behavioural question about working in a team, an embedded question about a student's strengths, a simple directive to tell the interviewer about a final-year project, or a question about his or her experience of managing one. Some discursive norms for talking about teamwork can be extrapolated from the unsuccessful answers in the examples above. First, as Mack's intervention underlines, the interviewee should differentiate his or her individual contribution from that of the team. This accords with the values of the new work order as explained by Campbell and Roberts (2007). Although the fact that the interviewee (a high-achieving student from Vietnam) was unable to recognise this as a norm without its being made sufficiently explicit seems at first to offer support for the cultural values hypothesis put forward by Wong and Lai (2000) – that coming from 'collective cultures' explains why engineering students produce inclusive 'we' in referring to team projects – evidence from similar interviews with Anglo-New Zealanders is available to refute their argument (Reissner-Roubicek 2010). Taken together, these cases highlight that the importance of discursive capital, including the ability to recognise inferential frameworks and procedures (Schnurr 2013) and the requirement for context-specific discursive skills (Iedema 2003), applies to novices across the board.

It also relates to the second core criterion: the need to synthesise personal, professional and institutional discourses (Roberts and Sarangi 1999; Roberts 2006; Campbell and Roberts 2007). That is, a teamwork answer needs to invoke hybrid identities by aligning the teller with institutional or corporate values as well as personalising the individual contribution to what is a collective professional activity. Mention of the word 'team' was enough to derail a 'strengths' answer in the case of Neela, where the interviewer's expectations of 'hard' rather than 'soft' skills (and professional, rather than personal, discourses) were not made explicit.

Third, talking about team members in any way other than 'professionally' – in other words, neutrally – is a potential minefield. Noting too how ready interviewers are to infer that teams at university are dysfunctional, by default this kind of talk bears out Adelswärd's (1988) finding that speaking generously of others is one factor bearing positively on success in job interviews. Speaking ungenerously of others can be unwittingly achieved, it seems, in the process of attempting to position oneself favourably.

The data show that interviewee strategies for talking about teamwork in these interviews were both elicited and evaluated with varying degrees of explicitness at different stages by the employers concerned. Mack, in Thanh's interview, moved dynamically from implicit to explicit evaluation whereas Bob and Phil, in Hari's and Neela's interviews respectively, were wholly explicit in the feedback stage, having previously been differently implicit during the interview stage. There is an intriguing relationship between this aspect of the talk and patterns of alignment between interlocutors. Additionally, there are interesting connections between the framing of the talk and associated activity roles. First, we see that interactional alignment does not necessarily signal ideological agreement, confirming Roberts et al.'s (2014) observations. The data illustrate one of the implications of this insight: that affiliative alignment by an interviewer does not necessarily signal a positive evaluation of the interviewee's response, certainly in respect of talking about team members.

In this light, the provision of interactional feedback (response tokens of various kinds) seems to have masked for students any cues that something was wrong with their answers. This lack of cueing that a repair or reformulation is needed aligns with the institutional mandate for fairness in real interviews in that it avoids giving one candidate more help than another. As Roberts and Campbell (2005, 2006) note, institutional requirements are also likely to be tightened for candidates when things go wrong. More generally, the goal of interactional feedback being to show 'active listening' (Holmes et al. 2013), sometimes consciously (Roberts et al. 2014), may lull the candidate into a false sense of security. This can be seen in all three examples in different ways. Interestingly, in the case of Hari it was the affiliative alignment by Bob in expressing his understanding of team members 'not pulling their weight' that did it. Neela, on the other hand, incorrectly inferred the meaning of Phil's embedded question about strengths, but his yes-plus or engaged response tokens contributed to reassure her she was going in the right direction with her answer about teamwork skills. Thanh's alignment at both levels with Mack meant that the abrupt frame-switch caught her unawares. While interviewers are sometimes attending really closely to the requirement to be impartial or to be mentors, at the same time, they are also acting (perhaps inconsistently) as conversational partners.

Strategies for enacting power reflect employers' other activity roles in mock interviews. These entail advising or mentoring. Mack, exceptionally, 'changes hats' (Goffman 1981) back and forth between his interviewer and mentor roles in switching the frame from interviewing to meta-communicative advising and back again, whereas Bob and Phil both maintain the interviewing frame and role until the feedback stage. In both frames and activity roles, the three employers' alignment with interviewees reflects the dynamic construction of power and their identities as expert professionals, co-constructing the students primarily as novices but also, in the case of Mack and Bob, as sometimes more equal than unequal through their expressions of affiliative alignment. However, turning to the feedback stage proper, although they sought to diminish it by mitigating their criticisms with softening 'conversational' or informal language, Bob's and Phil's revelations of their dissatisfaction with Hari's and Neela's answers inherently emphasised the power gap. Interestingly, they both used 'I' to foreground themselves as feeling dissatisfied rather than 'you' to front the students as having erred. This use of first-person singular has been contrasted with invoking the institutional voice in studies of evaluative feedback (e.g. Hyland and Hyland 2006). In the context of these mock interviews the strategy lifts the focus off the mistake-maker and simultaneously elevates the importance of the employers' personal opinions as gatekeepers.

In interpreting the employers' communicative strategies in this way, it is possible to see them as repressing and facilitating at the same time, suggesting these two ways of gatekeeping are not mutually exclusive. In volunteering to conduct mock interviews, employers go on record as trying to help students get 'through the gate', but this can be manifested in repressive gatekeeping, done at what seems to be quite a conscious level in order to fulfil the ultimate goal of being facilitative. It may be seen as facilitative to play a repressive role fully in order to provide a situated, authentic experience for apprenticeship. By virtue of their participation in the study, the IEEE employers sought to reflect on and improve their own interviewing practice as well as contribute to research with a view to helping students. These good intentions have helped expose patterns in graduate recruitment interviews that in part reflect the findings of Roberts and Campbell (2006) in respect of felicitous and infelicitous interviews. They show the likelihood of facilitative gatekeeping in the former and of repressive gatekeeping in the latter. Teamwork in particular invokes heightened gate-keeping behaviours and successful navigation of this boundary is crucial to novices constructing themselves as good team workers in line with competency discourses as these apply to graduate recruitment. They also need to understand that feedback and alignment practices in interviews may be motivated by many things, and may or may not be facilitative: in other words, that normal conversational rules do not in fact apply.

These insights also have important implications for those with an institutional stake in graduate employability, including careers practitioners working in higher education who are tasked with promoting it through professional skills training. Trainers and policy makers should reflect particularly on the evidence afforded by the discourse-analytic approach that the transition from university to the workplace is enacted linguistically, and can reveal how interlocutors co-construct and redefine their personal, social and professional identities dynamically through talk. Mock interviews provide a very specific window on employers as boundary-monitors that real interviews cannot offer – which the paired examples from the interview feedback stage underline. From an interactional perspective, these examples of boundary monitoring offer rich insights into the co-constructed nature of interviews and the interplay of multiple relevant identities for both interviewers and interviewees. What makes mock interviews with employers unique as a boundary-crossing event, however, is the underlying conflict and tension between the goals of facilitative and repressive gatekeeping, and unexpected twists and turns in the enactment of power so often triggered by the discourses surrounding teamwork.

Transcription conventions

.	downward intonation
,	rising intonation
?	high-rising intonation
He said *look here we're in a mess*	italics = direct speech being quoted
STRESSful	capital letters = heavily stressed syllable(s)
<u>probably</u> I can	underlined word = emphatic stress
::	elongated sounds
/	phrase unit boundary
(.)	pause of between half and a whole second
=	latching
wor-	broken-off word
[overlap	interrupted or overlapping speech starts
xxxx	indistinguishable word
((laughing))	paralinguistic feature

Notes

1. Those investigating job interviews as gatekeeping events through a sociolinguistic lens have regularly focused on the additional barrier faced by minority and born-abroad candidates (most recently, Kirilova 2013; Kuśmiercyk 2013). These studies have also typically focused on more experienced workers (Roberts and Sayers 1987; Roberts and Sarangi 1999; Kerekes 2006, 2007; Roberts and Campbell 2005, 2006). The results generally align with Sarangi's (1994: 187) finding that 'interviewees from minority groups, with some experience in a target culture, are as capable as native interviewees of providing "preferred" responses to the interviewer's indirect questions'.

2. The 'real' event was any interview for the hospitality industry that they might be called to in the future. Note that the questions asked by teachers playing interviewers were not behavioural questions, in other words this is not a structured, competency-based interview like a graduate interview. Such a forum style event

is similar to the way mock interviews with visiting employers were conducted at a Singapore faculty of engineering in Wong and Lai's (2000) study, and also how one employer elected to deliver a group training session in the present research context.
3. The mock interviews were conducted in several large rooms, usually four to a room, in the corners, which meant that the pairs of employers and students were far enough apart for a clear recording of any particular interaction to be collected. This also explains how the incident from the previous year described by Hari, among others, could have had any witnesses and of course why the interviewer might stand on a chair to make his pronouncement.
4. In fact, reflecting the superdiversity of university populations in cities such as Auckland, where the present study was located, many of the student participants in this study were minority/migrant but had also gained what Sarangi (1994) calls 'some experience in a target culture' through New Zealand higher education. This included working in project teams for academic credit. In terms of identities, however, all the students were novices in the professional sense, as they lacked familiarity with competency discourses and activity-specific norms. This, however, was because they were students on the threshold of professional work rather than because they are culturally different (Reissner-Roubicek 2010).

References

Adams, S. (2013), 'The 10 skills employers most want in 20-something employees', *Forbes*, 11 October, <http://www.forbes.com/sites/susanadams/2013/10/11/the-10-skills-employers-most-want-in-20-something-employees/> (last accessed 11 November 2016).

Adams, S. (2014), 'The 10 skills employers most want in 2015 graduates', *Forbes*, 12 November, <http://www.forbes.com/sites/susanadams/2014/11/12/the-10-skills-employers-most-want-in-2015-graduates/> (last accessed 11 November 2016).

Adelswärd, V. (1988), *Styles of success: on impression management as collaborative action in job interviews*, Linköping: Linköping University.

Akinnaso, F. N. and C. S. Ajirotutu (1982), 'Performance and ethnic style in job interviews', in J. Gumperz (ed.), *Language and social identity*, Cambridge: Cambridge University Press, pp. 119–44.

Archer, W. and J. Davison (2008), *Graduate employability: what do employers think and want?*, London: Council for Industry and Higher Education.

Boltanski, L. and E. Chiapello (2007), *The new spirit of capitalism*, London and New York: Verso.

Button, G. (1992), 'Answers as interactional products: two sequential practices used in job interviews', in P. Drew and J. Heritage (eds), *Talk at work: interaction in institutional settings*, Cambridge: Cambridge University Press, pp. 212–31.

Campbell, S. and C. Roberts (2007), 'Migration, ethnicity and competing discourses in the job interview: synthesizing the institutional and personal', *Discourse & Society*, 18: 5, pp. 243–71.

Careers NZ (2012), 'Skills employers are looking for', <http://www.careers.govt.nz/plan-your-career/not-sure-what-to-do/skills-employers-are-looking-for/#cID_115/> (last accessed 11 November 2016).

Cole, D. and M. Tibby (2013), *Defining and developing your approach to employability: a framework for higher education institutions*, York: Higher Education Academy.

Cornelissen, J. P. and M. D. Werner (2014), 'Putting framing in perspective: a review of framing and frame analysis across the management and organizational literature', *The Academy of Management Annals*, 8: 1, pp. 181–235.

De Fina, A. (2003), *Identity in narrative: a study of immigrant discourse*, Amsterdam: John Benjamins.

Diamond, A., L. Walkley, P. Forbes, T. Hughes and J. Sheen (2011), *Global graduates into global leaders*, Report commissioned by the Association of Graduate Recruiters (AGR), Council for Further Education (CFE) and Council for Industry and Higher Education (CIHE), London: National Centre for Universities and Business.

Ensink, T. (2003), 'Transformational frames: interpretive consequences of frame shifts and frame embeddings', in T. Ensink and C. Sauer (eds), *Framing and perspectivising in discourse*, Amsterdam: John Benjamins, pp. 63–90.

Erickson, F. and J. J. Schultz (1982), *The counselor as gatekeeper: social interaction in interviews*, New York: Academic Press.

Fugate, M., A. J. Kinicki and B. E. Ashforth (2004), 'Employability: a psycho-social construct, its dimensions, and applications', *Journal of Vocational Behaviour*, 65, pp. 14–38.

Gee, J. P., G. A. Hull and C. Lankshear (1996), *The new work order: behind the language of the new capitalism*, St Leonards, NSW: Allen & Unwin.

Goffman, E. (1981), *Forms of talk*, Philadelphia: University of Pennsylvania Press.

Gray, K. and A. Koncz (2014), 'The skills/qualities employers want in new college graduate hires', National Association of Colleges and Employers (NACE), 18 November, <http://www.naceweb.org/about-us/press/class-2015-skills-qualities-employers-want.aspx> (last accessed 11 November 2016).

He, A. W. (1995), 'Co-constructing institutional identities: the case of student counselees', *Research on Language and Social Interaction*, 28: 3, pp. 213–31.

Heritage, J. (1984), *Garfinkel and ethnomethodology*, Cambridge: Polity Press.

Hinchliffe, G. and A. Jolly (2011), 'Graduate identity and employability', *British Educational Research Journal*, 37: 4, pp. 563–84.

Holmes, J. (2007), 'Monitoring organisational boundaries: diverse discourse strategies used in gatekeeping', *Journal of Pragmatics*, 39, pp. 1993–2016.

Holmes, J., S. Marsden and M. Marra (2013), 'Doing listenership: one aspect of socio-pragmatic competence at work', *Pragmatics and Society*, 4: 1, pp. 26–53.

Holmes, L. (2013), 'Competing perspectives on graduate employability: possession, position or process', *Studies in Higher Education*, 38: 4, pp. 538–54.

Hyland, K. and F. Hyland (2006), *Feedback in second language writing: contexts and issues*, Cambridge and New York: Cambridge University Press.

Iedema, R. (2003), *Discourses of post-bureaucratic organization*, Amsterdam and Philadelphia: John Benjamins.

Jacoby, S. and E. Ochs (1995), 'Co-construction: an introduction', *Research on Language and Social Interaction*, 28: 3, pp. 171–83.

Kerekes, J. A. (2006), 'Winning an interviewer's trust in a gatekeeping encounter', *Language in Society*, 35, pp. 27–57.

Kerekes, J. A. (2007), 'The co-construction of a gatekeeping encounter: an inventory of verbal actions', *Journal of Pragmatics*, 39: 11, pp. 1942–73.

Kirilova, M. K. (2013), 'All dressed up and nowhere to go: linguistic, cultural and ideological aspects of job interviews with second language speakers of Danish', doctoral dissertation, University of Copenhagen Faculty of Humanities.

Knight, D. and S. Adolphs (2008), 'Multi-modal corpus pragmatics: the case of active listenership', in J. Romero-Trillo (ed.), *Pragmatics and corpus linguistics: a mutualistic entente*, Berlin: Mouton de Gruyter, pp. 175–90.

Kuśmierczyk, E. (2013), '"The only problem is finding a job": multimodal analysis of job interviews in New Zealand', PhD thesis, Victoria University of Wellington.

Levinson, S. C. (1979), 'Activity types and language', *Linguistics*, 17, pp. 365–99.

Lowden, K., S. Hall, D. Elliot and J. Lewin (2011), *Employers' perceptions of the employability skills of new graduates*, London: Edge Foundation.

Lyster, R. and L. Ranta (1997), 'Corrective feedback and learner uptake', *Studies in Second Language Acquisition*, 19: 1, pp. 37–66.

McCarthy, M. (2003), 'Talking back: "small" interactional response tokens in everyday conversation', *Research on Language in Social Interaction*, 36: 1, pp. 33–63.

Norrick, N. R. (2009), 'Interjections as pragmatic markers', *Journal of Pragmatics*, 41: 5, pp. 866–91.

Norrick, N. R. (2010), 'Listening practices in television celebrity interviews', *Journal of Pragmatics*, 42: 2, pp. 525–43.

Norrick, N. R. (2012), 'Listening practices in English conversation: the responses responses elicit', *Journal of Pragmatics*, 44: 5, pp. 566–76.

O'Keeffe, A. and S. Adolphs (2008), 'Response tokens in British and Irish discourse: corpus, context and variational pragmatics', in K. Schneider and A. Barron (eds), *Variational pragmatics: a focus on regional varieties in pluricentric languages*, Amsterdam: John Benjamins, pp. 69–98.

Reissner-Roubicek, S. (2010), 'Communication strategies in the behavioural job interview: the influence of discourse norms on graduate recruitment', unpublished PhD thesis, University of Auckland.

Reissner-Roubicek, S. (2012), '"The guys would like to have a lady": the co-construction of gender and professional identity in interviews between employers and female engineering students', in D. Van de Mieroop and J. Clifton (eds), *The interplay between professional identities and age, gender and ethnicity*, Special issue of *Pragmatics*, 22: 2, pp. 231–54.

Roberts, C. (1985), *The interview game and how it's played*, London: British Broadcasting Corporation.

Roberts, C., and S. Campbell (2005), 'Fitting stories into boxes: rhetorical and textual constraints on candidates' performances in British job interviews', *Journal of Applied Linguistics*, 2: 1, pp. 45–73.

Roberts, C. and S. Campbell (2006), *Talk on trial: job interviews, language and ethnicity*, Department for Work and Pensions Research Report no. 344, Leeds: Corporate Document Services, <http://webarchive.nationalarchives.gov. uk/20130314010347/http://research.dwp.gov.uk/asd/asd5/rports2005-2006/ rrep344.pdf> (last accessed 8 November 2016).

Roberts, C. and S. Sarangi (1999), 'Hybridity in gatekeeping discourse: issues of practical relevance for the researcher', in S. Sarangi and C. Roberts (eds), *Talk, work and institutional order: discourse in medical, mediation and management settings*, Berlin: Mouton de Gruyter, pp. 473–503.

Roberts, C. and P. Sayers (1987), 'Keeping the gate: how judgements are made in interethnic interviews', in K. Knapp, W. Enninger and A. Knapp-Potthoff (eds), *Analyzing intercultural communication*, Berlin, New York and Amsterdam: Mouton de Gruyter, pp. 111–35.

Roberts C., S. Atkins and K. Hawthorne (2014), *Performance features in clinical skills assessment: linguistic and cultural factors in the Membership of the Royal College of General Practitioners examination*, London: Centre for Language, Discourse and Communication, King's College London with the University of Nottingham.

Sarangi, S. (1994), 'Accounting for mismatches in intercultural selection interviews', *Multilingua*, 13: 1/2, pp. 163–94.

Sarangi, S. (2005), 'Social interaction, social theory and work-related activities', *Calidoscópio*, 3: 3, pp. 160–9.

Sarangi, S. (2010), 'Healthcare interaction as an expert communicative system', in J. Streeck (ed.), *New adventures in language and interaction*, vol. 196, Amsterdam: John Benjamins, pp. 167–98.

Schiffrin, D. (1994), *Approaches to discourse*, Oxford: Blackwell.

Schnurr, S. (2013), *Exploring professional communication: language in action*, London: Routledge.

Sniad, T. (2007), '"It's not necessarily the words you say . . . it's your presentation": teaching the interactional text of the job interview', *Journal of Pragmatics*, 39: 11, pp. 1974–92.

Tannen, D. and C. Wallat (1993), 'Interactive frames and knowledge schemas in interaction: examples from a medical examination/interview', in D. Tannen (ed.), *Framing in discourse*, Oxford: Oxford University Press, pp. 57–76.

TARGETjobs (n.d.), 'Teamwork skills', <http://targetjobs.co.uk/careers-advice/ skills-and-competencies/300764-teamwork-its-high-on-the-graduate-recruiters- wishlist/> (last accessed 8 November 2016).

Tranekjær, L. (2015), *Interactional categorization and gatekeeping: institutional encounters with otherness*, vol. 4, Bristol: Multilingual Matters.

Vic Careers (n.d.) *Employability skills survey*, Victoria University of Wellington, <http://www.victoria.ac.nz/st_services/careers/resources/employment_skills_ survey.aspx/> (last accessed 8 November 2016).

Wong, I. F. H. and P.-C. Lai (2000), 'Chinese cultural values and performance at job interviews: a Singapore perspective', *Business Communication Quarterly*, 63: 1, pp. 9–22.

Yate, M. J. (2008), *Great answers to tough interview questions*, 7th edn, London: Kogan
   Page.
Yate, M. J. (2015), *Ultimate CV: over 100 winning CVs to help you get the interview and
   the job*, 4th edn, London: Kogan Page.

5

'Doing Evaluation' in the Modern Workplace: Negotiating the Identity of 'Model Employee' in Performance Appraisal Interviews

Dorien Van De Mieroop and Stephanie Schnurr

1. Introduction

Developments and transitions have characterised modern-day organisations ever since the historic shift from the industrial worker to the knowledge worker has put increasing emphasis on employees' skills and knowledge.[1] This process has been referred to as the 'new work order' (Gee et al. 1996) and is characterised by several diverse tendencies. One of these tendencies is 'the dispersal of centralised authority and hegemony' (Gee et al. 1996: xiii), which implies that 'top-down hierarchies are replaced by "flat" allegedly egalitarian systems' (Angouri 2013: 577). In these 'flat' hierarchical systems, workers 'are expected to share the vision of the employer they work for' while also orienting to 'a set of core values – for example, equality, trust, collaboration, quality' (Sarangi 2005: 163). These transitions to seemingly flatter organisational structures (Geis et al. 1990) have also led to changes in management approaches. These have been increasingly oriented to the egalitarian ideal of the new work order and have put more and more emphasis on empowering rather than directing employees. This worker empowerment 'thus amounts to taking full responsibility and remaining accountable for what they [the employees] do (not) achieve' (Sarangi 2005: 163). So, employees are made responsible for 'motivating, disciplining and directing themselves' (Cameron 2000: 14). Many organisational practices, such as problem solving, and standardising procedures which were traditionally the responsibilities of individuals in senior positions are often redefined in the modern workplace as the collective responsibility of the team, thus illustrating the shift 'from top-down/bottom-up to the level of the team' (Angouri 2013: 577).

In turn, such a transition towards more participatory approaches has had profound effects on the professional identities of employees, that is, the ways in which they perceive themselves, and their roles and responsibilities in the wider context of their workplace (see Fairclough 1992). For example, in a study of a gaming machine factory and a teaching hospital, Iedema and Scheeres (2003) observed how structural changes in these workplaces led to challenges for the staff in conceptualising their (new) roles and constructing their (new) professional identities. In order to reflect the structural changes of their workplaces, members on all levels of the organisational hierarchy had to rethink their roles and responsibilities within the organisation, which also affected the status and privilege associated with certain roles.

However, these ideologies underlying current trends towards flatter organisational structures may sometimes contradict each other. While organisations may on the one hand propagate their employees' empowerment, on the other hand, they may also impose the company's vision and values upon them and hold them accountable when they fail to act and perform accordingly. These tensions between 'institutional and professional modes' relating to these new work order ideologies may 'have a societal basis', but they are 'routinely experienced at the interactional level' (Sarangi 2005: 163; see also Sarangi and Roberts 1999). So even though companies may propagate egalitarianism at a macro level, this is not necessarily true at a micro level. Holmes et al. (2011: 30–1) give an example of the reverse situation in which, in some organisations that seem to have a strict hierarchical structure 'identifiable in static measures with formal, organisational charts [. . .], these power asymmetries were less observable in the interactional practices of these organisations', in which 'egalitarianism [. . .] imbued their regular operations'. Hence, in line with these discursive approaches, we propose to explore some of the effects of organisations' structural transitions by scrutinising how these are – or *are not* – talked into being on the micro interactional level.

In this chapter we particularly zoom in on the organisational activity of performance appraisal. This is 'a general heading for a variety of activities through which organizations seek to assess employees and develop their competence, enhance performance and distribute rewards' (Fletcher 2001: 473). This may take the form of 'a line manager completing an annual report on a subordinate's performance' (Fletcher 2001: 473), but, due to new work order organisational changes, the use of such 'conventional top-down appraisal systems' has become 'more difficult' (Fletcher 2001: 480). This subsequently has given rise to a new 'genre', in which 'the goal of assessing an employee's performance is realized using interactive conventions that resemble those of a therapy or counselling session' (Cameron 2000: 15). As such, employees are given a voice in their own evaluation process and this approach thus orients to the egalitarian ideals of the new work order. In short, we define this genre of performance appraisal interviews as 'recurrent strategic interviews between a superior in an organization and an employee that focus on employee performance and development' (Asmuß 2008: 409). These interviews thus take place between an interviewer who represents the institution and who usually acts as a gatekeeper (Van De Mieroop and Schnurr 2014) and an interviewee who is a member of the same institution.

Moreover, these interviews at the same time contribute to creating and maintaining a specific institutional reality (see Van De Mieroop and Schnurr 2014). In other words, they more or less explicitly refer to specific institutional norms and practices thereby actively creating or talking into being – the potential changes in – the institution itself and what it means to be a 'good' member, thus making them crucial sites for identity construction. In particular, both interlocutors engage in the conjoint construction of their professional and institutional identities, not only in relation to each other, but also to the wider institutional context in which the interaction takes place.

Furthermore, since differing perceptions of employees' roles in the modern workplace typically surface during such interactions, identities are often explicitly negotiated between interlocutors. It is thus perhaps not surprising that performance appraisal interviews have also been referred to as 'a case of institutionalized identity work' (Adelswärd and Nilholm 2000: 548).

Importantly though, due to their evaluative nature, performance appraisal interviews are potentially face-threatening encounters that may actually contradict some of the ideologies underlying current trends towards flatter organisational structures. This is particularly true for instances of negative assessment, that is, those sequences in which the interviewers criticise the interviewees for a particular aspect of their performance (e.g. where the interviewees may not have met a particular target or where they do not adhere to institutional practices and procedures). In these potentially face-threatening sequences, on the one hand, employees engage in identity work as they have to position themselves in relation to the negative assessment or criticism by justifying and defending their identities as a particular kind of professional and as a valuable member of the institution. On the other hand, supervisors tend to voice these negative assessments in a careful way in order to prevent too much damage to the working relationship with the employees, as previous research from a conversation analytic perspective has demonstrated (Asmuß 2008; Clifton 2012). This is particularly understandable from the perspective of new work order ideologies orienting to ideals of egalitarianism, in which top-down evaluations and assessments of employees' behaviour often become increasingly unacceptable. These complexities make negative assessments a particularly interesting research topic for the discursive analysis of transitions in the modern workplace.

2. Identity and face

In this chapter we take a social constructionist stance and view identities as being conjointly constructed, enacted and negotiated among interlocutors as an interaction unfolds (see Jenkins 1996; Hall et al. 1999; Holmes et al. 1999; Postmes 2003). Thus, rather than understanding identity as something that people *are*, we conceptualise identity as something that people actively and conjointly *do* (Butler 1990; Widdicombe 1998: 191). Moreover, identities are relational phenomena that 'emerge only in relation to other identities' (Bucholtz and Hall 2005: 605; see also Hall et al. 1999). However, this conjoint construction of identities does not necessarily have to take place in harmony, and interlocutors may, of course, resist, challenge and undermine each other's attempts at portraying themselves and others in certain ways (Hall 2000: 17; see also Lytra 2009; Schnurr and Zayts 2011).

One of the processes through which identity construction takes place is face work (e.g. Hall 2000; Schnurr and Chan 2011). Although there exists a controversy among researchers as to what exactly 'face' means and what kinds of phenomena should fall under this term (Haugh and Hinze 2003: 1582), like most recent theorisations we build our understanding of face on Goffman's seminal definition of face as 'the positive social value a person effectively claims for himself [sic] by the line others assume he [sic] has taken during a particular contact' (Goffman 1967: 5).

Adapting this definition of face, Geyer (2008: 50) illustrates the link between face and identity by explaining that 'an interactant's face manifests itself as his or her interactional self-image, which is determined in relation to others, discursively constructed during a particular contact, and closely aligned with the participant's discursive identity'.

Given this relatively close relationship, it is perhaps not surprising that the concepts of identity and face have received a lot of attention (e.g. Locher 2008; Haugh 2009). And yet, the intricate ways in which they interact with each other are still relatively under-researched. Several researchers have pointed to similarities between the notions of identity and face. For example, Tracy (1990: 210) claims that 'face references the socially situated identities people claim or attribute to others' and Locher (2008: 515) proposes that 'the notion of face can stand for identity construction in more general terms'. Although it seems that there are certain cognitive similarities between the notions of face and identity (see Spencer-Oatey 2007: 644 for further discussion), this tendency to conceptualise face as a 'concern for identity' is problematic as it 'raises the question of how such research on face can be distinguished in a meaningful way from broader work on identity' (Haugh 2009: 3). Thus, in spite of some similarities between these concepts, we treat them as separate albeit related analytical constructs in our analysis below. Although the processes of doing face work and constructing identities are closely intertwined, they are not identical. Rather, as we have shown in our earlier work on co-leadership (Schnurr and Chan 2011), throughout an interaction interlocutors actively and dynamically construct and negotiate their own and each other's professional identities (which are, of course, closely interrelated) by orienting to their own and each other's face needs. In this sense, through doing face work and orienting to each other's face needs, interlocutors at the same time position themselves in relation to each other and do identity work.

3. Data and approach

Our analysis of negative assessments in performance appraisal interviews is based on five excerpts that were selected from a larger corpus of authentic spoken institutional interactions in Dutch, which contains, among other data types, ten performance appraisal interviews. The excerpts under discussion here come from performance appraisal interviews recorded in a Belgian medical laboratory. At this workplace, performance appraisal interviews are carried out annually. We particularly zoom in on two interviews because they each contain interesting negative assessment sequences. The interviews that we analyse here were conducted by the same interviewer, who is the head of one of the segments of the laboratory, and they each last for an hour or slightly more, so they are fairly similar in these respects. Both interviewees are relatively senior in the lab and they are also at the same hierarchical level as the interviewer, namely that of 'analyst one'. This means that even though all employees of the lab are trained chemical analysts, they have different hierarchical positions in the lab, namely either level 3, level 2 or level 1 analysts, representing respectively the lower, middle and upper category of the staff. The level 1 analysts (or 'analysts one') have additional managerial and administrative tasks and they are also responsible for a segment of the lab. The interviewer is also on this level, but she at the same time coordinates the entire lab.

While the interviewer and interviewee 1 are both in their forties, interviewee 2 will retire the following year. The latter makes this fact explicitly relevant a couple of times in the course of the interview, as discussed below. The topical discussion of both interviews is guided by a general questionnaire, which is based on the organisation's four main competencies (e.g. self-development and customer-orientedness), which are further divided into twenty-three sub-competencies (e.g. creativity, flexibility and patients' issues). The questionnaire is sent to all employees prior to the interview, who prepare their answers and send them back to the supervisor before the interview takes place (for a more detailed discussion, see Van De Mieroop and Vrolix 2014). Afterwards, the supervisor writes a report on the basis of the interview and this report is then sent back to the employees who can request amendments. Complementary to these data, an ethnographic interview was carried out with the interviewer. Insights gained from this ethnographic interview were used as background information that enhanced our in-depth understanding of the data.

In order to explore how interlocutors *do evaluation* in performance appraisal interviews, we take a discourse analytical approach to the data, as for example described by Holmes et al. (2011). This approach is strongly embedded in a social construction-ist view on the world, which 'frames communication as a process that is instrumental in the creation of our social worlds, rather than simply an activity that we do within them' (Holmes et al. 2011: 21). In practice, this means that for the analyses, we draw on contextual information – obtained through ethnographic interviews – as well as on micro-level analytic techniques to scrutinise the local interactional negotiation of meaning. In our case, the sequential characteristics and the 'association between an action's preference status and the turn shape in which it is produced' (Pomerantz 1984: 64) are of especial interest. Furthermore, we aim to integrate the three levels of analysis identified by De Fina (2003), namely the lexical, textual/pragmatic and inter-actional levels, to demonstrate the many ways in which identities are constructed and negotiated in relation to face work in the interactions under study. Finally, we under-take our analyses from a critical perspective, as we pay attention to the particular ten-sions that may arise due to the new work order ideals of egalitarianism and employee empowerment as discussed above.

4. Doing evaluation by constructing identities through face work

The two interviews we have chosen for closer scrutiny here are particularly interest-ing for our research question since the two interviewees differ considerably in their career plans, which they both express explicitly in their interviews. While interviewee 1 expresses her ambition to move further up the hierarchical ladder in the lab, inter-viewee 2 has no ambitions and explicitly stresses his upcoming retirement during the performance appraisal interview. We will now look into the way negative assessments are initiated by the interviewer in the interviews, and how these are discursively negotiated amongst the interlocutors in both interviews.

4.1 Interview 1

In the excerpts discussed in this subsection, the ambitious employee is being criticised for sending and receiving personal emails and text messages during her work hours. This topic is initiated in excerpt 1.1.

Excerpt 1.1 Interview 1, interviewee's pseudonym: Karen, interviewee's partner's pseudonym: Tim[2]

```
1   IR:    I wro:te down
2          'I am very pleased with your dedication.'
3   (0.7)
4   IR:    E:::::rm (.) 'I do sometimes have the ↑impression' (.)
5          ((deliberate cough))
6          a a £critical remark£=
7   IE:    =( [ )
8   IR:       ['that Karen during her job is also regularly
9          mailing and texting with her boyfriend Tim
10         or with other family members'=
11  IE:    =no text[ing.
12  IR:            ['Mind
13         your exemplary role in this.'
14  IE:    >I have to say< texting in any case not
```

The topic of sending and receiving personal messages is brought up by the interviewer in a mitigated and thus relatively face-saving way, who initiates it by reading out her notes. This is indicated by the explicit anticipatory framing (line 1), the shift to a reading voice (as reflected in the transcription by means of quotation marks in lines 2, 4, 8–10, 12–13) and the reference to the interviewee by means of her first name (line 8) instead of directly addressing her, for example by means of the second person singular pronoun. The interviewer first voices a very positive general evaluation of the interviewee (line 2). Then the pauses (lines 3, 4), lengthy hesitation (line 4), deliberate cough (line 5) and the 'smile voice' (Buttny 2001) in which the anticipatory framing of the upcoming talk as 'a critical remark' (line 6) is uttered, all function as postponing and softening devices. These give the utterance a dispreferred turn shape, and, together with the downplaying formulation of the introductory part of the criticism (line 4), they mitigate the potential face threat of the critical remark, which, in turn, is voiced in a rather direct and quite specific way (by naming addressees of the emails in lines 9–10).

The interviewee immediately latches on a response refuting one part of the criticism (line 11) thereby defending her own (and possibly threatening the interviewer's) face, but this is overlapped by the interviewer who continues to read out the final part of the negative assessment in her notes, as the reading voice clearly indicates. This is formulated as an imperative, as the verb form and the second person singular pronominal form directly addressing the interviewee demonstrate ('Mind your exemplary role in this', lines 12–13). The latter phrase proves to be very important in the course of this, as well as the next, interaction, and it is a translation of the Dutch *Let op je voorbeeldfunctie in deze*, in which the verb can be translated as 'mind' in the meaning of 'pay attention to'. Interestingly, this final part of the negative assessment links the criticism directly to the interviewee's professional identity as a model employee ('exemplary role', line 13), which is projected upon her by the interviewer. This role of the model employee can be related to the interviewee's position as an 'analyst one', who is thus in charge of a section of the lab and is responsible for her team of level 2 and 3 analysts, whom – this identity projection of the model employee suggests – she is thus supposed to 'lead by example'. Also, this concept of the 'model employee' reflects the new work order view on employees as sharing and incorporating the vision of their employer and the company's core values (Sarangi 2005: 163), so that they all *exemplify* the organisation.

The relation between the negative assessment and this particular identity projection will be developed further in the interaction as we discuss in more detail below, but first the interviewee repeats her rebuttal of part of the criticism (line 14) – thereby saving her own face – and in the lines following this fragment (lines 15–31) she starts listing the text messages and calls she regularly receives and accounts for them. Through this justification she tries to save her own face and at the same time she attempts to portray herself as a 'good' employee whose practices are in line with institutional rules regarding sending and receiving personal text messages and emails at work. These rules are not made explicit at this point, but from the rest of the interaction, we can deduce that there is an implicit agreement that a limited amount of personal communication is allowed as long as the 'job does not suffer from it' (line 38) and as long as employees do not frequently send text messages (discussed mainly in excerpts that are not shown here).

In excerpt 1.2, we see how the interviewer responds to this justification by the interviewee.

Excerpt 1.2 Interview 1

32	IR:	Sometimes it also strikes me that you
33		>when you then go you quickly close something or so<
34		and then I think '↑Hmmm'
35		but then I think 'Yes, is that important ↑now'=
36	IE:	=↓No::.=
37	IR:	=In itself I think it is not important
38		>because your job does not suffer from it< (.) •h
39	IE:	°°mm°°=
40	IR:	=but you have an exemplary ↓ro[le
41	IE:	[Yes no
42		bu[t
43	IR:	[so just mind that [as well.
44	IE:	[I send I send
45		indeed from time to time once a mail

Excerpt 1.2 starts with the interviewer's description of the interviewee's inappropriate behaviour, and more specifically that she closes certain documents on the

computer (presumably emails) when the interviewer walks in (line 33). Although this accusation is quite implicitly formulated (line 33) and the frequency of this behaviour is hedged from the start ('sometimes', line 32), this criticism is nevertheless potentially face-threatening to the interviewee. It is framed by the interviewer as something that 'strikes' her (line 32, original: *soms valt mich det ook op*) and that is a cause for reflection in this institutional context. This is shown by the enactment of the 'constructed dialogue' (Tannen 1989) reporting on the thoughts of the interviewer in lines 34–5. The last quote contains a question, to which first the interviewee (line 36) and then the interviewer respond negatively (line 37). The latter then accounts for this negative answer in the subsequent line (line 38). But as both the initial limiting frame 'in itself' (line 37), which already sets up the potential for a contrastive follow-up statement, and the final audible in-breath (line 38) indicate, this is not the end of the interviewer's turn. By means of a very silently voiced continuer (line 39), the interviewee then displays an orientation to the second part of the interviewer's turn. This is latched on by the interviewer, who immediately frames it as contrasting to the previously attributed lack of importance (line 37) by means of the conjunction 'but' (line 40).

In the following turns the interviewer engages in explicit identity work: she again attributes the identity of an exemplary employee to the interviewee and uses it as an important reason for the criticism. In other words, portraying the interviewee as 'exemplary' is an ambiguous move as it not only attends to and strengthens the interviewee's face by constructing a positive professional identity for her, but it also at the same time threatens the interviewee's face – by highlighting her failure to achieve this 'model identity' – and challenges the interviewee's professional identity to some extent by reminding her of the obligations that this 'exemplary role' brings with it. So the interviewer emphasises that the interviewee's relatively independent status as an employee – typical of her hierarchical position as a level 1 analyst, but also of the general empowerment of new work order employees – also implies a number of responsibilities, to which she appeals in lines 40 and 43. The second part (line 43) is formulated in competition with the partially overlapping bid for the floor by the interviewee (lines 41–2). The formulation of this reason clearly echoes the previously read out notes from excerpt 1.1 ('mind your exemplary role', lines 12–13).

The interviewee responds to this by admitting that she sends an email 'from time to time' (line 45), hence emphasising the small number and frequency of this forbidden activity. This is agreed to by the interviewer who stresses her initial and frequent use of the hedge 'sometimes' when formulating this criticism. The discussion then moves to the fact that the interviewee keeps her mobile phone with her in the workplace. The latter accounts for this by stressing that she does not use it but only keeps it with her for her sense of safety. The interviewer expresses her understanding of this, thus showing that the rules about keeping a mobile phone with oneself in the workplace constitute a bit of a grey area, but she then contrasts it with the behaviour of other employees, as can be seen in line 84 in excerpt 1.3.

Excerpt 1.3 Interview 1
84   IR: But (.) <others> take it with them
85   for other reasons=

```
 86  IE:    =Ye[s
 87  IR:        [and you are nevertheless an analyst one
 88         who is looked at just like
 89         I am looked at as as as unit mana[ger
 90  IE:                                      [m[m
 91  IR:                                         [and our
 92         (1.0)
 93  IR:    e::::rm (.) be↑haviour (.)
 94         and w and and what we say
 95         is also put on bigger [scales
 96  IE:                          [°yes yes right°
 97  IR:    than of others
 98  IE:    °°ye[s°°
 99  IR:        [So just simply MIND tha[t
100  IE:                                [yes=
101  IR:    =that you have an exemplary role in this.
102  IE:    mm
```

Using the conjunction 'but' (line 84), the interviewer again sets up a contrast. This is further emphasised by means of the immediately following pause and the markedly slower pronunciation of the word 'others', which is, in turn, stressed further by the use of the mirroring adjective 'other' in line 85. By referring to 'others', the interviewer constructs different (opposing) subject positions for the interviewee on the one hand, and other institutional members on the other. This kind of identity work becomes more explicit a few lines later when she constructs the interviewee's professional identity by categorising her as 'an analyst one' (line 87) and the indefinite article in this phrase, 'produces the category as something with known-in-common meanings' (Stokoe 2009: 77). By using the contrasting adverb 'nevertheless' (*toch* in Dutch, line 87) the interviewer continues to contrast the interviewee with 'other' institutional members. The interviewer then draws a comparison between the interviewee and herself by describing the ways in which she is regarded in her function (lines 88–9). By stressing the resemblance between the interviewee and herself by means of the booster 'just' (line 88) in collocation with 'like', the interviewer orients to the interviewee's face, constructs her own identity as colleague, and also sets up an in-group between them. In particular, from line 91 onwards, this in-group between herself and the interviewee is created, as marked by the use of the first person plural pronominal form ('our', line 91; 'we', line 94) and by referring to shared experiences (e.g. how they are both regarded more critically because of their professional roles). She contrasts that again with the way 'others' (line 97) are regarded, thus setting up an 'us versus them' dichotomy between herself and the interviewee on the one hand, and other employees on the other hand.

From line 96 onwards, the interviewee expresses her agreement with this (lines 96, 98, 100), and the interviewer then closes the topic by another appeal to the interviewee's projected identity as 'model employee' (lines 99, 101). This appeal is an almost verbatim repetition of her initial formulation, which was read out loud from her notes, and this is especially marked because of the repetition of *in deze* (translated as 'in this', line 13, excerpt 1.1 and line 101 in excerpt 1.3), which is a typical feature of written language in Dutch rather than spontaneous oral discourse. The discussion of this topic comes to an end when the interviewee expresses an acknowledgement in the final line of the excerpt. After this excerpt, the interviewer closes the topic by explicitly stating that she is making adjustments to her notes regarding the fact that texting is not an issue, by which it is implied that the issue of sending personal emails remains in the interviewee's file (subsequent to this excerpt).

The excerpts from this interview nicely illustrate some of the complexities of the relationship between face and identity on the one hand, and identity negotiations against the backdrop of changing institutional values and norms on the other. In particular, as our analyses have shown, it is striking that the ways in which the interviewer formulates a negative assessment of the interviewee are so strongly – and almost immediately – related to the institutional expectations of a 'good' employee, as voiced in the identity projection of the 'exemplary'/'model' employee. Interestingly, the interviewer exploits the identity of a 'model employee' here as a justification of her criticism and as a means to construct an in-group with the interviewee, as such demonstrating the general applicability of these institutional expectations for all employees of the same 'analyst one' category (as opposed to employees of a different category; see excerpt 1.3). This in-group construction between the interviewer and the interviewee, as well as the appeal to the employee's responsibilities in this particular institutional role, are quite emblematic for the tensions typical of new work order workplaces, in which evaluators on the one hand align with evaluees rather than exploit their hierarchically higher position as could be expected in more traditional, hierarchically structured workplaces, while on the other hand still holding them accountable for their behaviour and registering this negative evaluation in their file (as made explicit by the interviewer after excerpt 1.3) even though the interviewee's 'job does not suffer from it' (line 38). Finally, as we have shown, this identity of the model employee performs ambiguous functions in this context as it not only provides the (alleged) reason for the criticism but at the same time also functions as a mitigation mechanism which potentially minimises the threat of the criticism on the interviewee's face, thus showing the interviewer's orientation to 'doing evaluation' as a problematic activity.

In this interview, the identity projection of model employee upon the interviewee is quite successful, which may be related to the interviewee's professional ambitions which require an almost spotless record. This is quite different in the case of interview 2, in which the interviewee is about to retire and has explicitly stated his lack of interest in being evaluated. We discuss this performance appraisal interview in the next section, in which we show how the interviewee rejects the identity of model employee – which is potentially threatening his own and the interviewer's face – by subverting the interviewer's attempts to use this identity as a way of criticising his performance while at the same time saving his face.

4.2 Interview 2

In the excerpts that we have chosen from this interview, the interviewer utters a negative assessment of the interviewee's repeated refusal to fill in a certain type of form. Both, the latter's refusal and the former's explicit criticism of this fact, are potentially face-threatening acts which in the context of the performance appraisal interview may pose challenges to the interlocutors' professional and institutional identities.

Excerpt 2.1 Interview 2

```
1    IR:    •hh E:::rmm (1.0) what I thought was less ( ),
2           because of course I also think something is less ((good)).=
3    IE:    =°°That will [be so.°°
4    IR:                 [That I you
5           that I have to motivate you to fill in the ↑RI.
6           I don't know whether you have done it after all, >we had
7           talked about it in the middle management consultations<
8           and you say 'I am not going to fill that ↑in'
9    IE:    I have not filled that in.
10   IR:    ((hits the table with her flat hand))=
11   IE:    =No.
12   (0.7)
13   IR:    SLAP!
14          >But okay, I have written it down anyway,
15          I thought that was less good.<
16   IE:    Yes.
```

In lines 1–2, the interviewer voices a preliminary to her negative assessment. The initial audible in-breath, the hesitation and the pause immediately give this turn a dispreferred turn shape. Also, next to voicing the preliminary (line 1), the interviewer provides an additional account (line 2) that implicitly frames the upcoming criticism as typical of the genre of appraisal interview (hence the 'of course', *natuurlijk* in Dutch, in line 2) and as only one element ('something', line 2) as opposed to the many positive evaluations that were discussed during the interview. The interviewee quietly acknowledges this in line 3, which is overlapped by the interviewer's formulation of her criticism in line 4. This criticism concerns a specific form, the 'RI', which members of the middle management – such as the interviewee – are expected to fill in but of which the latter has declared in an earlier meeting he would not do this. Interestingly, the interviewer does not formulate a direct accusation of negligent behaviour (which would be: 'you haven't filled in the RI'), but she frames it as a problem because an additional encouragement is needed to make sure the interviewee displays the correct behaviour. She thereby considerably mitigates the potential face-threat of the criticism. However, in the subsequent line, the interviewer repeats her criticism by sketching the context in which the interviewee had made a bold statement displaying his unwillingness to fill in the RI. She thereby challenges his face more explicitly and also portrays him as somebody who deliberately does not conform to institutional practices (in this case: filling in the form when requested). In particular, this statement is enacted by the interviewer in line 8 by means of direct reported speech, and this, together with the shift to the present verb tense in the quotative ('say', line 8), adds vividness to her story, but it also implicitly attributes an unmitigated, highly face-threatening, refusal to the interviewee.

In responding to these accusations, the interviewee does not justify himself or provide explanations but he simply states that he did not comply with what was expected of him (line 9), thus mirroring the preceding direct quote. He thereby not only challenges the institutional norms but also considerably threatens the interviewer's face. The interviewer responds to this twice paralinguistically: first, she hits the table with her flat hand, in reaction to which the interviewee latches a negative particle repeating his refusal (line 11), and second, after a brief pause (line 12), she loudly mimics the sound of a slap in the face (line 13). As such, she marks the interviewee's unmitigated refusal as a face threat and she also replies to it in highly face-threatening (and quite physical) ways. So by the rapidly shifting turn shapes from dispreferred to preferred while voicing these face-threatening utterances, the interlocutors here shift to an orientation to argumentation as context (Kotthoff 1993) instead of to 'normal' conversation.

Interestingly though, the interviewer at this point does not pursue the topic further, but quickly closes it (lines 14–15) as marked by the initial concluding particle 'okay' and she refers to the institutionalised nature of the assessment through her notes (line 14) that were made before the interview. She thus seems to return to the initial situation without outlining any future actions, which is acknowledged by the interviewee in line 16, and she seems to accept the interviewee's non-adherence to the institutional expectations. This could be seen as an orientation to the new work order idea of employee empowerment and independence, while it is at the same time a failure of the system as this employee challenges the organisation's vision, thus uncovering the tensions related to contradictory ideologies as discussed in the introduction.

However, the interviewer's acceptance of the interviewee's refusal turns out to be only temporary, as in the next line, in excerpt 2.2, she re-initiates the topic of the RI by providing arguments that further appeal to behaviour change in the interviewee.

Excerpt 2.2 Interview 2
17 IR: I think you have an exemplary ro[le hey
18 IE: [Uhu.
19 IR: as as analyst one.
20   Erm (.) especially regarding as well, because
21   I see you sitting in that dump the hours of fertility hey,
22   I would like to that there comes nevertheless a window
23   with top light hey, so that you would have more (.) window
24   it would be important if you mention that,
25   if you mention that if you also [there
26 IE: [Mmm
27 IR: e:rm would fill in that ↓RI.
28 IE: There is no money there for that for the moment,

```
29           that is already well known.=
30    IR:    =No but okay e:::rm, when e::rm
31           when an RI is filled in regarding
32           certain pressure poi[nts then they will
33    IE:                     [Mmm.
34    IR:    sooner be in↑[clined than when that is not filled in
35    IE:                   [°↑Yes°
36    IR:    Erm (.)
```

In excerpt 2.2, the interviewer appeals to two main arguments. First, she attributes an 'exemplary role' to the interviewee and relates this to his position as 'analyst one' (lines 17, 19). By linking these two, the interviewer projects an identity of 'model employee' upon the interviewee in a similar way as in interview 1. She thereby not only attends to his face needs, but also, and more importantly, by setting higher standards for the interviewee's professional behaviour, she reminds him of the responsibilities and duties that come with his professional role. This, in a way, also mitigates her previous negative assessment of the interviewee's failure to fill in the RI form since she implies that it is *because* of his professional role that the interviewee is expected to display model behaviour and that failure to do so is particularly bad because the standards for him are higher than for a *normal* employee.

Moreover, after a false start (line 20), the interviewer appeals to a collective identity by showing empathy for the interviewee's work situation, and in particular for the lack of a window (lines 20–3) in his workspace. She describes the latter as a 'dump' (*kot* in Dutch, line 21) and expresses her wish (line 22) to improve the interviewee's work situation. As such, she does 'stake inoculation' since she demonstrates that she is not acting out of self-interest (Potter 1996: 125), and she displays her good character (Clifton and Van De Mieroop 2010) thereby attending to the potentially damaged identity of *good* supervisor and colleague. She then relates this to the topic at hand, namely filling in the RI, after a number of reformulations (lines 24–5) and a hesitation (line 27).

However, rather than going along with the interviewer, the interviewee immediately rebuts her attempts by factually asserting the lack of financial means for her suggested changes (line 28–9). Although the interviewee's refusal of compliance is relatively face-threatening to the interviewer – as it challenges her line of argument and does not lead to the intended solution – she acknowledges this rebuttal. After a few hesitations (line 30), she reformulates her request to fill in an RI, this time relating it to a more general statement about what RIs are useful for. This generalising character is clearly shown through the repeated use of the passive voice (lines 31, 34) that avoids attributing any agency to the interviewee. She also implicitly constructs a collective identity with the interviewee here by setting up a contrastive group ('they' in line 32), which vaguely refers to the hospital management in charge of allocating funds. As such, she creates an 'us versus them' opposition between the analysts (including the interviewee and herself) on the one hand and the hospital managers on the other hand. She thereby aligns with the interviewee and stresses collectivity. However, these strategies do not lead to an explicit agreement by the interviewee and after a brief hesitation (line 36) the interviewer initiates the next topic on the agenda thereby closing the current topic.

What is particularly interesting about this fragment, then, is the fact that the interviewee resists the identities that the interviewer attempts to project onto him. As a consequence, the interviewer's attempts to mitigate the potential face threat of this negative assessment by doing identity work do not lead to an agreement or compliance. In particular, rather than accepting his role as a model employee and as a member of the same in-group as the interviewer, the interviewee boldly refuses to comply with the interviewer's demands in rather face-threatening ways. In this interview, thus, both interlocutors set up and negotiate their own and each other's professional and institutional identities by doing face work (i.e. challenging as well as attending to their face needs) but without agreeing on them. Also, this interview illustrates that the supervisor refrains from voicing a bald on-record criticism that forces the employee to carry out the required tasks or from punishing him in one way or another for his refusal to cooperate. This, one could argue, is in line with the egalitarian ideals of the new work order in which employees are empowered to make certain decisions themselves. However, it may also simply be a way for the interviewer to maintain working relationships with this interviewee, who, as he claimed himself at the start of the interview, has nothing to lose anyway as he will retire soon after the interview. So it is in the interviewer's own interest not to criticise the interviewee explicitly, and instead, she does a lot of identity work in order to manoeuvre the latter into a position of acceptance of the institutional expectations. In spite of various attempts by the supervisor, this remains unsuccessful, thus leading to a situation of strong employee empowerment, which, at the same time, challenges the organisation's vision and is thus not in line with new work order ideologies. This outcome is quite exceptional in comparison with the other performance appraisal interviews in our data and it can be hypothetically explained by the virtually untouchable status of the employee due to his approaching retirement.

5. Discussion and conclusion

In this chapter we have looked at the relatively new but increasingly relevant genre of performance appraisal interviews in the modern workplace. Due to their evaluative function and their close link to organisational norms and practices, performance appraisal interviews are crucial sites where identity work takes place, and where insights can be gained about the discursive processes through which interlocutors construct, negotiate and sometimes reject their various identities – always in close relation with each other and their institution. With its focus on developing employees' competence and performance in a collaborative bottom-up – instead of the traditional top-down – manner, the introduction of such interviews can be seen as a direct result of structural changes in organisational hierarchies and transitions towards more participative and empowering organisational practices, as Fletcher (2001) observed. However, whether changes towards a more egalitarian approach of performance appraisal on the macro-level are also reflected in micro-level interactional practices remains to be seen (e.g. Holmes et al. 2011), and this has been the focus of our analyses here.

Our analyses have illustrated how these identities are constructed and negotiated through interlocutors orienting to each other's face needs. By voicing potentially face-threatening criticisms, the interviewer displayed a clear orientation to her institutional role and as such constructed her identity as supervisor who is able to explicitly voice negative assessments since she is in a hierarchically higher position than the interviewees, upon whom the identity of subordinate was projected at the same time. The interconnectedness of these processes clearly illustrates the relational character of identities (Bucholtz and Hall 2005). Crucially, the construction of this hierarchical difference through these negative, and potentially face-threatening, assessments is contradictory to the egalitarian ideals of the new work order as well as to the relatively close hierarchical position all interlocutors held (as 'analysts one'). It is hence not surprising that it was strongly mitigated through face work – especially that which was particularly oriented to attending to interlocutors' positive face needs.

Although the specific criticisms uttered by the interviewer differed in terms of their objects and the responses they generated, in all cases the negative assessments were explicitly linked to – as well as downgraded by means of – professional and institutional identities. The interviewer projected a positive professional identity upon the interviewees and also constructed a collective institutional identity including both interlocutors which highlighted their relative hierarchical closeness. These two identities are indexed (cf. Ochs 1993; Bucholtz and Hall 2005) differently in our data. The first one is mainly constructed by projecting the identity of the model employee upon the interviewees. While this identity attends to positive face needs, it is also used to account for the reasons why the interviewee's conduct is problematic. The second, collective, identity construction relies quite strongly on pronominal usage. Pronouns have been observed to be 'coherent indication[s] of the speaker's presentation of self' (De Fina 1995: 382) in relation to others. Through her use of pronouns the interviewer sets up an 'us versus them' dichotomy which enforces the construction of a collective in-group of 'analysts one'. Interestingly, the antagonists of these in-groups varied significantly in the interviews and included other employees (interview 1) and hospital management (interview 2), thus showing the versatile nature of this discursive feature.

These constructions of identities, in turn, appeal to the face needs of the interlocutors. First, by projecting a positive professional identity upon the interviewees, they are complimented and their importance within the organisation is emphasised. Second, by constructing a collective identity between herself and the interviewees, the interviewer highlights the points on which both interlocutors agree or share the same position. This is supported by setting up a contrast with a particular out-group, thereby drawing further attention to the similarities between interlocutors. By highlighting these similarities and minimising the differences, the interviewer also attends to the interviewees' face needs and effectively orients to and boosts 'the positive social value' (Goffman 1967: 5) of the interviewee. Importantly, however, this collective identity projection also does identity and face work for the interviewer, since by placing herself and the interviewee in the same in-group, the interviewer constructs her identity as a colleague, thus downplaying the hierarchical difference that was talked into being by voicing the negative assessment. Given the relative hierarchical closeness of the interlocutors, this is perhaps not surprising, and so it would be interesting to further investigate whether similar processes occur when the hierarchical difference between the interviewer and the interviewees is significantly larger. Anyhow, in this case, this construction of a collective identity partially restores the face threat that was constructed through the negative assessment. This identity of colleague versus supervisor shifts back and forth dynamically during the interaction and the interviewer selectively draws on both at different points.

The interviewer's use of both identities and her attempts to involve the interviewee in negotiating the content of the performance appraisal interview can thus be interpreted as a reflection of the transitions towards flatter organisational structures in line with new work order ideologies relating to employee empowerment and egalitarianism. Indeed, this relatively new genre of performance appraisal interviews is quite emblematic of these organisational changes since it is characterised, on a general level, by more collaborative processes of employee evaluation, and, on a more particular level regarding these interviews, by a strong mitigation of the supervisor role and its related activities – namely, voicing criticism. This mitigation is talked into being by several different means, as discussed above, and it may result in either successful (in the case of interview 1) or unsuccessful (in the case of interview 2) bids for a change in the professional practices of the employees, thus demonstrating the supervisor's orientation to a more collaborative way of *doing evaluation*. As discussed elsewhere, these collaborative processes are further reinforced by the writing-up of the interview to which both interviewer and interviewee contribute (see Van De Mieroop and Schnurr 2014). Furthermore, our analyses also uncovered the tensions relating to this new work order ideal of employee empowerment, as it implies that employees are expected to have incorporated the organisation's vision and values. Whenever they challenge these, either implicitly by covertly sending personal messages or explicitly by overtly refusing to fill in a particular form, they are reprimanded by the supervisor, even though the latter agrees that changes in behaviour would not affect their work in any way. This clearly demonstrates that employees are only 'empowered' as long as they accept and remain within the boundaries set out by the organisation and that 'things are very different' whenever these boundaries are challenged.

Although this study was necessarily exploratory in nature, it demonstrates the importance of looking at relatively new genres that have arisen as a consequence of structural transitions in the modern workplace and of critically scrutinising to what extent the actual micro-level interactions reflect these macro-level organisational changes. It is through these new and relatively under-researched genres, like the performance appraisal interview, that actual organisational realities are talked into being and are collaboratively negotiated on a turn-by-turn basis. Hence these genres provide a rich site for future research on the complexities of identity construction and negotiation in relation to the ongoing processes of transitions in the workplace.

Appendix: original excerpts

Excerpt 1.1

1	IR:	Ich han opgeschrè:ven
2		'Ik ben zeer tevreden over de inzet van diech.'
3	(0.7)	
4	IR:	Eu:::::hm (.) 'Waal han ich soms de ↑indruk' (.)

```
5              ((deliberate cough))
6              een een £kritische kanttekening£=
7      IE:     =( [ )
8      IR:        ['dat Karen tijdens werk auch met haar vriend Tim
9              regelmatig zit te mailen en te sms'en
10             of met ander familieleden'=
11     IE:     =Sms'en ne[et.
12     IR:              ['Let op
13             je voorbeeldfunctie in deze.'
14     IE      >Ich mot zeggen< sms'en sowieso neet
```

Excerpt 1.2

```
32     IR:     Soms valt mich det ook op of dat se
33             >get wen se dan effe get wegclicks of zoe<
34             en dan denk ich van '↑Hmmm'
35             maar dan dink ich 'Ja, is het noe belang↑rijk'=
36     IE:     =↓Nè::.=
37     IR:     =Op ziech vind ich het neet belangrijk
38             >want dien werk lijdt der neet onder< (.) •h
39     IE:     °°mm°°=
40     IR:     =maar du has een voorbeeld↓func[tie
41     IE:                                    [Ja nè
42             ma[ar
43     IR:       [dus let der ge[wuun ook op.
44     IE:                      [Ich stuur ich stuur
45             inderdaad waal af en toe eens een mail
```

Excerpt 1.3

```
84     IR:     Maar (.) <anderen> nemen em
85             om andere redenen met=
86     IE:     =Jo[a
87     IR:        [en du bes toch een analist één
88             woe hen gekeken wordt net zo wie
89             noa miech als als als unitmanager gekè[ken
90     IE:                                          [m[m
91     IR:                                            [en os
92     (1.0)
93     IR:     eu::::hm (.) ge↑drag (.)
94             en w- en en wat we zaggen
95             wèrd auch op een grotere [balans gelagd
96     IE:                              [°joa joa klopt°
97     IR:     wie van anderen
98     IE:     °°jo[a°°
99     IR:        [Dus LET doa geweun effe o[p
100    IE:                                  [joa=
```

101 IR: =det se een voorbeeldfunctie in deze has.
102 IE: mm

Excerpt 2.1

1   IR: •hh Eu:::hmm (1.0) wat ich minder ( ) vond,
2   want ich vin natuurlijk ooch get minder.=
3   IE: =°°Dat z[al waal.°°
4   IR: [Dat ich dich
5   dat ich dich mot motiveren om de RI in te ↑vullen.
6   Ich weet niet of se dat toch has gedoan, >we hadden
7   toen 'n het middenkaderoverleg over gehad<
8   en du zegs 'Dat goan ich neet ↑invullen'
9   IE: Dat heb ich neet ingevuld.
10 IR: ((hits the table with her flat hand))=
11 IE: =Nè.
12 (0.7)
13 IR: ZWATSCH!
14   >Maar goed, ich hou het waal opgeschrèven,
15   dat vond ich minder good.<
16 IE: Ja.

Excerpt 2.2

17 IR: Ich vind du has een voorbeeldfunct[ie hè
18 IE: [Uhu.
19 IR: als als analist één.
20   Euhm (.) vooral met betrekking ook, want
21   ich zien de uren fertiliteit zit in dat hok hè,
22   ich zou graag dat doa toch een raam met bovenlicht
23   kom he, dus da de wat meer (.) raam zoudt hebben
24   zou het belangriek zien als se dat vermeldt,
25   als se dat vermeld als se [da ooch
26 IE: [Mmm
27 IR: eu:h die RI zous in↓vullen.
28 IE: Doa is dar geen geld veur voorluipig,
29   dat is al goed bekend.=
30 IR: =Nee maar goed eu:::h, went eu::h
31   went er een RI wordt ingevuld over
32   bepaalde knelpun[ten dan zullen ze
33 IE: [Mmm.
34 IR: eerder ge↑[neigd zeen dan went dat neet ingevuld is
35 IE: [°↑Ja°
36 IR: Euhm (.)

Transcription conventions

(.)	brief pause
(0.7)	timed pause
↑now, ↓no	onset of noticeable pitch rise or fall
40 IR ro[le	
41 IE [Yes no	square brackets '[' aligned across adjacent lines denote the start of overlapping talk
No:::	colons show that the speaker has stretched the preceding sound
( )	uncertain transcription due to audio problems
39 IE °°mm°°=	
40 IR =but	the equals sign shows an example of latching, which means that there is no discernible pause between a speaker's or, as in this case, two speakers' turn(s)
MIND, SLAP	words that are fully written in capitals are pronounced more loudly (capitals at the beginning of sentences do not have this specific meaning)
° yes yes right°, °°mm°°	words between degree signs are quieter, words between double degree signs are even quieter
> But okay, I have written it down anyway, I thought that was less good.<	inwards arrows show faster speech
<others>	outwards arrows show slower speech
£ critical remark£	the words between £ signs are spoken in a 'smile voice' which has a markedly higher pitch and an intonational contour comparable to laughing during speaking but without any laughter tokens
((deliberate cough))	description of something difficult to transcribe phonetically
•hh	audible in-breath

Notes

1. We are greatly indebted to Eveline Vrolix for collecting and making an initial transcription of the data.
2. The original Dutch fragments in the appendix were translated into English as literally as possible, so that the sequential aspects of the interaction, which would be lost in a less literal translation, were retained. This may sometimes result in non-standard grammar and word order, which can make the transcripts a bit difficult to follow. The interviews were transcribed following the main guidelines of the Jeffersonian transcription system. However, in order to enhance the readability of the fragments, we also integrated standard punctuation (e.g. capitals, full stops and commas).

References

Adelswärd, V. and C. Nilholm (2000), 'Who is Cindy? Aspects of identity work in a teacher–parent–pupil talk at a special school', *Text & Talk*, 20: 4, pp. 545–68.

Angouri, J. (2013), 'The multilingual reality of the multinational workplace: language policy and language use', *Journal of Multilingual & Multicultural Development*, 34: 6, pp. 564–81.

Asmuß, B. (2008), 'Performance appraisal interviews: Preference Organization in assessment sequences', *Journal of Business Communication*, 45: 4, pp. 408–29.

Bucholtz, M. and K. Hall (2005), 'Identity and interaction: a sociocultural linguistic approach', *Discourse Studies*, 7: 4–5, pp. 585–614.

Butler, J. (1990), *Gender trouble: feminism and the subversion of identity*, New York: Routledge.

Buttny, R. (2001), 'Therapeutic humor in retelling the clients' tellings', *Text*, 21: 3, pp. 303–27.

Cameron, D. (2000), *Good to talk: living and working in a communication culture*, London: Sage.

Clifton, J. (2012), 'Conversation analysis in dialogue with stocks of interactional knowledge: facework and appraisal interviews', *Journal of Business Communication*, 49: 4, pp. 283–311.

Clifton, J. and D. Van De Mieroop (2010), '"Doing" ethos – a discursive approach to the strategic deployment and negotiation of identities in meetings', *Journal of Pragmatics*, 42: 9, pp. 2449–61.

De Fina, A. (1995), 'Pronominal choice, identity, and solidarity in political discourse', *Text*, 15: 3, pp. 379–410.

De Fina, A. (2003), *Identity in narrative: a study of immigrant discourse*, Amsterdam and Philadelphia: John Benjamins.

Fairclough, N. (1992), *Discourse and social change*, Cambridge: Polity Press.

Fletcher, C. (2001), 'Performance appraisals and management: the developing research agenda', *Journal of Occupational and Organisational Psychology*, 74: 4, pp. 473–87.

Gee, J. P., G. Hull and C. Lankshear (1996), *The new work order*, St Leonards: Allen & Unwin.

Geis, F. L., V. Brown and C. Wolfe (1990), 'Legitimizing the leader: endorsement by male versus female authority figures', *Journal of Applied Social Psychology*, 20, pp. 943–70.

Geyer, N. (2008), *Discourse and politeness: ambivalent face in Japanese*, London: Continuum.

Goffman, E. (1967), *Interaction ritual: essays on face-to-face behavior*, Garden City, NY: Anchor Books.

Hall, C., S. Sarangi and S. Slembrouck (1999), 'The legitimations of the client and the profession', in S. Sarangi and C. Roberts (eds), *Talk, work and institutional order: discourse in medical, mediation and management settings*, Berlin and New York: Mouton de Gruyter, pp. 293–322.

Hall, S. (2000), 'Who needs "identity"?', in P. du Gay, J. Evans and P. Redman (eds), *Identity: a reader*, London: Sage, pp. 15–30.

Haugh, M. (2009), 'Face and interaction', in F. Bargiela-Chiappini and M. Haugh (eds), *Face, communication and social interaction*, London: Equinox, pp. 1–30.

Haugh, M. and C. Hinze (2003), 'A metalinguistic approach to deconstructing the concepts of "face" and "politeness" in Chinese, English and Japanese', *Journal of Pragmatics*, 35: 10–11, pp. 1581–611.

Holmes, J., M. Stubbe and B. Vine (1999), 'Constructing professional identity: "doing power" in policy units', in S. Sarangi and C. Roberts (eds), *Talk, work and institutional order: discourse in medical, mediation and management settings*, Berlin and New York: Mouton de Gruyter, pp. 351–85.

Holmes, J., M. Marra and B. Vine (2011), *Leadership, discourse and ethnicity*, Oxford: Oxford University Press.

Iedema, R. and H. Scheeres (2003), 'From doing work to talking work: renegotiating knowing, doing, and identity', *Applied Linguistics*, 24: 3, pp. 316–37.

Jenkins, R. (1996), *Social identity*, London: Routledge.

Kotthoff, H. (1993), 'Disagreement and concession in disputes: on the context sensitivity of preference structures', *Language in Society*, 22: 2, pp. 193–216.

Locher, M. A. (2008), 'Relational work, politeness, and identity construction', in G. Antos and E. Ventola (eds), *Handbook of interpersonal communication*, Berlin: Mouton de Gruyter, pp. 509–40.

Lytra, V. (2009), 'Constructing academic hierarchies: teasing and identity work among peers at school', *Pragmatics*, 19: 3, pp. 449–66.

Ochs, E. (1993), 'Constructing social identity: a language socialization perspective', *Research on Language and Social Interaction*, 26: 3, pp. 287–306.

Pomerantz, A. (1984), 'Agreeing and disagreeing with assessments: some features of preferred/dispreferred turn shapes', in J. M. Atkinson and J. Heritage (eds), *Structures of social action: studies in conversation analysis*, New York: Cambridge University Press, pp. 57–101.

Postmes, T. (2003), 'A social identity approach to communication in organizations', in A. Haslam, D. van Knippenberg, M. Platow and N. Ellemers (eds), *Social identity at work: developing theory for organizational practice*, New York and Hove: Psychology Press, pp. 81–97.

Potter, J. (1996), *Representing reality: discourse, rhetoric and social construction*, London: Sage.

Sarangi, S. (2005), 'Social interaction, social theory and work-related activities', *Calidoscópio*, 3: 3, pp. 160–9.

Sarangi, S. and C. Roberts (eds) (1999), *Talk, work and institutional order: discourse in medical, mediation and management settings*, Berlin and New York: Mouton de Gruyter.

Schnurr, S. and A. Chan (2011), 'Exploring another side of co-leadership: negotiating professional identities through face-work in disagreements', *Language in Society*, 40: 2, pp. 187–210.

Schnurr, S. and O. Zayts (2011), 'Be(com)ing a leader: a case study of co-constructing professional identities at work', in J. Angouri and M. Marra (eds), *Constructing identities at work*, Houndmills: Palgrave Macmillan, pp. 40–60.

Spencer-Oatey, H. (2007), 'Theories of identity and the analysis of face', *Journal of Pragmatics*, 39: 4, pp. 639–56.

Stokoe, E. (2009), 'Doing actions with identity categories: complaints and denials in neighbor disputes', *Text & Talk*, 29: 1, pp. 75–97.

Tannen, D. (1989), *Talking voices: repetition, dialogue, and imagery in conversational discourse*, Cambridge: Cambridge University Press.

Tracy, K. (1990), 'The many faces of facework', in H. Giles and W. P. Robinson (eds), *Handbook of language and social psychology*, Chichester: John Wiley, pp. 209–26.

Van De Mieroop, D. and S. Schnurr (2014), 'Negotiating meaning and co-constructing institutionalisable answers: leadership through gate-keeping in performance appraisal interviews', *Journal of Pragmatics*, 67, pp. 1–16.

Van De Mieroop, D. and E. Vrolix (2014), 'A discourse analytical perspective on the professionalization of the performance appraisal interview', *International Journal of Business Communication*, 51: 2, pp. 159–82.

Widdicombe, S. (1998), 'Identity as an analysts' and a participants' resource', in C. Antaki and S. Widdicombe (eds), *Identities in talk*, London: Sage, pp. 191–206.

6

Negotiating Social Legitimacy in and across Contexts: Apprenticeship in a 'Dual' Training System

Stefano A. Losa and Laurent Filliettaz

1. Transitions from school to work in a 'dual' apprenticeship system

This chapter advances a new perspective for approaching the role of discourse and interaction in vocational education and training (VET), a perspective that sees these ingredients not as peripheral components of the training curriculum, but rather as central mediating tools for vocational learning.

The chapter focuses on apprenticeship programmes in the context of Switzerland, where the dominant form of training consists of a complex combination of school-based and practice-based learning. According to such a 'dual' training system, apprentices experience a plurality of training sites. They move back and forth between vocational schools or training centres, where they are introduced to both technical and general content, and ordinary workplaces, where they acquire practical skills and encounter the specific requirement of work production tasks. For many years, apprenticeship programmes following the scheme of the dual system have regularly been reported as efficient strategies for securing employment and supporting smooth transitions from school to work (Dubs 2006). However, recent research also shows that accomplishing the transition between learning sites such as vocational schools and workplaces is not always a benign experience, but provides apprentices with numerous challenges and, often, contradictory expectations. Depending on the occupations and the geographical areas, between 20 per cent and 40 per cent of apprentices who enter the dual VET system do not complete their apprenticeship within the stated terms of their contracts (Stalder and Nägele 2011). Of these, 9 per cent change occupation, 11 per cent have to repeat a year, 7 per cent change training company, and 7 per cent drop out from the apprenticeship system without having any immediate alternative pathway. Recent studies have investigated the causes leading to young people dropping out or making changes in apprenticeship programmes (Lamamra and Masdonati 2009). These studies depict a nuanced portrait of the dual VET system and show that transitions from school to work are often far from smooth and unproblematic. They conclude that poor working conditions, low support by trainers and unsatisfactory workplace relations emerge as the main causes leading to dropout.

In this particular context, we propose that apprentices are not only exposed to vocational knowledge in the range of contexts in which training takes places, they also encounter specific discourse practices and face numerous and often implicit or invisible expectations regarding the ways these discourses may be enacted and conducted. It is by engaging with these discourse practices that apprentices gain access to knowledge, develop practical skills and may adopt legitimate social positions within the multiple communities they belong to during their training. These language and communication skills are neither transparent nor self-evident. Like other components of vocational training, they must be observed and, most importantly, learnt. Some apprentices are very successful in identifying and acquiring the specific discursive demands underlying the range of practices included their training programme. Others are not and may encounter challenging experiences in their journey to a VET qualification (Filliettaz et al. 2013; Losa et al. 2014).

In a research programme conducted at the University of Geneva, these various ideas were elaborated and discourse analytic methods were implemented to address vocational education issues (Filliettaz et al. 2008; Filliettaz 2010a, 2010b, 2010c). Analysing discourse and verbal interaction among apprentices, trainers and workers, it is proposed, can contribute to a better understanding of the complex learning processes associated with initial vocational training and illuminate the multiple challenges faced by apprentices when accomplishing the transition from school to work.

In this chapter, we focus on the relationship between trainers and apprentices within dedicated training centres and workplaces, and wish to highlight how discursive and interactional processes can lead participants to establish legitimate, recognised and valued social positions within specific communities of practice. Adopting an interactional perspective on social recognition and impression management, we address the following range of questions. How do apprentices negotiate their participation in communities of practice? How do they actively contribute to their legitimacy in face-to-face interaction? What kinds of semiotic resources do they use to do so? Reciprocally, we are also interested in investigating the perspective of trainers and experienced workers. How do trainers shape interactional participatory practices for apprentices? What sorts of resources are afforded to them and how may these specific resources support or hinder social recognition for apprentices?

A contrasted data analysis based on audio-video recordings recently collected in the Geneva area shows how various apprentices may respond differently to the specific requirements set towards communicative tasks. Depending on the contexts in which they engage, complex social expectations emerge, regarding how apprentices should participate in interaction. By contrasting the contexts of a training centre and a workplace, we question the continuities and discrepancies between learning experiences, and illustrate how the 'crossing of boundaries' is very much a matter of interactional accomplishment by participants themselves.

2. Participation and social recognition in interaction

2.1 Communities of practice and boundary crossing

Vocational training practices have been extensively studied within educational research. However, such practices have been examined from an interactional perspective only in relatively recent times, which has led a number of scholars to approach vocational learning processes as relational practices and joint accomplishments (Filliettaz 2010a; Kunégel 2005; Mayen 2002). Central to this field is the pivotal work of Lave and Wenger (1991) on communities of practice. Communities of practice are defined as 'groups of people who share a concern or a passion for something they do and learn how to do it better as they interact regularly' (Wenger-Trayner and Wenger-Trayner 2015: n.p.). Accordingly, learning contexts such as workplaces and schools can be considered as communities of practice when people mutually engage around a joint enterprise by drawing on 'a shared repertoire of communal resources' for learning, like 'language, routines, sensibilities, artefacts, tools, stories, styles' (Wenger 2000: 229).

In relation to VET contexts, it is generally acknowledged that school and work are two fundamentally different and separate realities, each with its own histories, objectives, practices and standards. From that perspective, participants (i.e. apprentices, colleagues, experts, mentors) are facing two distinct communities of practice, associated with different forms of participation and learning. Consequently, it is assumed that school-based learning is quite different from workplace learning and at odds with what an apprentice will need at work. As noted by Hodkinson:

> school-based learning fails, because the context and practices of the school dominate the content that is to be taught. Put differently, school pupils learn how to be pupils – how to participate in the peculiar community of practice that is school. This includes learning to give answers that a teacher wants to hear and learning to pass examinations . . . This is quite different . . . from learning in everyday life or at work. (Hodkinson 2005: 523)

In other words, 'successful participation at work is learned whilst being at work, and cannot be prepared for in a college setting' (Hodkinson 2005: 523).

However, during the last fifteen years, various authors (Wenger et al. 2002; Tuomi-Gröhn et al. 2003; Hodkinson 2005; Akkerman and Bakker 2012) have attempted to rethink the relationship between school and work in the field of vocational education and training. These authors aim to understand the complexity of such a relationship, which seems to be based on the crossing of boundaries rather than upon a clear separation of these two contexts. Indeed, the increasing movement of people, practices and ideas across different professions and disciplines (Tsui and Law 2007), as well as the functioning of vocational education and learning devices themselves, has led to rethinking and redefining the analytical relevance of the boundary across communities of practice. In reality, learning through collective practices involves heterogeneous and unequal forms of participation and mutual relationships amongst participants, even within a single community of practice. Heterogeneity and complexity among learning and training communities emerge across several dimensions, such as boundary cross-ing, actors' non-engagement within their roles, multiactivity, and so on.

In this regard, Akkerman and Bakker propose adopting a new perspective on learning conditions at the crossing of boundaries (boundary crossing) between school and work:

> the notion of boundary crossing urges us to consider not only how schools prepare for students' future work practices, but simultaneously how current work experiences of students during school trajectories are exploited for learning to become a professional. Consequently, work is not to be seen as a context outside the educational practice, but as part of the schooling process. Thinking about boundary crossing leads to questions about how and to what extent continuity is maintained despite sociocultural differences between school institutes and local workplaces. (Akkerman and Bakker 2012: 155–6)

According to Akkerman and Bakker, this approach aims to foster elements of continu-ity rather than difference and leads to taking into account two dimensions in particular: the 'epistemic culture' within schools and workplaces; and the 'identity positions' of apprentices in and across the two contexts. Epistemic cultures may encounter tensions between schools and workplaces, where attitudes often consider the overly theoreti-cal perspective of teachers as disconnected from more applied, practical and implicit forms of knowledge as they are used in professional practice. Thus, 'From a boundary-crossing perspective then, the challenge is to find a way to interrelate these different types of epistemologies in favour of the learning process of the apprentice' (Akkerman and Bakker 2012: 156). Regarding identity positions as well, it is necessary to consider the ambiguous or even paradoxical position of the apprentice (learner vs. worker) as a potentially privileged mediating position to navigate between the two communities of practice. As suggested by Akkerman and Bakker (2012: 156), 'This ambiguous posi-tion can lead to insecurity, but also creates the potential to act as a broker, meaning that one can introduce elements of one practice into another.'

By adopting a close look not only within specific training contexts but also beyond and across contexts, the boundary-crossing approach allows for renewed attention to practices and modalities of participation that apprentices and other participants are required to produce in learning situations. In particular, such an approach takes account of the fact that participation practices are diverse and should not to be seen as bound to one specific community of reference, whether the school or the profes-sional context. Instead, discourses, practices and values may cross different contexts, depending on the ways they are enacted by participants. Therefore, it seems necessary to consider the complexity and plurality of standards that can be locally mobilised by apprentices and other participants involved in vocational training. More specifically, if the distinction between vocational schools and workplaces has institutional validity, it seems appropriate to question such a 'duality' from the perspective of the participants themselves and their participation practices. To what extent do their participatory practices differ or coincide between and across these institutional contexts?

2.2 Participation and learning in and across contexts

In the field of vocational education and training, the issue of participation has mainly been approached in terms of identity positioning and belonging to a professional community of practice. This is particularly apparent in Lave and Wenger's (1991) core concept of 'legitimate peripheral participation'. This concept

> provides a way to speak about the relations between newcomers and old-timers, and about activities, identities, artifacts, and communities of knowledge and practice. It concerns the process by which newcomers become part of a community of practice. (Lave and Wenger 1991: 29)

Participation is thus addressed in terms of the identity process unfolding over a certain period of time and depending on the progress of the learner (newcomer) in its formative path within the community of practice up to his or her recognition as full member. Learning is deeply connected to becoming a legitimate member of a community of practice. For apprentices, this requires participation in joint activities and being able to 'position [themselves] in a complex network of relations involving other apprentices, teachers, trainers and co-workers' (Filliettaz 2010a: 30). Here, legitimacy is about the recognition and the acceptance of the apprentice's novice identity from an old-timer trainer. In other words, trainers expect apprentices to act in a consistent and relevant way according to their ratified learner position. Thus, individuals involved in a learning process need to interactively align themselves to what is normatively expected according to the social role they take on. This draws attention to the fact that groups or communities of practice that are organised around professional practice – whether in training situations or work environments – not only share a repertoire of learning resources such as language, peculiar sensitivities, tools and specific skills, as mentioned above, they also share a repertoire of normative and behavioural expectations including norms, beliefs, values, attitudes, and individual and role-based engagement. Depending on these expectations, specific ways to talk, to communicate and to participate with others and within the group are perceived as more appropriate than others.

Developing these perspectives, Billett (2001, 2004) shows how individual engagement and agency are central components of participation and learning within communities and workplace environments, and how these components interact with social and contextual ingredients. In particular, Billett's work pays attention to contextual and social conditions that may have an impact on learning opportunities. He focuses on the forms and qualities of guidance processes through which experts provide support to newcomers in work production tasks and considers learning as the consequence of 'participatory practices' enacted by learners and through which they may get access to work opportunities allowing them to progress. Following Billett, participatory practices consist of two interdependent factors: social factors and individual ones. Social factors are characterised by the range of resources afforded by work environments (i.e. forms of guidance and expertise, material resources). Individual factors relate to the ways novices elect to engage with work activities and with the resources afforded to them. From this perspective, it becomes relevant to investigate how novices and experts involved in interaction participate and position themselves and how this positioning contributes to the expansive or restrictive nature of learning environments (Fuller and Unwin 2003). Being involved in a valued and recognised way may have strong implications in terms of access to knowledge and membership within learning communities of practice.

All these contributions have in common that they see participation in communities of practice as a reciprocal process or joint actions (Clark 1996; Goffman 1959), in which participants must constantly and mutually negotiate their roles, expressions, faces and ultimately their legitimacy. Participation is thus regarded as an interactional practice (or interactional participatory practices) and defined as 'a mutual orientation the interactants manifest to each other and the reciprocal engagement they display toward a joint activity' (Filliettaz et al. 2009: 99). However, in vocational education and training contexts characterised by a plurality and a combination of communities of practice, the repertoire of normative and behavioural expectations recognised as valuable may be multiple or even contradictory. Therefore, the question arises: how do participants cope with such a plurality? How do they build their legitimacy in and across contexts? What normative frameworks will be selected as contextually salient? These questions consider how participants themselves define the boundaries across contexts and how they determine the locally salient normative expectations that need to be recognised.

2.3 Legitimation as an interactional accomplishment

As mentioned above, gaining access to knowledge and developing practical skills requires apprentices to participate in social practices and become legitimate members of communities of practice. Reciprocally, vocational school teachers and workplace mentors and supervisors must also maintain their positions as experts and need to be recognised as legitimate references. In other words, participants involved in face-to-face interactions (both learners and trainers) are expected to behave in a contextually consistent and valuable way. From an interactional perspective, participants in a learning process need to interactively align themselves to what is normatively expected according to the effective social role. Therefore, participation practices in vocational training contexts are relevant resources to detect actors' agency about the ways they build their social recognition and legitimacy in interactions.

In contemporary sociology, social recognition has been defined in terms of social and civil rights and associated with other societal phenomena like multiculturalism, ethnicity, democratic participation and sexuality (Taylor 1994; Fraser 1995, 2000; Honneth 1996). Within social psychology, social recognition has a long research tradition, conceptualised in terms of basic needs and background motivation sources for the development of one's individual self (Mead 1967) and explaining individual behaviour. Thus, according to Jacobsen and Kristiansen (2009: 50–1), social recognition has been either approached as an abstract philosophical issue or referred to as the 'person's subjective perception of being recognized by his/her surroundings'. They argue, however, that 'the intermediary realm between self and others constituted by actual people engaging with each other in actual face to face interaction has been neglected' (Jacobsen and Kristiansen 2009: 51). By focusing on the trainer–trainees relationship within vocational training centres and workplaces, we intend to explore legitimacy and legitimation as face-to-face recognition processes. To understand recognition as driven by 'interactional, situational or interpersonal' factors (Jacobsen and Kristiansen 2009: 51), we adopt a Goffmanian perspective on social recognition. Goffman (1959, 1963) distinguishes between 'cognitive recognition' and 'social recognition'. The former refers to 'a process by which one individual "places" or identifies another, linking the sight of him with a framework of information concerning him' (Goffman 1963: 112–13). The latter is more concerned with 'the process of openly welcoming or at least accepting the initiation of an engagement, as when a greeting or a smile is returned' (Goffman 1963: 113).

Applied to vocational educational and training contexts, these two forms of recognition seem particularly suited to investigate legitimation processes occurring in and across contexts. Such legitimation processes involve both cognitive and social dimensions. Indeed, in vocational training relationships, apprentices, teachers, trainers, mentors, and so on are cognitively recognised and 'placed' within relevant categories (i.e. as members of specific communities of practice). They are cognitively recognised as persons of a certain kind: an apprentice, a vocational teacher, a workplace supervisor, and so on. Cognitive recognition is thus 'the process through which we socially or personally identify the other' (Goffman 1963: 113). However, since these individuals belong to several communities of practice in which different roles and identities are mobilised and different values, positions and norm expectations are referred to, social identifications may be perceived as inadequate or displaced. Consequently, participants have to locally negotiate or navigate between these multiple identities and/or references. Such negotiations are particularly relevant for learners in vocational education and training programmes because, as described by Akkerman and Bakker (2012: 156), they are 'at the periphery of both practices and face simultaneously a "neither/ nor" and a "both/and" situation of belonging to communities'. For learners, such an 'in-between' position could potentially generate contradictions. Indeed, 'Apprentices find themselves in an ambiguous position, being a student and novice who is learning yet at the same time a professional who is expected to know and act' (Akkerman and Bakker 2012: 156). Therefore, it is possible that an apprentice is recognised as an 'expert' of his or her work in the context of the school community and at the same time as a 'novice' in the workplace context, or vice versa. Regarding trainers, similar tensions may arise, when, as noted by Lave and Wenger (1991), trainers feel their authority threatened by apprentices becoming full participants.

The ways participants identify others is directly linked with how they interact with them or about them. Participants are expected to socially recognise each other and align their behaviour to 'social, ceremonial and indeed interactive rules and norms of engagement with others in actual social interaction' (Jacobsen and Kristiansen 2009: 59). In other words, according to the relevant context, specific cognitive recognition outputs and identifications may be face-threatening if revealed or made explicit without any form of tact. Thus, legitimation processes are largely based on the symbolic interplay between participants and the management of their 'faces'. Adopting

Goffman's perspective, participants in social encounters display a certain valuable image of their self and consistently work to orient the impression they make on other participants. Individuals are able to act as a certain type of person or enact specific roles through verbal and body language especially. However, when acting, people also give off expressions that are mostly involuntary or uncontrolled. Conveying and maintaining the self-image they want to display appears to be complex work, particularly because the recognition of one's face largely depends on others' judgement.

Using this framework, our aim is to apply a microscopic approach to vocational education and training participatory practices. By adopting an interactional analysis perspective on legitimation/delegitimation participatory practices, we see engagement and participation in activities and social interactions within communities of practice as key contributions to learning as well as to the construction of legitimate identities.

3. Analysing apprenticeship in a 'dual' training system: methodology and data

To investigate legitimation practices in vocational training interactions, we adopt a discursive and interactional perspective. Such a framework combines several analytic frameworks and disciplines. As mentioned above, Goffman's dramaturgical and interactional perspective (Goffman 1959, 1963, 1974) provides a means to finely describe the ways through which participants shape their relationship and negotiate a joint understanding of the local context in which they engage. Highlighting interactional processes of contextual recognition and legitimacy can thus be described and analysed as impression management. From this standpoint, Goffman's dramaturgical perspective (Goffman 1959, 1963, 1974) provides analytic tools of particular importance for our analysis. First, the notions of 'face' and 'face work' highlight how individuals in interaction are bound to the symbolic recognition they will afford one another and to the need to consistently negotiate their self-impression. Second, the concept of 'participation framework' captures the interactional involvement of participants and the ways this involvement may be constantly reframed. In addition to Goffman's analytic categories, contributions from the ethnography of speaking and interactional sociolinguistics (Gumperz 1982) are also central to our analysis. This latter perspective enables us to account for the complex relations linking contextual information with participants' interactional behaviour in general and the production of speech in particular. Gumperz emphasises the contextual dimension not determined by external aspects but rather constructed by actors themselves through 'contextualisation cues' that manifest to others how the ongoing encounter is interpreted and understood. Moreover, insights from pragmatics and interactional linguistics (Filliettaz et al. 2008; Mondada 2004) are used to analyse and understand how speech and language convey meanings that are necessarily situated and emerging from the ongoing interaction process. Finally, multimodal discourse analysis (Kress et al. 2001; Norris 2004; de Saint-Georges 2008) is also used to take into consideration the wide range of semiotic resources used by participants as a complement to verbal communication (gestures, gaze, body positions, interactions with objects and the material environment, etc.). Although these different methodological frameworks come from various disciplinary currents, their articulation is widely compatible and complementary due to the same epistemological orientation centred on an empirical approach of language practices in their contextual usages and because of their underlying ethnographic approach to data production.

Empirical material used in this chapter is part of a larger research project (Filliettaz et al. 2008, 2009, 2010; Filliettaz 2010a, 2010b, 2010c) that aimed at tracing contrasting trajectories of participation in order to better understand the processes of learning and identity construction in the context of transition from school to work.[1] Data collection involved ethnographic observations of a cohort of forty apprentices engaged in three different technical trades: car mechanics, automation and electric assembly. This ethnographic perspective allowed us to observe and document situations of vocational training in naturally occurring conditions in the Geneva area and in the various settings involved in the dual training system: vocational schools, private training centres and workplaces. With the consent of participants, ordinary training activities were video-recorded by researchers. In addition to audio–video recording and ethnographic observations, other empirical sources of information were collected, consisting primarily of field notes, research interviews and various written documents. Special attention was paid to training interactions in which apprentices were involved in vocational learning tasks with a variety of experts, ranging from vocational teachers working in vocational schools, to dedicated trainers hired by training centres, to experienced employees available in the workplace. Apprentices were mainly male adolescents, aged between fifteen and eighteen years old. They were observed during both the first and fourth years of their apprenticeship, namely at the beginning and at the end of their training programme.

4. Examples of legitimation through participatory practices

In this section, a detailed analysis of excerpts of data will illustrate how participation in interaction may consist, for apprentices and experts, of negotiating legitimate positions through legitimation and delegitimation participatory practices. To this end, we use two case studies selected from the available data set. The two case studies refer to two different apprentices – Rodrigo (ROD) and Victor (VIC) – both enrolled in an apprenticeship programme in automation, but observed in two different training sites during their first year of training: a training centre in the first case; and the workplace for the second. In addition, in order to illustrate the diversity of the two training sites, both case studies were selected to show how apprentices may face difficulties or unforeseen events that challenge their positions in training centres as much as in workplaces. By illustrating how ROD and VIC interact with different sorts of experts in these diverse training contexts, we demonstrate how participants manage their mutual relationship and achieve recognition and legitimacy in interaction.

The data and analysis aim to identify diverse and constantly changing participation formats and to understand how these participation formats exert an influence, in terms of both (1) access to work-related knowledge and (2) the position of participants in specific communities of practice. Using this process, we question the 'boundaries' between these learning sites and observe how participants themselves may or may not cross these boundaries in and through their interactions.

4.1 Negotiating a legitimate learner's position in a training centre

The first case study refers to the context of a training centre in which first-year apprentices in automation spend the first six months of their apprenticeship programme, before experiencing the production conditions of workplaces. The objective of the training courses is to provide apprentices with basic technical skills in mechanics, electronics and electricity. The sequences of interaction we use occur approximately three to four months after the beginning of the training course. They relate to a period of training specifically dedicated to the learning of electric wiring. The activity setting underlying these sequences can be described as an individual practical exercise consisting of producing a basic electric command system named 'motor controller' according to explicit technical specifications. Apprentices are asked to build a command system, starting from an electric diagram. This kind of exercise is based on typical tasks that automation specialists are expected to accomplish in the workplace.

The analysis focuses on the interaction between the trainer in charge of the electricity workshop (MON) and an apprentice (ROD). ROD is not progressing as quickly as other apprentices in the workshop. Moreover, the quality of the work he is producing is often not positively assessed by the trainer. In the period of time preceding the transcribed excerpts, MON observed the command system produced by ROD and considered that the wiring was not properly aligned and did not follow the given instructions (see Figure 6.1). He asked ROD to start the wiring all over again. A couple of minutes later, MON comes back to ROD's desk and congratulates ROD for his improvements. This is where excerpt 1 starts.[2]

Excerpt 1 'we will go and see how your boss works' (218, 39:54–40:17)
1　　MON:　((*approaches ROD and observes his work*)) yes that's much better than before\
2　　ROD:　i am doing it properly now\
3　　MON:　did you see the electric unit next-door/ ((*points with his right thumb toward the electric station of the workshop*)) [Figure 6.2]
4　　ROD:　no\
5　　MON:　you want me to show you the electric unit next-door/

Figure 6.1 Electric command system built by ROD before MON asks him to start again.

Figure 6.2 The trainer proposes to go and see the electric station of the workshop.

6	ROD:	a Scheffer one/ [name of the company in which ROD works]
7	MON:	yep\ have you already seen it/
8	ROD:	no\
9	MON:	yes and you work for Scheffer don't you/
10	ROD:	yes i am with Scheffer
11	MON:	come on then we will go and see how your boss works
12		((*MON and ROD leave the mechanics workshop to visit the electric station*))

The first excerpt shows how, through mechanisms of legitimation and delegitimation, changes in the interactional participation practices locate learners in specific communities of practice. Consequently, it also shows how identities are locally built and socially accomplished through micro-negotiation of participation practices.

At the beginning of the excerpt, the trainer (MON) positively assesses ROD's work ('yes that's much better than before', line 1) as accomplished so far, although tacitly suggesting that improvements are still possible. In line 2, ROD ratifies MON's statement but reframes the trainer's assessment by self-evaluating his own work as 'proper' ('i am doing it properly now'). In turn, the trainer reframes ROD's self-evaluation by suggesting that he watch a real electric unit, located in the electric station of the workshop ('did you see the electric unit next-door', line 3). After admitting not having looked at it yet, ROD identifies and categorises ('a Scheffer one', line 6) the electric unit as the one built by Scheffer, the name of the company that has hired ROD as an apprentice. Responding to the sudden reference to the workplace community of practice, the trainer MON instigates an interesting reframing of ROD as a member of such a community ('yes and you work for Scheffer don't you', line 9). Then, after ROD's confirmation about his membership in Scheffer (line 10), MON invites the apprentice to visit the electric station ('come on then we will go and see how your boss works', line 11).

Interestingly, significant changes in the participatory configuration appear at this moment. ROD's wiring activity is suspended by the trainer's proposal that he watch the electric unit, and the activity frame of a wiring task carried out individually is momentarily interrupted. In this new activity frame, ROD is offered an 'observer's' position, guided by the trainer, and located in a different space.

This shift in the participatory practice has important consequences in terms of social recognition and legitimation processes. What at the beginning was labelled as an 'electric unit' is categorised at the end of the excerpt as 'how your boss works'. By reframing ROD's self-evaluation and inviting him to discover what a 'real' electric unit looks like, MON places the apprentice in a specific position, within the community of learners in the training centre: his work is certainly remote from professional standards as they apply in practice; it is still at the periphery of what it should look like. At the same time, as will be seen in greater detail in excerpt 2, the trainer also positions ROD as a member not only of a learners' community of practice, but also of a community of workers. His identity as an employee of Scheffer is explicitly made visible ('you work for Scheffer') and reference is made to 'how the boss works'.

After entering the electric station of the workshop, the trainer opens the electric unit and draws ROD's attention to various properties of the device.

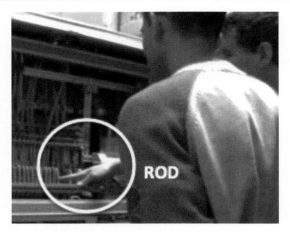

Figure 6.3 The trainer opens the electric unit and points to wires.

Excerpt 2 'that's the kind of work your boss expects' (218, 41:00–42:00)

[. . .]

31	MON:	can you see how the wires are installed/ [Figure 6.3]
32	ROD:	oh yeah/ wouaou the same height/
33	MON:	and each time they make a sort of loop so that there is enough wire in case they need additional wire for a modification ((*designs a loop with his finger*))
34	MON:	OK/ it looks nice doesn't it/
35	ROD:	yeah yeah\
36	MON:	everything is well aligned/ . everything is magnificent/ . right it's not exactly the same as your own wiring earlier is it/
37	ROD:	no it's not the same\ ((*laughs*))
38	MON:	did you see how nice it is all the wires bam bam bam
39	ROD:	yeah\
		[. . .]
47	MON:	so that's the kind of work your boss expects\
48		((*MON and ROD leave the electric station and move back to the mechanics workshop*))

The opening of the electric unit affords new resources in terms of access to professional knowledge and social recognition. As indicated in excerpt 1, the trainer places the apprentice in an 'observer's' position. In line 31, MON starts to draw ROD's attention to the specific way wires are installed and aligned within the electric unit ('can you see how the wires are installed', line 31). He points to material artefacts that are illustrations of a legitimate professional practice, by stressing the aesthetic nature of the wiring: 'OK it looks nice doesn't it' (line 34); 'everything is well aligned, everything is magnificent' (line 36). This aesthetic categorisation of the wiring as 'nice' and 'magnificent' is accomplished in contrast with ROD's own work, in the context of the learning task: 'right it's not exactly the same as your own wiring earlier is it' (line 36).

Pointing to the aesthetic aspects of the electric unit also has important consequences in terms of social recognition and legitimation. By categorising ROD's work as 'not the same' as the real electric unit on display, MON is positioning the apprentice as a legitimate peripheral participant within the learners' community of practice of the training centre. Interestingly, ROD ratifies sequentially the trainer's assertions: 'oh yeah' (line 32); 'yeah yeah' (line 35) 'no it's not the same ((laughs))' (line 37); 'yeah' (line 39). In doing so, he seems to align to the legitimate but peripheral position assigned to him by MON. Moreover, through explicit reference to the workplace community of practice and by comparing ROD's work with Scheffer's professional wiring, the trainer also implicitly positions the apprentice as a peripheral participant within the workplace community of practice. This repositioning appears as particularly salient when ROD expresses how he understands the content of the electric unit. By responding 'oh yeah wouaou the same height' (line 32), ROD ascribes specific categories to the wiring and to what he sees as a professional way to arrange wires. Interestingly, the trainer does not recognise such a statement as fully relevant and orients towards distinct features of the electric unit: the fact that loops are used as a reserve in case additional wire is needed (line 33). ROD's learning and workplace peripheral participation in particular is definitively made relevant by the trainer with his final statement: 'so that's the kind of work your boss expects' (line 47).

In terms of legitimation processes, it is also interesting to notice how the trainer performs such a repositioning of the apprentice. Indeed, before the explicit assessment of ROD's work as 'not the same' (line 37), MON avoids direct face-threatening acts such as direct orders (for example, 'you must do this or that'). Instead, he sensitively draws the apprentice's attention to other models of work and prompts him towards a means to transform his own way to wire. Expressions such as 'oh yeah wouaou' could then be considered as ways for ROD to express relevant learning-driven discoveries. In sum, the trainer acts as 'broker' (Wenger 1998; Akkerman and Bakker 2012) in this particular context: through his participation in interaction, he crosses the physical and symbolic boundary of the training setting and uses the material artefact of the 'real' electric unit as a way to invite the workplace inside the learning situation. By doing so, MON relates ROD's developing skills to professional standards, with his reference to 'how your boss works'. ROD's learning identity is clearly challenged at this point by the community of the workplace, a community he does not yet belong to, but whose material accomplishments are exhibited as resources for learning to work.

4.2 Keeping the apprentice in a workplace marginal position

If vocational training situations are not hermetic to workplace contexts, it should also be observed that workplace training practices may borrow participation formats that are typical of learning and instruction processes. To illustrate this, we turn to a second case, observed in the same trade of automation, but related to the training context of the workplace. The situation involves Victor (VIC), a first-year apprentice, and an experienced technician, Norbert (NOR). NOR is not a professional trainer but an ordinary worker, who supervises the work of the apprentice during a three-month internship in the production department of a large industrial company producing electric generator devices.

In the two sequences transcribed below, VIC and his supervisor work together at the end of the production line in an area where the electric generators are tested before leaving the production site. The testing procedure comprises a long list of routine tasks and measures that have to be accomplished in a strict order to make sure all the parts of the generator produced are functioning properly. In the analysis, we draw attention to how VIC and NOR jointly accomplish the testing procedure and how they negotiate specific legitimate participant positions in interaction.

Excerpt 3 takes place at the very beginning of the testing procedure. The apprentice and his supervisor are standing in front of the generator and the apprentice prepares to switch on.

Excerpt 3 'what's the problem?' (220, 05:30–07:35)

1	VIC:	can i switch on now/ ((*VIC touches the main switch and looks at NOR*)) [Figure 6.4]
2	NOR:	first you should check the battery here
3		now you can press on the green button\
4	VIC:	OK\ ((*VIC presses on the main switch, but nothing happens*))
5		a time relay/
6	NOR:	no no it should be on now\ . try again/
7	VIC:	((*VIC presses on the green button again, but nothing happens*))
8	NOR:	((*NOR steps into the electric generator and makes verifications*)) [Figure 6.5]
9	VIC:	what's the problem/
10	NOR:	((*NOR goes back into the electric generator and makes verifications*))

In the first part of the sequence, the apprentice (VIC) has direct access to the testing procedure. He attempts to start the generator under the supervision of an experienced

Figure 6.4 VIC touches the main switch of the generator and addresses NOR: 'can i switch on now'.

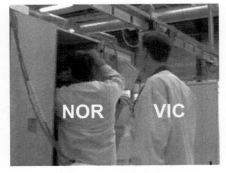

Figure 6.5 NOR steps into the electric generator and makes verifications.

worker (NOR). The leading position of VIC in carrying out the activity is made possible through the strong guidance provided by NOR. Indeed, VIC elicits ratification from NOR before taking action ('can I switch on now', line 1), and NOR responds by providing instructional guidelines ('first you should check the battery here', line 2; 'now you can press on the green button', line 3). Such a participation configuration has important implications for VIC in terms of his identity and membership of the professional community of practice. By affording him the opportunity to lead the ongoing activity, NOR recognises VIC as 'worker' in the making. As stressed by the close guidance provided by NOR and his configuring role in the ways the testing procedure unfolds sequentially, VIC's participation appears as largely 'attenuated' or mediated by the expert. In other words, VIC seems to be recognised as a legitimate participant in the testing procedure, but peripheral to the community of practice and, thus, still in a 'learner's' position.

At the precise moment when the apprentice switches the start button, an unanticipated 'event' occurs: the generator does not turn on (line 4). Interestingly, the emergence of such an event transforms the participatory practices of the apprentice and his supervisor. To deal with the current situation, NOR, the supervisor, adopts a leading position and takes over a close investigation of the generator (line 8), whilst the apprentice (VIC) stands back and becomes an 'observer' of what is happening. NOR no longer produces verbal instructions oriented towards VIC and does not respond to VIC's questions ('what's the problem', line 9). The reframing of the participation practices between VIC and NOR produces a redistribution of the roles and the situated identities endorsed by participants at this stage. NOR re-endorses the role of 'worker' while VIC loses access to the ongoing task. In other words, VIC is placed aside of the work production task and he is not addressed any more as a guided learning worker by his supervisor.

During the next five minutes, NOR keeps on checking the electric generator visually without saying a word but observed by VIC. In spite of his efforts, the generator still does not switch on. After a while, NOR explains to the apprentice that a more systematic troubleshooting procedure has to be conducted. He grabs a folder including the electric diagram of the generator as well as an electric meter device and starts to test all the connecting points in a specific order.

Excerpt 4 'i think it comes from the print' (220, 13:12–14:45)

12	NOR:	[Figure 6.6] until here it's OK now we will check XT-122.4
13	VIC:	yes\
14	NOR:	((*NOR uses the electric meter device to check the contact*))
15		here you have nothing\ . OK that's normal\
16	VIC:	mhmm\
17	NOR:	the contact is open\ . press on now/
18	VIC:	((*VIC presses on the main switch but nothing happens*))
19	NOR:	still nothing\
20	VIC:	right so the problem comes from here\
21	NOR:	((*points to the electric diagram*)) here you have the 26\ so the problem comes either from the button
22	VIC:	yes\

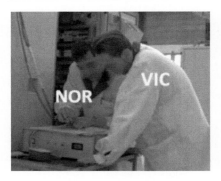

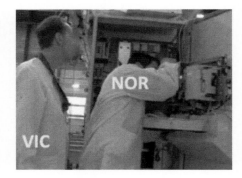

Figure 6.6 NOR and VIC are checking the
electric diagram.

Figure 6.7 NOR takes an electric torch and
observes the electronic board located behind
the main switch.

23   NOR: or from the print\ . i think it comes from the print\ often these prints are a
              bit messy\
24   VIC: mhmm\
25   NOR: let's have a look\ . wait a minute\
26   ((*takes an electric torch and observes the electronic board located behind the main
              switch*)) there is a bad connection here\ [Figure 6.7]
27   VIC: mhmm\
28   NOR: all sorted/ ((*stands up and puts away the flashlight*)) one contact is lacking\
29   VIC: so it's the print\
30   NOR: yes\ we have to change it\

As in excerpt 3, the participation configuration characterising the relation between
the apprentice (VIC) and his supervisor (NOR) appears as highly asymmetrical: it is
again the supervisor who carries out the troubleshooting procedure, by accomplishing
specific testing steps in a sequential and systematic order. However, unlike what happened immediately after the emergence of the event, NOR performs the activity in a
'public' way as he explicitly addresses the apprentice. VIC is selected as the addressed
speaker by NOR ('here you have nothing OK that's normal', line 15). NOR provides
information about various aspects of the troubleshooting procedure. For instance, he
explains forthcoming actions ('let's have a look', line 25), anticipated consequences
('here you have nothing OK that's normal', line 15) and diagnostic hypotheses ('i think
it comes from the print often these prints are a bit messy', line 23). VIC aligns with
these participation stances and endorses an active role of ratified recipient: he listens
to NOR's explanations (lines 16, 18, 24, 27), expresses ratifications (lines 13, 22), and
he rephrases his own understanding of the situation ('right so the problem comes from
here', line 20; 'so it's the print', line 29).

Interestingly, the participatory practices accomplished by NOR and VIC at this
stage have clear consequences in terms of access to professional knowledge. By enacting and commenting on the steps through which a troubleshooting procedure can be
carried out, the supervisor makes visible elements of procedural knowledge and the

specific concepts related to it (Billett 2001). In other words, NOR affords a learning opportunity to VIC in the sense that he does not exclusively addresses a practical production problem individually, but deploys numerous resources to transform this production problem into a meaningful experience addressed to the apprentice.

In terms of social positioning and legitimacy, complex situated identities are endorsed by participants in excerpt 4. NOR, for instance, positions himself as an experienced worker within the professional community: he displays expertise in dealing with a complex production situation. At the same time, however, he endorses a trainer's role as he shapes the activity as interpretable to the apprentice. Reciprocally, VIC is also led to endorse multiple positions in this excerpt. While he is positioned as a marginal member within the professional community of practice since he no longer has direct access to the relevant work, he is nevertheless recognised as a legitimate participant within the community of learners trained in the workplace.

This second case study clearly illustrates that participatory practices, as observed in workplace contexts, do not necessarily consist of strict work production tasks. Participants may invite training and learning practices within workplace contexts, even when carrying out routinised work procedures. As illustrated by the data and analysis, there are several ways for participants to transform production practices into learning opportunities: trainers may guide learners through the experience of conducting work-related actions (see excerpt 3), or they may display these actions as meaningful experiences for apprentices, by making encapsulated work-related knowledge visible (see excerpt 4). However, while work is certainly permeable to training practices and learning opportunities, it should be emphasised how fragile the conditions for crossing such boundaries are. As illustrated by the unexpected event emerging during the testing procedure, the real conditions in which work unfolds in practice can quickly challenge legitimate learners' positions and marginalise the role of apprentices in real work production tasks.

5. Discussion and conclusions

Whether in training centres or in workplaces, acting in a valuable and legitimate way for an apprentice results from a complex process of negotiation and co-construction, involving teachers, trainers and/or the supervising workers. Through the two selected case studies, our analysis shows that apprentices often have to face difficulties or unexpected events in training situations. For example, their work can be assessed as inappropriate, as in ROD's case, or technical troubles may emerge and interrupt routinised work scenarios, as in VIC's experience. These events or difficulties often introduce changes in participation practices and in the roles and positions endorsed by apprentices in the ongoing activities. More specifically, they often initiate a shift from direct access to practice towards observers' positions in which apprentices are addressed as recipients of explanations or demonstrations. Interestingly, these changes in the participation configuration have implications in terms of legitimacy because they transform the ways apprentices are recognised and positioned with regard to ongoing activity frames.

Thus, it appears that participants involved in training and/or in work interactions are provided with access to a plurality of identities, which place them in different communities of practice. As shown with the two apprentices of our case studies, legitimate participation may involve both the community of learners and the community of workers. Reciprocally, professional trainers or workplace supervisors also alternate between workers' and trainers' positions, depending on the ways in which they engage in ongoing activities with apprentices. In other words, the negotiation of social legitimacy in and across contexts often leads participants to cross boundaries. In the first excerpt, taken from the context of a training centre, MON, the trainer, explicitly brings to the apprentice's attention work-based references and norms. In the second excerpt, taken from the context of a workplace, the supervising worker, NOR, turns a troubleshooting procedure into a training opportunity for the apprentice, VIC.

By adopting a fine-grained interactional analysis, it appears that the forms of participation across institutional boundaries are not individually intended and enforced but rather constantly negotiated between participants involved in the ongoing interaction. Such boundaries are not fixed and linked to specific places but rather constructed by the participants who give them contextual saliency. Our analysis shows how participants use discursive and multimodal resources in interaction to establish links between the different epistemological spaces and to cross borders. Such resources can be mobilised in different ways: (1) by referring explicitly to institutional categories related to specific communities of practice ('so that's the kind of work your boss expects'); or (2) by accomplishing specific forms of participation in interaction.

Finally, the interactional approach adopted here brings new perspectives to the social issues related to transitions from school to work and to the difficulties often faced by young people when engaging in apprenticeships. Indeed, apprentices in a dual training system are not only confronted with different institutional spaces associated with distinct normative expectations, they are also expected to navigate across permeable borders even within these institutional settings. Such considerations point to the complexity of participation practices and identity positioning at work within a dual training system. If transitions are not as smooth as expected for an important proportion of apprentices, it is perhaps because the process of crossing boundaries in and through discourse and interaction requires complex skills and competences, which are neither taught nor explicitly detected. The precise contribution of a discursive lens to vocational education and training is to give greater visibility to the sorts of hidden challenges faced by youths when negotiating boundaries at work.

Transcription conventions

.   pause
/   rising tone
\   falling tone
((*action, movement or gesture*))   non-verbal behaviour

Notes

1. This research programme was been sponsored by the Swiss National Science Foundation (SNF) under references PP001-106603 and PP00P1-124650. It benefited from the contributions of Prof. Ingrid de Saint-Georges, Dr Barbara Duc and Dr Stefano Losa.
2. All the excerpts presented in this chapter are translated from French to English.

References

Akkerman, S. F. and A. Bakker (2012), 'Crossing boundaries between school and work during apprenticeships', *Vocations and Learning*, 5, pp. 153–73.

Billett, S. (2001), *Learning in the workplace: strategies for effective practice*, Crows Nest, NSW: Allen & Unwin.

Billett, S. (2004), 'Workplace participatory practices: conceptualising workplaces as learning environments', *The Journal of Workplace Learning*, 16: 6, pp. 312–24.

Clark, H. H. (1996), *Using language*, Cambridge: Cambridge University Press.

de Saint-Georges, I. (2008), 'La multimodalité et ses ressources pour l'enseignement – apprentissage', in L. Filliettaz, I. de Saint-Georges and B. Duc (eds), *'Vos mains sont intelligentes!': interactions en formation professionnelle initiale*, Université de Genève: Cahiers de la Section des Sciences de l'Education, 117, pp. 117–58.

Dubs, R. (2006), *An appraisal of the Swiss vocational education and training system*, Bern: HEP Verlag.

Filliettaz, L. (2010a), 'Interaction and miscommunication in the Swiss vocational education context: researching vocational learning from a linguistic perspective', *Journal of Applied Linguistics and Professional Practice*, 7: 1, pp. 27–50.

Filliettaz, L. (2010b), 'Dropping out of apprenticeship programs: evidence from the Swiss vocational education system and methodological perspectives for research', *International Journal of Training Research*, 8: 2, pp. 141–53.

Filliettaz, L. (2010c), 'Guidance as an interactional accomplishment: practice-based learning within the Swiss VET system', in S. Billett (ed.), *Learning through practice: models, traditions, orientations and approaches*, Dordrecht: Springer, pp. 156–79.

Filliettaz, L., I. de Saint-Georges and B. Duc (2008), *'Vos mains sont intelligentes!': Interactions en formation professionnelle initiale*, Université de Genève: Cahiers de la Section des Sciences de l'Education, 117.

Filliettaz, L., I. de Saint-Georges and B. Duc (2009), 'Interactions verbales et dynamiques de participation en formation professionnelle initiale', in M. Durand and L. Filliettaz (eds), *Travail et formation des adultes*, Paris: Presses universitaires de France, pp. 95–124.

Filliettaz, L., I. de Saint-Georges and B. Duc (2010), 'Skiing, cheese fondue and Swiss watches: analogical discourse in vocational training interactions', *Vocations & Learning*, 3: 2, pp. 117–40.

Filliettaz, L., S. Losa and B. Duc (2013), 'Power, miscommunication and cultural diversity: applying a discourse analytic lens to vocational education practices', in I. de Saint-Georges and J.-J. Weber (eds), *Multilingualism and multimodality: current challenges for educational studies*, Rotterdam: Sense Publishers, pp. 153–81.

Fraser, N. (1995), 'From redistribution to recognition: dilemmas of justice in a "post-socialist" age', *New Left Review*, 212, pp. 68–93.

Fraser, N. (2000), 'Rethinking recognition', *New Left Review*, 3, pp. 107–20.

Fuller, A. and L. Unwin (2003), 'Learning as apprentices in the contemporary UK workplace: creating and managing expansive and restrictive participation', *Journal of Education and Work*, 16: 4, pp. 407–26.

Goffman, E. (1959), *The presentation of self in everyday life*, New York: Doubleday.

Goffman, E. (1963), *Behavior in public places: notes on the social organization of gatherings*, New York: Free Press.

Goffman, E. (1974), *Frame analysis: an essay on the organization of experience*, New York: Harper & Row.

Gumperz, J. J. (1982), *Discourse strategies*, Cambridge: Cambridge University Press.

Hodkinson, P. (2005), 'Reconceptualising the relations between college-based and workplace learning', *Journal of Workplace Learning*, 17: 8, pp. 521–32.

Honneth, A. (1996), *The struggle for recognition: the moral grammar of social conflicts*, Cambridge, MA: MIT Press.

Jacobsen, H. M. and S. Kristiansen (2009), 'Micro-recognition: Erving Goffman as recognition thinker', *Sosiologisk Årbok*, 3: 4, pp. 47–76.

Kress, G., T. Charalampos, J. Ogborn and C. Jewitt (2001), *Multimodal teaching and learning: the rhetorics of the science classroom*, London: Continuum.

Kunégel, P. (2005), 'L'apprentissage en entreprise: l'activité de médiation des tuteurs', *Education permanente*, 165, pp. 127–38.

Lamamra, N. and J. Masdonati (2009), *Arrêter une formation professionnelle: mots et maux d'apprenti-e-s*, Lausanne: Antipodes.

Lave, J. and E. Wenger (1991), *Situated learning: legitimate peripheral participation*, Cambridge: Cambridge University Press.

Losa, S. A., B. Duc and L. Filliettaz (2014), 'Success, well-being and social recognition: an interactional perspective on vocational training practices', in A. C. Keller, R. Samuel, M. M. Bergman and N. K. Semmer (eds), *Psychological, educational, and sociological perspectives on success and well-being in career development*, Dordrecht: Springer, pp. 69–98.

Mayen, P. (2002), 'Le rôle des autres dans le développement de l'expérience', *Education permanente*, 139, pp. 65–86.

Mead, G. H. (1967), *Mind, self, and society: from the standpoint of a social behaviorist*, Chicago: University of Chicago Press.

Mondada, L. (2004), 'Temporalité, séquentialité et multimodalité au fondement de l'organisation de l'interaction: le pointage comme pratique de prise du tour', *Cahiers de linguistique française*, 26, pp. 269–92.

Norris, S. (2004), *Analyzing multimodal interaction: a methodological framework*, London: Routledge.

Stalder, B. E. and C. Nägele (2011), 'Vocational education and training in Switzerland: organisation, development and challenges for the future', in M. M. Bergman,

S. Hupka-Brunner, A. Keller, T. Meyer and B. E. Stalder (eds), *Youth transitions in Switzerland: results from the TREE panel study*, Zurich: Seismo, pp. 1–39.

Taylor, C. (1994), 'The politics of recognition', in A. Gutmann (ed.), *Multiculturalism: examining the politics of recognition*, Princeton: Princeton University Press.

Tsui, A. B. M. and D. Y. K. Law (2007), 'Learning as boundary-crossing in school–university partnership', *Teaching and Teacher Education*, 23: 8, pp. 1289–301.

Tuomi-Gröhn, T., Y. Engeström and M. Young (2003), 'From transfer to boundary-crossing between school and work as a tool for developing vocational education: an introduction', in T. Tuomi-Gröhn and Y. Engeström (eds), *Between school and work: new perspectives on transfer and boundary-crossing*, Amsterdam: Pergamon, pp. 1–18.

Wenger, E. (1998), *Communities of practice: learning, meaning and identity*, New York: Cambridge University Press.

Wenger, E. (2000), 'Communities of practice and social learning systems', *Organization*, 7: 2, pp. 225–46.

Wenger, E., R. McDermott and W. Snyder (2002), *Cultivating communities of practice*, Boston: Harvard Business School Press.

Wenger-Trayner, E. and B. Wenger-Trayner (2015), 'Introduction to communities of practice: a brief overview of the concept and its uses', <http://wenger-trayner.com/introduction-to-communities-of-practice/> (last accessed 7 November 2016).

Part II Transitions *within* a Profession

7

Multilingualism and Work Experience in Germany: On the Pragmatic Notion of 'Patiency'

Kristin Bührig and Jochen Rehbein

1. Crossing: leaving for Germany

In the Introduction to this volume the editors identify several subjects of relevance with respect to the topics of boundary marking.[1] One of them is 'how individuals scrutinise their own understanding of how things work' within the process of crossing boundaries, be it between different countries, between different languages, or socialising into a new group.

In a worldwide perspective, crossing boundaries comes hand in hand with complex urbanisation by which living, working and talking together is becoming more and more abstract, opaque as well as multifaceted, and so the societal structures are increasingly difficult to grasp not only for the immigrant but also for the domestic citizen (Rehbein 2010). Closely examined, by the process of urbanisation, leaders (entrepreneurs) and clerks, white- and blue-collar workers, agents and clients of institutions and other actants are equally subjected to the objective determinants of the social space of action, its contrariness, vicissitudes and unpredictabilities as are those who cross the boundaries and have to discern the objective determinants in the new urban framework from the very first (Zikic et al. 2010).

In view of globalised societies being in a state of flux, it seems that we are dealing with two antagonistic types of activities connected to different 'actancies'. Intervening 'actancy', the first type, based on planning and decision-making and aiming at the restructuring of the space of action, is generally known as 'agency' (e.g. von Wright 1968; Goldman 1970; Davidson 1971; Rehbein 1977; Ahearn 2001; Duranti 2004; Helfferich 2012). The second type, which requires accommodation to objective social structures, involves perception, processing of new experiences (Ehlich and Rehbein 1977) and mental restructuring. In what follows, we focus on the concrete analysis of the second type of actancy based on narrative fragments, stemming from interviews with Turkish migrant workers which were conducted in the early 1980s in Germany's Ruhr region.

The reason why we rely on these early data has to do with the specific history of mass immigration into Germany. Let us briefly recall the situation of immigrants leaving Turkey for Germany in the late 1960s and early 1970s. All the workers from our interviews reported that once having passed the physical examination and an elementary knowledge test at the so-called *Anwerbungsstellen* (recruitment offices) in Turkey, they had to wait for a letter of invitation which ordered their often imminent departure but without giving them any idea of what kind of work they would have to do and where.

Thus, the entrance to their new working career can be described in Baumann's (2005) term as 'liquid lives', where 'the conditions under which people act [. . .] change faster than it takes the ways of acting to consolidate into habits and routines' (Baumann 2005: 1).[2] As Baynham (2006: 376) states in his study on Moroccan economic migrants in London: 'Narratives of migration and settlement are narratives in which, almost by definition, settled and stable senses of self are unsettled and challenged.'

Although our interviewees' biographies differ with respect to their professional education, they were all so-called blue-collar workers with originally no knowledge of German. Yet, in the 1970s and 1980s, their respective workplaces required monolingual communication in German; yet the immigrant workers were not provided with any German classes. Apart from communication with other Turkish migrants, our interviewees were thus confronted with situations of muteness; the successive acquisition of German as a second language took place during work time in more or less 'empractical' (i.e. on-the-spot) speech situations (Bühler 1934: 176–7; Bührig 1996; Rehbein 2007a).[3]

Our interviewees' narrations illuminate the particular problems of the work constellations in the 1970s, which are dominated by the typical reactions of a hegemonic society towards needed but clearly alien people with foreign ways of speaking and acting. As things have changed today, we hold it to be a desideratum to deal with the situation of this earlier generation of migrant workers, not only from a general linguistic point of view but also with regard to language acquisition as such. Deplorably, most early studies of second language acquisition do not consider the societal conditions of language acquisition (cf. Clahsen et al. 1983; Perdue 1993), nor do they take into account what it means for the learners if their participation in their everyday working life is restricted by their limited communication.

2. Social structures, identity and biographical interviews

Our data stem from twelve biographical interviews. The conversations with the interviewees took place after work at the workers' homes, with other family members present, and lasted about three hours each. Another participant apart from the authors was a Turkish student who had established the contact and also acted as interpreter. The aim was to create an atmosphere which would enable attentive listening as well as the narration of extraordinary experiences at the workplace.[4]

As a starting point for our analysis, we consider 'structuration theory' as outlined by Giddens (1984), within which he rejects the notion that human activity solely depends on agency. Block, in turn, supports Giddens's claim that individuals rather develop their sense of self in close interaction with their particular environments:

'their environments provide conditions and impose constraints whilst they act on that same environment, continuously altering and recreating it' (Block 2006: 38).

It is this process of interaction which can be understood as a source of the ambivalence and conflicts which in their lifelong projects individuals have to cope with in their 'search for answers to fundamental questions which all human life in some way addresses' (Giddens 1991: 47). As Block points out, the individuals' ongoing search for 'ontological security' (to quote Giddens again) motivates them to reconcile their current sense of self and their accumulated past, with a view to dealing with what awaits them in the future (Block 2006: 35).

This perspective on Giddens's argument can be used as an anchor point for referring to Bourdieu (1985). He points out that the perception of the social world implies an act of construction of reality to be performed in everyday practice. The respective categories of perception can be understood as a result of this incorporation of objective structures of the '*espace social*'. They are responsible for accepting the world as it is instead of struggling against it; they build up schemata for perception and experience which cannot be expressed offhandedly, or whose expression cannot be taken for granted (Rehbein 2007b: 139).

In contrast to Bourdieu's radical concept of determination, our interviews suggest the possibility of reflection in narrative discourse. The interview situation turns out to be an opportunity for the interviewees to defend themselves against prefabricated 'roles' and 'identities', or 'images' and scopes of action that were ascribed to them in the past. In our analysis below, we show how the interviewees manage this defence by investigating the usage of reported speech, formulaic expressions and restaging practices. For this reason, the interviewees' utterances have to be interpreted beyond their literal wording.

It is clear that the interviewees are not just telling a story. Rather, in recounting their work experiences they enter into a process of reflecting on these experiences as well as questioning their ascribed identities; thus, they acquire an understanding of how things work. Within this process, the interviewees display a specific form of coping with their experiences, a form which we call 'patiency'.

Let us give a preliminary working definition: in opposition to 'agency', 'patiency' is to be understood as a type of actancy (1) which is characterised by the receptivity of the actant with regard to the societal reality as well as the discursive co-construction in the linguistic interaction, (2) where the actant is not able to determine the conditions of his or her actions, that is, the field of control, and (3) which is characterised by perception and processing of experience up to the level of consciousness. We will return to the definition of 'patiency' after the discussion of the data (section 7 below).

Due to the quality of patiency as a process, we cannot demonstrate its several aspects without looking at lengthy sections of the interviews. However, for the sake of brevity, we will present only the relevant parts which constitute the quintessential moral (Rehbein 1982); in our interviews this is sarcastic submission or disillusion. It is remarkable that, by analysing the transcribed examples, it turns out that the discursivity of the narration corresponds to the processuality of patiency.

3. Sarcastic submission

The first example shows how the migrant worker qualifies the process of accommodation to the linguistic norms of the new society. It stems from an interview with a Kurdish woman who grew up in Turkey to whom a German widow offered the opportunity to work as a waitress in a so-called *Wirtschaft* (inn). She accepted the offer although she was not able to speak any German. However, after a while she succeeded in understanding the German customers. Her strategy for improving her German was to ask questions like 'what do you call this?' and then to write down the German answer in order to learn the respective expression or utterance by heart. In her narration, the Germans appear as teachers; conversely, she was ascribed the role of a pupil who would be immediately corrected if she made a mistake. The fragment in example 1 illustrates this process.

Example 1 'Corrections'
R: interviewer, German academic; K: working person, Turkish with Kurdish background, f.; A: Ayşe, Turkish-German student, interpreter, f.; Com: comment.

[180]

	/411/
R [v]	Hm˙

	/412/	/413/
K[v]	Ging das. Und die deutsche Jungens und mit deutsche(s)
K[TL]	*And the German boys came in with German girl(s), (we had*

[181]

K[v]	Mädchen reingekommen sind, immer (hatten wir), wenn ich ma(l) eine
K[TL]	*always), when I made a mistake regarding language,*

[182]

K[v]	Fehler gemacht hab, mit Spr/ Sprache, dann haben (die) gesagt: "Nein,
K[TL]	*then they used to say: "No,*

[183]

	/414/
R [v]	Hm̌˙
	/415/

K[v]	• dat is falsch" und "dat is richtig" un(d) so, ne? Hab immer bei
K[TL]	*that is wrong" and "that is right", and so on, ok? I've have always*

[184]

	/416/ /417/
R [v]	Hm̌˙ Hm̌˙
	/418/ /419/

K[v]	aufgeschrieben, ne? Und haben sie immer... • • Hab (im/ m/
K[TL]	*written this down, ok? And they have always... • • I've (for)*

[185]

K[v]	äh) Beispiel hab ich immer (am) Telefon gesagt "Wiedersehen", ne?
K[TL]	*example I've always said in the telephone "See you/ meet you again, ok?*

[186]

/420/

K[v]	Und (da) haben sie gesagt, "Nein, mußt du sagen: 'Wiederhören'"!
K[TL]	*And then they have said, "No, you have to say "talk to you again"!*

[187]

/421/ /423/ /426/

R [v]	Ach so! ((lacht)). Ja.
R[TL]	*I see! Yes.*

/422/ /424/ /425/ /427/

K[v]	Ne? So das. ((lacht)). Ja, ich)/ ich konnte nich sagen, (*
K[TL]	*Ok? That's how it went.((laughs)) Yes, I/I could not say, (*
A[v]	((lacht belustigt))
A[TL]	*((laughs amusedly))*

[188]

/428/ /429/

R [v]	Aber das sagen doch auch Deutsche! Sagen manchmal am Telefon
R[TL]	*But even Germans say so! Say sometimes on the*
K[v]	) auf Wiedersehen, ne?
K[TL]	*) meeting you again, ok?*

[189]

/431/

R [v]	"auf Wiedersehen" oder "Wieder (*)". ((--------- lacht----
R[TL]	*telephone "see you again "or ( ) again". ((-----------*

/430/ /432/

K[v]	Ja, ich ((lacht)) ich weiß nicht. Aber äh (also)
K[TL]	*Well, I ((laughs)) don't know. But uh (well)*

[190]

/433/

R [v]	--------)). Ja.
R[TL]	*laughs -------------)).*
K[v]	immer zu mir gesagt: "Nein, muß am Telefon immer sagen". En
K[TL]	*they always told me: "No, you always have to say so on the telephone". A*

[191]

/434/

R [v]	Hm̃ Hm̃ Hm˙ Hm˙ Ja.

/435/

K[v]	paar/ (n) paar mal hab ich immer gesagt "Wiedersehen" und so, ne?
K[TL]	*couple/ (a) couple of times I've always said "See you" and stuff, okay?*

[192]

		/437/
R [v]		Hm˙
	/436/	
K[v]	Aber haben die mir gesagt: "Nein, (muß' sagen) Wiederhören".	
K[TL]	*But they've said to me: "No, (you've to say), talk to you again!"*	

[193]

	/438/	/439/
K[v]	Dann hab ich (das auch noch)…	((lacht)). Ich hab' gesag(t), hab' ich
K[TL]	*Then I have (this too even)…*	*((laughs))I've said, thereby, I've learnt*

[194]

		/440/
R [v]		((lacht)).
R[TL]		*((laughs))*
		/441/
K[v]	noch ein Wort dabei gelernt.	(lacht)).
K[TL]	*another word even.*	*((laughs))*

The analysis starts with segment 413 in score area 180. The example clearly shows that in light of the interviewee's command of German, some of the customers conceive of themselves as experts in the German language. This apparently is a role that encourages the customers to confront the interviewee with particular norms of the German language. In doing so, the customers also give self-initiated corrections and thus they – presumably unrequested – interfere with the interviewee's (linguistic) action processes. From research on repairs and corrections (e.g. Schegloff 2000), we know that corrections in everyday conversations which are not initiated by the primary speaker may cause trouble in interaction as they are understood as a type of impolite frontier crossing, as a violation of the primary speaker's 'field of control' (Rehbein 1977; Rehbein and Fienemann 2004). However, this is not a point that our interviewee makes herself. She accepts the correction without protest: in other words, she accepts the role of obedient pupil, though her portrayal clearly contains some sarcasm, which is apparent in her tone.

The interviewee uses reported speech to describe the situation. In contrast to the poor command of German that she attests herself, the interviewee copies the customers' dialect (prosody and pronunciation of deictic elements in the so-called Ruhr-German *dat* (that); see segment 413). Thus, she demonstrates to a high degree her (actual) language awareness and linguistic proficiency. In doing so within her narration, the interviewee vividly restages the situations of correction.

Subsequently she gives another example (segments 419–20): she uses the German formulaic expression 'see you again' for both: saying goodbye to customers in the inn as well as closing a phone call. The zealous customers' correction which says that she has to use 'talk to you again', first causes amusement signalled by laughter on the interviewer's part, and then leads him to point out that even Germans use 'see you' when closing phone calls (segments 428, 429). The interviewer's amusement presumably results from the obtrusive character of the customers' correction. The point that even Germans use 'see you' when talking on the phone clearly indicates that this correction is not relevant and casts doubt on the customers' overall teaching behaviour. Overall, the narrative conveys the impression that the corrections are not performed in order to improve the interviewee's German. Rather, she becomes an object of observation and language dressage and an addressee (one might be tempted to say 'victim') of the customers' self-presentation.

4. Disillusion

The second example illustrates how the migrant worker gains insight into social structures at the workplace. The interviewee complains that he is constantly appointed to different workplaces within the company, and that he, especially as a foreign worker, suffers from the negative effects of the generally increasing lack of work. Similar to example 1, the interviewee in example 2 uses reported speech to recount his experiences, so that one cannot speak of a 'subject-centred narration' (no *Ich-Erzählung*).

Example 2 'Why?', 'Must' (*'Warum?'*, *'Muss'*)
I1: interviewer 1, German academic; V: working person, Turk, 1. generation, 40, father, m.;
V [IL]: interlinear translation of Turkish utterances of V; M: Turkish woman, wife of V,
mother (M), f.; M [IL] interlinear translation of M's Turkish utterances

[54]

		/251/			
I1 [v]		Hm˙			
			/253/	/254/	/255/
V [v]	wieder arbeiten.		O...	Äh...	Ondan sonra/ un dann
V [IL]					Danach
V[eg]					Ondan sonra/ and then
		/252/			
M [v]		Grev yapmışlar yani geldikleri zamanda.			
M [IL]		Sie haben gestreikt also, als sie gekommen sind.			

[55]

			/256/		/257/
V [v]	Firma Arbeit sechs Jahre da.		((3 s))( ) (Imma da) ( ).		Gute Arbeit (
V[eg]	company work six years there		((3s)) { }(always there)( ).		Good work (
					/258/
M [v]					Parası az
M [IL]					Geld zu

[56]

		/259/	/261/			/264/
I1 [v]		Aha!	Ja.			Nix richtig?
I1[eg]		Uhm	Yes.			Nothing proper?
			/260/	/262/	/263/	/265/
V [v]	) da.		Firma.	Ama • nix riktig machen da.	((4 s))	
V[eg]	) there.		Company.	Ama • nothing right do there.	((4s))	
M [v]	diye [aktı.					
M [IL]	wenig, hat er (sie) gelassen.					
Com	[supposedly: bıraktı = hat gelassen (has let)					

[57]

		/266/			
I1 [v]		Hm˙			
			/267/		/268/
V [v]	Firma, ja.		Einmal hija da, • einmal hija, • einmal da, • einmal da.		• Ganz
V[eg]	Company, yes.		Once here there, • once here, • once there, • once here.		•

[58]

	/269/	/270/	/272/		/274/
I1 [v]	So?	Hm, hm˙	Hm˙	Hm˙	Ah ja.
I1[eg]	So?				Uh
			/271/	/273/	
V [v]	diese • riktig machen.		Un dann: "nix kollega!	Hija arbeiten!"	
V[eg]	*Totally this right make.*		*And then: "nothing colleague! • Here work!"*		

[59]

		/277/		
I1 [v]		Hm˙		
I1[eg]	yes			
	/275/	/276/	/278/	/279/
V [v]	Warum?	((4 s)) Ja, muss!	Un dann schlek spregen.	Un dann ab…
V[eg]	*Why?*	*((4s)) Yes, must!*	*And then bad speak.*	*And then off…*

[60]

	/281/			/283/	/285/	
I1 [v]	Hm˙ Hm˙			Hm˙	Hm˙	
	/280/		/282/		/284/	/286/
V [v]	((2 s))	Warum?	((5 s)) Diese ganz riktig Arbeit.		Ja.	Un dann warum
V[eg]	*((2s))*	*Why?*	*((5s)) This totally right work.*		*Yes.*	*And then why*

[61]

		/287/			
I1 [v]		Hm˙			
		/288/		/289/	/290/
V [v]	"wieda • i die Arbeit."	((5 s)) Un dann alles klar, ja.	•	Ja, • muss.	((2 s))
V[eg]	*"work over there."*	*((5 s)) And then all clear, yes.*	• *Yes,*	• *must.*	*((2s))*

[62]

	/291/	/293/		/295/
I1 [v]	Hm˙	Hm˙		Hm,
		/292/	/294/	
V [v]	Ich bin Ausländer.	Ama Deutschen alles klar.	Deutsche imma arbeitet.	
V[eg]	*I am foreigner.*	*Ama Germans all clear.*	*Germans allways works.*	

[63]

		/297/		/300/	/302/
I1 [v]	hm, hm̃˙	Hm˙		Hm˙	Hm˙
	/296/		/298/	/299/	/301/
V [v]	Ich bin Ausländer.		Denn hau ab!	((4 s))	Warum ab?
V[eg]	*I am foreigner.*		*Then get lost!*	*((4s))*	*Why lost?*

[64]

		/304/		
I1 [v]		Hm˙ Hm˙		
	/303a/	/303b/	/305/	
V [v]	Un dann wieda arbeiten.	• Muss.	Un dann • Meister komm da, ne?	
V[eg]	*And then work again.*	• *Must.*		

The analysis starts with segment 255 in score area 54. In the example, the Turkish immigrant relates experiences about his being given the run-around by his colleagues in unskilled workplaces. As throughout the discourse, example 2 shapes according to 'narrative episodes' as follows:

1. A connecting element introducing a new episode: An episode starts with an 'and then' ('*ondan sonra/un dann*') (segment 255) by which it is linearly bound to the preceding discourse and which can be regarded as a pragmatic transfer from Turkish.[5]

2. A topic: The topic of the episode is given in 'company work six years there … always there. Good work there … company' ('*Firma Arbeit sechs Jahre … imma da. Gute Arbeit da … Firma*') (segments 256–60).

3. The state of affairs, or the constellation of the episode: The claim is that although the storyteller works correctly, he is given the run-around: '*Ama*

> • nothing right do there' ('*Ama nix riktig machen da*') (segment 262), 'Once here there, • once here, • once there, • once there. [K. B., J. R. – Although:] • Totally this • right make' ('*Einmal hija da*, • *einmal hija*, • *einmal da*, • *einmal da*. [K. B., J. R. – Although:] • *Ganz diese* • *riktig machen*') (segments 267–8).[6]

4. Events, verbal and non-verbal actions: The worker relates events and actions using reported speech by quoting his colleagues: 'no colleague! • Here work!' ('*nix kollega!* • *Hija arbeiten!*') (segments 271, 273); later he summarises the orders of his colleagues directed at him: 'And then bad speak. And then off . . .' ('*Und dann schlek spregen. Un dann ab . . .*') (segments 278, 279); another order: 'work over there!' ('*wieda* • *i die Arbeit*') (segment 286); at the end of the episode he quotes a general order: 'Then get lost' ('*Denn hau ab!*').[7]

5. Comment(s) about points 3 and 4 (assessments and other knowledge structures): With the question 'why' ('*Warum?*') (segment 275), the Turkish worker interrogatively starts his comment with which he draws upon the subjective consequences; he does this repetitively in segments 286, 289, 301. He accomplishes, then, the comment with his own laconic answer: 'must' ('*Muss*') in segments 276, 289 and in segment 303b at the end of the episode. A further answer is: 'I am a foreigner' ('*Ich bin Ausländer*') (segments 290, 296), or another similar statement: '*Ama* Germans all clear. Germans always works' ('*Ama Deutschen alles klar. Deutsche imma arbeitet*') (segments 292, 294).[8]

Through his narrative, the Turkish worker characterises himself as somebody who permanently has to follow the speech action type of request/order of his German co-workers. In his comment, which reflects the events and actions told, 'why?' ('*warum?*') plays an important role because, by means of intonation and prosody, the interrogative element invites the hearer to look for an answer, thus creating shared understanding and complicity; in other words: 'why?' ('*warum?*') is a thematic cry inviting the listener to form partisanship with the storyteller concerning the scandal that is being verbalised.

'Why?' ('*Warum?*'),[9] then, is a rhetorical question underlining the propositional content which follows. 'Why?' ('*Warum?*') has two discursive dimensions: the discourse preceding it is set as a topic (so '*warum?*' is a topicaliser), while the discourse after 'why?' ('*warum?*') has the function of a complex predicate. According to this analysis, 'why?' ('*warum?*'), then, has the role of a connective (Bührig 2007) which links theme and rheme, and which, at the same time, provides to the connected theme and rheme a structure of knowledge (here an assessment or, even, a sentential knowledge; see Ehlich and Rehbein 1977 for this term) as the storyteller conveys the impression that the related actions and events have an everlasting 'always' character.

The answers to 'why?' ('*warum?*'), that is, the following propositional content, are succinct: 'must' ('*Muss*') (segment 276), 'This totally right work' ('*Diese ganz riktig Arbeit*') (segment 282), 'all clear' ('*alles klar*') (segment 288), 'must' ('*muss*') (segment

289), 'I am a foreigner' ('*Ich bin Ausländer*') (segment 290), '*Ama* (but) Germans all clear' ('*Ama Deutschen alles klar*') (segment 292), 'Germans always works' ('*Deutsche imma arbeitet*') (segment 294), 'I am a foreigner' ('*Ich bin Ausländer*') (segment 298) and 'Must' ('*Muss*') (segment 303b). In these answers, the Turkish worker signals that his related actions indicated a strong compliance. In particular, the repeated modal 'must' ('*muss*') signals subordination under an abstract necessity, and the sentential speech formula 'I am a foreigner' ('*Ich bin Ausländer*') pointing to the advantages of the German nationality of his fellow workers articulates the *causa actionis* to which he is submitted.

Thus, in example 2, theme and rheme are not only linked by 'why?' ('*warum?*') as a connective element, but it is just the imputing function of this 'why?' ('*warum?*') that governs the illocutionary force of the whole propositional content of what follows. In this sense, 'why?' ('*warum?*') governs theme, rheme and their connection as an interactionally constructed matrix (of a matrix construction) (see Rehbein 2007c).

By means of this narrative device, namely, rhetorical 'why?' ('*warum?*') together with the modalised answer, the whole episode (which gets a linear one-after-the-other connectivity by the episodes connected by 'and then' ('*und dann*')) positioned as a comment acquires an additional impression of unavoidability and coerciveness of events and actions to which the storyteller applies himself in constructing the story. Thus, the Turkish worker depicts his own role as being subjected to German co-workers' speech actions and to the hierarchical structures of the company where the immigrant worker is at the bottom and subjected to the words and orders of Germans. As an immigrant worker, one is by default an acted-on person, not an acting one.

Against this background the worker's repeatedly used expression 'must' ('*muss*') also deserves closer examination because it reveals some ambiguity. It is a modal indicating an absolute necessity or obligation. Morpho-syntactically, 'must' ('*muss*') is a finite form of the third person singular present, but here it lacks the – for German – mandatory personal pronoun in the subject position. Maybe, the worker is influenced by Turkish *mecbur* (compulsion) which is, grammatically speaking, a noun phrase predicate and not a verb. Also, 'must' ('*muss*') is not marked prosodically as the imperative-like answer to the question 'why?' ('*warum?*') and therefore it cannot be part of a (reported) discourse among the actants at the workplace. Consequently, it should be read as the narrator's own comment embedded in a quoted dialogue with his colleagues. Used in this way 'must' ('*muss*') gets the quality of a predicate, that is, rheme, of 'sentential knowledge' (see Ehlich and Rehbein 1977) to which the theme has to be inferred from what has been said before. So, 'must' ('*muss*') discloses a synthesis of the worker's repetitive experiences and narratively processes his disillusion concerning the possibility of ever actively changing his workplace conditions. Yet, its discursive appearance here is a citation within a question – answer format: 'Why?', 'Must' ('*Warum?*', '*Muss*'), instead of an explicit comment.

Thus through the tenor of his narration, the Turkish immigrant characterises his experiences as a mode of 'suffering', which is the opposite of 'agency'.

5. Fortune

The third example relates the migrant worker's experience that hazard permeates the workplace. First, the interviewer R asks the Turkish miner B about his everyday duties at the workplace, and he continues with an enquiry about the specific dangers of the job. The interviewee, B, responds with sentential knowledge 'the mine always dangerous' ('*das* • • • *Zeche imma gefährlich*') (score area 1), adding a maxim of action: 'There(fore) pay attention' ('• *Des(halb) (äh) aufpassen.*'). When, in a follow-up question, the interviewer zooms in on potentially hazardous incidents, B comes up with a, to him, unforeseen occurrence involving an exploded hose (score area 2 onwards).

Example 3 'Dangerous work'
R: interviewer 1, German academic; RTL: translation tier of R; B: working person, 40, f.; BTL: translation tier of B; A: Ayşe, Turkish-German student, interpreter; ATL: translation tier of A; Com: Comment.

[1]

B [v]		((1,5s)) Ja, das • • •
BTL		*Yes, the • • mine*
R [v]	Und ähm • • • äh w/ äh is die Arbeit gefährlich?	
RTL	*And ah • • • ah w/ ah is the job dangerous?*	

[2]

B [v]	Zeche imma gefährlich! • Des(halb) (äh) aufpassen.		
BTL	*always dangerous!*	*There(fore) (ah) pay attention.*	
R [v]	Gefährlich! Jă.	Jă. • • Is da schon mal	
RTL	*Dangerous! Yes.*	*Yes. • • Has there*	

[3]

B [v]	• • • I hab das einmal das Unfall gehabt. Das • • [hier.	
BTL	*• • • I have had that an accident once.*	*That • • [here.*
R [v]	was passiert?	
RTL	*something already happened?*	

[4]

B [v]	• • Und Schlau krieg... ((2s)) • • • Einmal Schlau pack • • äh w/ äh kaputt.
BTL	*• • And hose got...* ((2s)) *• • • Once hose took • • ah w/ ah kaput.*
com	*[points supposedly to a scar.*

[5]

B [v]	((1s)) Hochdruckschläuche, nech?	• • Glaube das v/v/v/
BTL	*((1s)) High pressure hoses, yes?*	*• • Think that f/f/f four*
R [v]		Ach so!
RTL		*I see!*

[6]

B [v]	vierhundert ATÜ.	Nech? • So äh • • Druck.	Imma "bum
BTL	hundred bar.	Yes? • So ah • • pressure.	Always "bong
R [v]	• • Hm̌˙		• • Hm̌˙
RTL	• • uhu		• • uh huh

[7]

B [v]	bum bum bum". Auf einnmal: "bwumm". Kaputt!		Ih hab Glück
BTL	bong bong bong. Suddenly: "boing".	Broken!	I was lucky.
R [v]		• Hm̌˙	
RTL		• uh huh	

[8]

B [v]	gehabt. • Des einmal s/ äh gesehn, nech?	Aber so.
BTL	• This once s/ ah sawn, yes?	But so.
R [v]		Hm̌˙ Ach so! Sie ham...
RTL		uh huh I see! You have...

[9]

B [v]	• • Ich bin kipp, ne, da so. Und da, • • da kuck meine Kopp! • • Äh •
BTL	• • I fell down, yes, like this. And then • • there look my head! • • Ah •
R [v]	Hm̌˙ Hm̀hḿ˙
RTL	uh huh uh huh uh huh

[10]

B [v]	äh • das hier krieg nur. Aber viellich i bin so stehn, né, • • • nich
BTL	ah • this here got only. But perhaps I was standing like this, yes, didn't
R [v]	Hm̌˙ Hm̌˙
RTL	uh huhuh huh

[11]

B [v]	gesehn, ne? • • • Dann vielleicht die Augän kaputt.
BTL	see, yes? • • • Then perhaps my eyes bust.
R [v]	• • • Und Sie
RTL	• • • And you
A [v]	Hm̌˙ Hm̌˙
ATL	uh huhuh huh

[12]

B [v]	Aba Gulü/ Glück gehabt. Das hier • • • äh...		• • Jă.
BTL	But luck/ was lucky. This here • • • ah...		• •
R [v]	haben gesehen, wie das so... ((5s)) Der Schlauch is, • is geplatzt?
RTL	saw how this so... ((5s)) The hose did, • did burst?

[13]

B [v]	
BTL	Yes.
R [v]	Hm̌˙ Hm̌˙ • • Das ham Sie grad gesehen auch, wie s so
RTL	uh huh uh huh • • That's what you just saw, too, how this came
A [v]	• Hm̌˙
ATL	• uh huh

[14]

B [v]		Jă.	I gesehn de so.	Einmal: "bum bum bu". So,
BTL		*Yes.*	*I seen this so.*	*Once "bong bong bo".* *Like*
R [v]	aufgegangen...	Hm̆˙		
RTL	*loose...*	*uh huh*		

[15]

B [v]	ne? Einmal: "[schupp". ((4s)) Kaputt! • • Jà. Einmal hier passiert. Und
BTL	*this,yes? Once "snap". ((4s)) Broken! • • Yes. Once happened here. And*
com	*[melodic voicing*

[16]

B [v]	((3s)) einmal das hier. • • Glaube dieser Finger. • Das sswischen der Ro/
BTL	*((3s)) once this here. • • Think this finger. • This between the pi/*

[17]

B [v]	Rohre. Aber ((3s)) das nich schlimm. Aber hier. ‿Das is seks Woche
BTL	*pipes. But ((3s)) that not bad. But here. ‿This is six weeks*

[18]

B [v]	Krankinhaus.			
BTL	*hospital.*			
R [v]		Im Krankenhaus!	Sechs Wochen!	Oh je! Hm̀hm̆˙
R T L		*In hospital!*	*Six weeks!*	*Oh dear! uhu, uhu*
A [v]				Hm̆˙
ATL				*uh huh*

The interviewee B renders the factual circumstances of his accident via onomatopoetic expressions '*bum bum bum*' (score areas 6–7, 14). Onomatopoetic expressions such as the ones B uses belong to the category of expressive linguistic procedures of the linguistic 'tinge' field, according to Functional Pragmatics theory (Bühler 1934; Ehlich 1991). They enable the storyteller not only to imitate sounds of the workplace but to render a scenic restaging of the material constellation underlying the action and event structure (cf. Redder 1994; Fienemann 2006; Rehbein 2013). In example 3, B's expressive procedures replicate the acoustic perception of the accident, namely, the sound of the high-pressure hose exploding.

The actual course of the accident is summarised by B saying that he escaped only by good fortune: 'I was lucky. This once s/ ah sawn, yes?' ('*Ih hab Glück gehabt. Des einmal s/ äh gesehn, nech?*') (score areas 7–8). Furthermore, he exemplifies the range of his fortune by means of an alternative scenario (score areas 9–10), which suggests a potential eye injury if he had been in a different position and therefore been unable to perceive the exploding hose.

In this fragment the interviewee does not appear as an active actant in his statements. At first, the main point of his narrative is the hoses and their properties, then the sounds which B perceives but which he does not take as a trigger for actively changing his focus of action (for the distinction between 'perception' and 'reception', see Rehbein 1977). B's verbalisation does not offer a clear indication concerning the exact point in time when the complete/actual reception of the incident sets in (as is apparent in his comment 'broken' ('*kaputt*') (score areas 4, 7), that is, whether in the risky situation itself or rather later on. Against this backdrop B is still at the mercy of the contingencies of his space of action, namely, the preconditions of his workplace.

If we regard as the organising principle of B's story the dangers connected with working in a mine which he illustrates in response to the interviewer's enquiry, then: 'being fortunate' as well as the communicative emphasis of perceived incidents can be classified as a component of a certain type of narrative:[10] characteristic of this particular species of narrative is B's 'passive role' in the depicted incidents.[11]

Unlike a 'tale of woe' (see Rehbein 1980), in B's narrative the existing workplace conditions gain their own momentum, and due to their function of delineating the action space they subject the actant and prestructure his actions. If the action space transforms into a source of danger, you can only trust your good fortune. In light of this constellation, the discursive processing of his workplace experiences by the passive actant adds up to a 'fortune' narration (for this type of storytelling, see Fienemann 2006) with the specification of an 'observer story'.

6. Domains of 'patiency'

In the transcripts discussed, a number of characteristics of a certain type of social actant emerged which can be summed up according to their relevant domains.

First, with regard to the 'domains of interaction' and that of 'reference to reality', the narrator appears as the recipient of ascriptions which cannot be evaded (example 1), as a person who is continuously ordered about (example 2), or as a person whose action space is determined by random events instead of by planning (example 3).

Second, with regard to the domain of the 'structures of narration and depiction', that is, the domain of the forms of discourse, the narrator appears as an actant who is subordinated to the action space of the workplace. As can be seen in example 3, the narration is characterised by a twofold reduction of the actant's role, namely, (1) his remaining stuck in mere perception, and (2) his helplessness in the face of imminent hazards. In this vein, the connectivity of actions and occurrences as related gains a linearised structure and, thus, a certain ineluctability (especially in examples 2 and 3). Accordingly, the narrator in example 1 is exposed to the taunts of the native speaker majority, because of her allegedly immigrant accent, and remains defenceless.

Third, with regard to the 'domain of processing experiential knowledge', the actants start from a limited consciousness of constellation, but gain more insight in the course of their narration. In example 2, the narrator develops opposition against being ostracised and demands a formal notice; in example 1, the narrator eventually succeeds in ironising the native speakers; and in example 3, the narrator, by means of restaging, characterises his workplace as being contingency-prone. In such cases, the experience of impotence with respect to the workplace conditions leads to an increasing consciousness of constellations and, at the same time, it offers the chance of processing one's experiential knowledge by patiency. This domain, therefore, counts as the critical domain of patiency as it allows for a characteristic 'synthesis of experiences' within a diachronic as well a cumulative structure which eventually may revert to a productive processing of knowledge.

Therefore, in accordance with this analysis, we term the passive actant – as the counterpart to the active actant – the 'patient actant'.

7. 'Patiency' as a basic concept for analysing workplace boundaries

The analysis of the transcribed conversations identifies a number of phenomena which are not conceived or narrated as actions of an autonomous actant with plans and decisions of his or her own (von Wright 1971; Rehbein 1977; Ehlich and Rehbein 1986; Bührig 2005; Schlosser 2015). These results contribute to the vivid debate on the concept of 'agency': as Helfferich (2012) points out, it is useful to consider active and passive forms of 'agency' without delimiting 'agency' as object of research. Nevertheless, 'agency' is also attested as the predicate of 'a source of increasing strain and confusion in social thought' (cf. Emirbayer and Mische 1998: 962), respectively 'a red herring in social theory' (cf. Loyal and Barnes 2001). Scherr (2012) contributes to this debate with a diagnosis which places the debate on 'agency' within the huge range of social theories that deal with the relationship between social structures and the given individual; as a result of deliberating these theories, he concludes that each form of social action process in modern societies means to move between heterogeneous contexts, to recognise and to know the heterogeneous repertoires and to update them in accordance with the specific contexts (Scherr 2012: 116–17).

Needless to say, this chapter is not the place to join in this debate of sociological theories. From our analysis, however, we would like to distil the following idea at the interface between sociological and linguistic research: whereas 'agency' in the sense of Giddens is (the ideal of) the availability of all social conditions of (linguistic) actions by the self-determined subject, or agent,[12] in the domain of 'patiency', complex social activity is to be comprehended not so much through decision-making, social actants' identities and their negotiation, or through their struggle for self-determination and so forth. Rather, social actants' identity could be seen as receptivity when facing their conflicting experiences and as their looking for a balance in order to cope with these. In working, which means in the case of immigrants crossing borders, immigrants are being acted on and are not subjects practising free will to keep their identity. It should be emphasised, moreover, that 'patiency' is not to be identified with Bourdieu's idea of a quasi-total determination of the subject (*'agent'*) by structures of all sectors of society (*'champs'*) and their interplay (see Bourdieu 1980, 1985; Bourdieu et al. 1993). That is why it is necessary to look for a concept which can define these dimensions of subjectivity with higher precision.

The concept of 'patiency' is not a static one, as, for example, 'passivity'. Rather, it becomes obvious that the subject within the multilingual network of the modern social and working conditions of cities has lost a central component of the space of action, that is, the field of control. According to action-theoretic Functional Pragmatics, social subjects are embedded in spaces of action which have several (subjective and objective) dimensions (see Rehbein 1977), and one of these dimensions is the field of control. It is the loss of the field of control as one main structural component of the process of working that the narrating subjects try to recapture within the communicative stage of intercultural discourse (Rehbein 2006) when reflecting on their experiences, which, in turn, are characterised by patiency.

Transcription conventions

( )	incomprehensible parts of utterances with guessed extension (single parentheses)
(xxxxx)	guessed parts of utterances
((laughs))	descriptions of actions in the transcription tier
/	repair
. . .	break-off of an utterance
•, • •, • • •	pause symbols (very short, short, half a second)
((1s))	1 second pause
[	(in the transcription tier) indicates comments in a tier below
‿	liaison
hm˙	raised dot (interjections)
tones	hḿ, á (rising), hm̀, à (falling), hm̂ (rising, falling), hm̌ (falling, rising), hm̄ (progressive)
[180]	bracketed numbers on the left-hand side count score areas of the transcript
/411/	numbers above transcription tiers count segments

Notes

1. We are highly grateful to Ivika Rehbein-Ots for making suggestions regarding the English formulations in this chapter.
2. The classic Marxian *industrielle Reservearmee.*
3. At the time of our interviews, German functioned at the workplaces as a lingua franca (*Verkehrssprache*) in the same way as English in English-speaking countries (see Clyne 1994 for the situation in Australia and in New Zealand). With workers communicating in the lingua franca, linguistic irritations arise from the fact that the immigrant workers transmit into

the lingua franca the pattern knowledge of acting and speaking, and the action structures of their own home languages, by means of an intercultural apparatus.

4. The conversations comprise about fifty hours in all and were transcribed by means of Semi-interpretative Working Transcription (HIAT) with the transcription program EXMARaLDA (cf. Ehlich and Rehbein 1976; Ehlich 1993; Rehbein et al. 2004; Kameyama and Rehbein 2012; Rehbein 2012). The English interlinear version does not try to translate the German spoken immigrant language into English foreigner talk; instead, it is meant to express accurately the meaning of what is being said.

5. Cf. also '*Un dann*' ('and then') in segments 271, 278, 286, 288, 303a, 305; cf. also Turkish '*ama*' ('but') as a connective in segments 262, 292; also 'must' can be retraced to Turkish *mecbur* ('forced') in comparable modal constructions (see below). Rehbein and Fienemann 2004 argue that L2-phenomena like these which can easily be traced back to their counterparts in the L1 (here Turkish) are due to 'pragmatic transfer'.

6. L2-speech formulae of target-language German counterparts can be found in these formulations: >*mal hier, mal da*<, >*hab alles richtig gemacht*< (where finite German constructions are transformed into infinite L2-constructions): these are L2-models or L2-convergences of target-language German speech formulae (see Rehbein 1987 in detail).

7. The reported speech of his co-workers has the structure of an L2-*situative* speech abstracted from the empractical German '(target-)language of the workplace' (for this distinction, see Bühler 1934; Rehbein 2007a).

8. From a sociolinguistic point of view, the German variety of this Turkish worker can be categorised as a 'mixed language' (see Bakker and Matras 2003 for this term) composed of transferred pragmatic elements from (Turkish) L1, of multiple (German) L2-formulaic expressions converging with speech formulae of target-German (Rehbein 1987), and of reported speech of his co-workers, which show the structure of foreigner-talk German L2-situative speech modelling the empractical German target-language of the workplace. This mixture of three 'reference models' of language should not to be confounded with codeswitching. Rather, it is a phenomenon of creative multilingual synthesis of diverse elements of diverse languages.

9. Interestingly, nearly the same discursive device exists in Turkish with '*niçin?*' or '*neden?*' ('why?'), with which speakers used to elicit hearers' expectations (Ehlich and Rehbein 1972) to answers given by themselves in the form of short stories carrying a high, compelling illocutionary force. It seems to be a rhetorical questioning device in Turkish narrative discourse, too. Thus, '*warum?*' ('why?') in example 2 is conceptually based on an L1-counterpart and, therefore, is a pragmatic transfer as well (see Rehbein and Fienemann 2004).

10. In the literature on narratives, it has been noted (e.g. by Quasthoff 1980) that there are so-called observer stories, which is the case if somebody recounts an incident he or she was not involved in. These observer stories may be

realised in an ironic fashion if an actant who originally was involved in the retold incident assumes the perspective of an observer, as shown by Bührig (2003) (see also Goffman 1981 and Goodwin 2007 on 'footing'; Bührig and Rehbein 2000).

11. With Janet Holmes (2006), one could state that the worker constructs his or her identity in context, that is, as somebody who is immersed in the action and event structures of his or her workplace.

12. The same holds true for the beginning of linguistic pragmatics: similarly to Giddens, Austin (1962) and Searle (1969) regard the performers of a speech act to be active agents in their own right. Yet, in our data we find speech acts which cannot be traced back to an autonomous actant. Here, the actants do not make decisions, nor do they form plans, neither do they have command of a control field which is a critical element of the dimensions of the action space (see Rehbein 1977). What is more, their actions are not consistently anchored in what Bühler (1934) calls an origo, a hic-et-nunc-point in the constellation of the action.

References

Ahearn, L. M. (2001), 'Language and agency', *Annual Review of Anthropology*, 30, pp. 109–37.

Austin, J. L. (1962), *How to do things with words*, Cambridge, MA: Harvard University Press.

Bakker, P. and Y. Matras (2003) 'Mixed languages: reexamining the structural prototype', in P. Bakker and Y. Matras (eds), *The mixed language debate: theoretical and empirical advances*, Berlin: Mouton de Gruyter, pp. 151–76.

Baumann, Z. (2005), *Vivid life*, Cambridge: Polity Press.

Baynham, M. (2006), 'Performing self, family and community in Moroccan narratives of migration and settlement', in A. De Fina, D. Schiffrin and M. Bamberg (eds), *Discourse and identity*, Cambridge: Cambridge University Press, pp. 377–97.

Block, D. (2006), 'Identity in applied linguistics', in T. Omoniyi and G. White (eds), *The sociolinguistics of identity*, London: Continuum, pp. 34–49.

Bourdieu, P. (1980), *Le sens pratique*, Paris: Éditions de Minuit.

Bourdieu, P. (1985), *Sozialer Raum und 'Klassen'. Leçon sur la leçon. Zwei Vorlesungen*, Frankfurt am Main: Suhrkamp.

Bourdieu, P., G. Balazs, S. Beaud, S. Broccolichi, P. Champagne, R. Christin, R. Lenoir, F. Œuvrard, M. Pialoux, A. Sayad, F. Schultheis and C. Soulié (1993), *La misère du monde*, Paris: Éditions du Seuil.

Bühler, K. (1934), *Sprachtheorie. Die Darstellungsfunktion der Sprache*, Jena: Fischer (published in English as *Theory of language: the representational function of language*, trans. D. F. Goodwin, Amsterdam and Philadelphia: John Benjamins, 1990).

Bührig, K. (1996), *Reformulierende Handlungen. Zur Analyse sprachlicher Adaptierun-gsprozesse in institutioneller Kommunikation*, Tübingen: Narr

Bührig, K. (2003), 'Zur Strukturierung von Diskurs und Hoererwissen: auf jeden Fall im alltaeglichen Erzählen und in der Hochschulkommunikation', in L. Hoffmann (ed.), *Funktionale Syntax. Die pragmatische Perspektive*, Berlin and New York: Mouton de Gruyter, pp. 249–69.

Bührig, K. (2005), '"Speech action patterns" and "discourse types"', *Folia Linguistica*, 39: 1–2, pp. 143–71.

Bührig, K. (2007), 'Konnektivpartikel', in L. Hoffmann (ed.), *Handbuch der deutschen Wortarten*, Berlin and New York: Mouton de Gruyter, pp. 525–46.

Bührig, K. and J. House (2007), '"So, given this common theme . . .": linking constructions in discourse across languages', in J. Rehbein, C. Hohenstein and L. Pietsch (eds), *Connectivity in grammar and discourse*, Amsterdam and Philadelphia: John Benjamins, pp. 345–65.

Bührig, K. and Rehbein, J. (2000), *Reproduzierendes Handeln. Übersetzen, simultanes und konsekutives Dolmetschen im diskursanalytischen Vergleich*, Working Papers on Multilingualism, Series B (no. 6), Hamburg: University of Hamburg Collaborative Centre of Multilingualism 538.

Clahsen, H., J. M. Meisel and M. Pienemann (1983), *Deutsch als Zweitsprache: Der Spracherwerb ausländischer Arbeiter*, Tübingen: Narr.

Clyne, M. (1994), *Inter-cultural communication at work: cultural values in discourse*, Cambridge: Cambridge University Press.

Davidson, D. (1971), 'Agency', in R. B. Binkley, R. Bronaugh and A. Marras (eds), *Agent, action, and reason*, Oxford: Blackwell, pp. 73–98.

Duranti, A. (2004), 'Agency in language', in A. Duranti (ed.), *A companion to linguistic anthropology*, Oxford: Blackwell, pp. 452–73.

Ehlich, K. (1991), 'Funktional-pragmatische Kommunikationsanalyse', in D. Flader (ed.), *Verbale Interaktion. Studien zur Empirie und Methodologie der Pragmatik*, Stuttgart: Metzler, pp. 127–43.

Ehlich, K. (1993), 'HIAT: a transcription system for discourse data', in J. A. Edwards and M. D. Lampert (eds), *Talking data: transcription and coding in discourse research*, New York and London: Psychology Press, pp. 123–48.

Ehlich, K. and J. Rehbein (1972), 'Erwarten', in D. Wunderlich (ed.), *Linguistische Pragmatik*, Wiesbaden and Frankfurt am Main: Athenaeum, pp. 99–114.

Ehlich, K. and J. Rehbein (1976), 'Halbinterpretative Arbeitstranskriptionen (HIAT)', *Linguistische Berichte*, 45, pp. 21–41.

Ehlich, K. and J. Rehbein (1977), 'Wissen, kommunikatives Handeln und die Schule', in H. Goeppert (ed.), *Sprachverhalten im Unterricht*, Munich: Fink, pp. 36–113.

Ehlich, K. and J. Rehbein (1986), *Muster und Institution (Patterns and institutions)*, Tübingen: Narr.

Emirbayer, M. and A. Mische (1998), 'What is agency?', *American Journal of Sociology*, 104, pp. 962–1023.

Fienemann, J. (2006), *Erzählen in zwei Sprachen. Diskursanalytische Untersuchungen von Erzählungen auf Deutsch und Französisch*, Münster: Waxmann.

Giddens, A. (1984), *The constitution of society: outline of a theory of structuration*, Cambridge: Polity Press.

Giddens, A. (1991), *Modernity and self-identity: self and society in the late modern age*, Cambridge: Polity Press.

Goffman, E. (1981), 'Footing', in *Forms of talk*, Oxford: Blackwell, pp. 124–59.

Goldman, A. (1970), *A theory of human action*, Englewood Cliffs, NJ: Prentice-Hall.

Goodwin, C. (2007), 'Interactive footing', in E. Holt and R. Clift (eds), *Reporting talk: reported talk in interaction*, Cambridge: Cambridge University Press, pp. 16–46.

Helfferich, C. (2012), 'Einleitung: Von roten Heringen, Graebern und Bruecken. Versuch einer Kartierung von Agency-Konzepten', in S. Bethmann, C. Helfferich, H. Hoffmann and D. Niemann (eds), *Agency. Qualitative Rekonstruktionen und gesellschaftstheoretische Bezüge von Handlungsmächtigkeit*, Weinheim: Beltz Juventa, pp. 9–39.

Holmes, J. (2006), 'Workplace narratives, professional identity and relational practice', in A. De Fina, D. Schiffrin and M. Bamberg (eds), *Discourse and identity*, Cambridge: Cambridge University Press, pp. 166–87.

Kameyama, S. and J. Rehbein (2012), *Segmentation of HIAT-formatted transcripts in EXMARaLDA-PartiturEditor 1.5. Step-by-step instructions how to use the function 'insert utterance numbers' (2nd draft)*, mimeo, Hamburg: University of Hamburg and Ankara: Middle East Technical University.

Loyal, S. and B. Barnes (2001), 'Agency as red herring in social theory', *Philosophy of Social Science*, 31: 4, pp. 507–24.

Perdue C. (ed.) (1993), *Adult language acquisition: cross-linguistic perspectives*, vols 1 and 2, Cambridge: Cambridge University Press.

Quasthoff, U. (1980), *Erzählen in Gesprächen*, Tübingen: Narr.

Redder, A. (1994), '"Bergungsunternehmen" – Prozeduren des Malfelds beim Erzählen', in G. Bruenner and G. Graefen (eds), *Texte und Diskurse*, Opladen: Westdeutscher Verlag, pp. 238–64.

Rehbein, J. (1977), *Komplexes Handeln. Elemente zur Handlungstheorie der Sprache*, Stuttgart: Metzler.

Rehbein, J. (1980), 'Sequentielles Erzählen. Erzählstrukturen von Immigranten bei Sozialberatungen in England', in K. Ehlich (ed.), *Erzählen im Alltag*, Frankfurt am Main: Suhrkamp, pp. 64–108.

Rehbein, J. (1982), 'Biographisches Erzählen', in E. Lämmert (ed.), *Erzählforschung*, Stuttgart: Metzler, pp. 51–73.

Rehbein, J. (1987), 'Multiple formulae: aspects of Turkish migrant workers' German in intercultural communication', in K. Knapp, W. Enninger and A. Knapp-Potthoff (eds), *Analyzing intercultural communication*, Berlin: Mouton de Gruyter, pp. 215–48.

Rehbein, J. (2006), 'The cultural apparatus: thoughts on the relationship between language, culture and society', in K. Bührig and J. D. ten Thije (eds), *Beyond misunderstanding: the linguistic reconstruction of intercultural discourse*, Amsterdam and Philadelphia: John Benjamins, pp. 43–96.

Rehbein, J. (2007a), 'Narrative Verarbeitung des Arbeitsplatzes. Wiedergaben, Erläuterungen und Konnektivität in Gesprächen mit türkischen Arbeitern', in

S. Kameyama and B. Meyer (eds), *Mehrsprachigkeit am Arbeitsplatz. Forum Angewandte Linguistik*, Frankfurt am Main: Lang, pp. 7–55.

Rehbein, J. (2007b), 'Sprachpragmatische Ansätze in der interkulturellen Kommunikation', in J. Straub, A. Weidemann and D. Weidemann (eds), *Handbuch interkulturelle Kompetenz und Kommunikation*, Stuttgart: Metzler, pp. 131–43.

Rehbein, J. (2007c), 'Matrix constructions', in J. Rehbein, C. Hohenstein and L. Pietsch (eds), *Connectivity in grammar and discourse*, Hamburg Studies on Multilingualism, 5, Amsterdam and Philadelphia: John Benjamins, pp. 419–47.

Rehbein, J. (2010), 'Llengües, immigració, urbanització: elements per a una lingüística dels espais urbans del plurilingüisme – Sprachen, Immigration, Urbanisierung – Elemente zu einer Linguistik städtischer Orte der Mehrsprachigkeit', in P. Comellas and C. Lleó (eds), *Recerca i gestió del multilingüisme. Mehrsprachigkeitsforschung und Mehrsprachigkeitsmanagement*, Münster, New York and Berlin: Waxmann, pp. 44–111.

Rehbein, J. (2012), *Transcribing spoken language in HIAT-format under EXMARaLDA/Partitur. Editor, version 1.5. Step by step instructions for practical use*, mimeo, Ankara: Middle East Technical University.

Rehbein, J. (2013), 'Homileïc discourse – convening for talking . . . [Homileïscher Diskurs – zusammenkommen, um zu reden . . .]', in F. Kern, M. Morik and S. Ohlhus (eds), *Relating as a form [Erzählen als Form]: Festschrift für Uta Quasthoff*, Berlin and New York: Mouton de Gruyter, pp. 74–91.

Rehbein, J. and J. Fienemann (2004), 'Introductions – being polite in multilingual settings', in J. House and J. Rehbein (eds), *Multilingual communication*, Hamburg Studies on Multilingualism, 3, Amsterdam and Philadelphia: John Benjamins, pp. 223–78.

Rehbein, J., T. Schmidt, B. Meyer, F. Watzke and A. Herkenrath (2004), 'Handbuch für das computergestützte Transkribieren nach HIAT', in *Working Papers on Multilingualism*, series B, no. 56, Hamburg: University of Hamburg Collaborative Research Institute (SFB 538) – Multilingualism.

Schegloff, E. A. (2000), 'Overlapping talk and the organization of turn-taking for conversation', *Language in Society*, 29, pp. 1–63.

Scherr, A. (2012), 'Soziale Bedingungen von Agency. Soziologische Eingrenzungen einer sozialtheoretisch nicht aufloesbaren Paradoxie', in S. Bethmann, C. Helferrich, H. Hoffmann and D. Niemann (eds), *Agency. Qualitative Rekonstruktionen und gesellschaftstheoretische Bezuege von Handlungsmächtigkeit*, Weinheim and Basel: Beltz Juventa, pp. 99–121.

Schlosser, M. (2015), 'Agency', in *The Stanford encyclopedia of philosophy*, Fall 2015 edn, ed. Edward N. Zalta, <http://plato.stanford.edu/archives/fall2015/entries/agency/> (last accessed 8 November 2016).

Searle, J. R. (1969), *Speech acts*, Cambridge: Cambridge University Press.

von Wright, H. G. (1968), *An essay in deontic logic and the general theory of action*, Amsterdam: North-Holland.

von Wright, H. G. (1971), *Explanation and understanding*, Ithaca, NY: Cornell University Press.

Zikic, J., J. Bonache and J.-L. Cerdin (2010), 'Crossing national boundaries: a typology of qualified immigrants' career orientation', *Journal of
Organizational Behavior*, 31, Special issue, *New Directions for Boundaryless Career*,
pp. 667–86.

8

The 'Internationalised' Academic: Negotiating Boundaries between the Local, the Regional and the 'International' at the University

Anne H. Fabricius

1. Introduction

With mobility in the workplace ubiquitous nowadays, the negotiation of boundaries in professional contexts has become a focus area for sociolinguistic research.[1] When individuals move abroad, as many exchange students do during young adulthood, they are placed beyond a local comfort zone, and experience what Cushner (2007: 29) characterises as 'physical and psychological transitions that engage the cognitive, affective, and behavioural domains'. The interesting question that arises, then, is whether and to what extent this type of experience can become part of a later identity as a professional. Much of the work on boundary crossing and boundary negotiation in the present volume concerns the analysis of everyday interactions in the workplace; in this chapter, however, I analyse a reflective interview, and show how linguistic details as well as themes in some of the stories that are told can afford insights into the boundary crossing and boundary setting that are the focus of this volume.

The analytical case in point in this chapter is an interview with a university teacher and researcher whose history (at an English-speaking high school as an exchange student) was perceived to be part of what made him an experienced and competent English-medium instructor at the university. One is not after all born an internationally oriented academic; one becomes one, and in the current global and economic climate 'cosmopolitanism' is often celebrated as a desirable norm, a trope which is found in many public discourses (Otsuji and Pennycook 2010). With that backdrop, the present chapter arises from a wider study with an interest in a sociolinguistic view of personal and professional biographies and how they contribute to professional development and performance as 'an international academic'. The intention of the data analysis presented here is to show how the internationalised university as professional context is negotiated by one speaker in boundary defining and boundary crossing. We take the theoretical stance expressed in Auer (1998: 1) that 'code-switching has and creates communicative and social meaning, and is in need of an interpretation by co-participants as well as analysts'. When explicit and conscious internationalisation as an agenda enters a professional context, as it has done strongly in Danish higher education in recent years, participants must continually position themselves within that context, and literally find their place, both in their micro-level language use and in their expressed attitudes and reflections, when these are being elicited, as they are in the present research. The overall aim of the project was to examine the linguistic and cultural ways in which 'the international' can be tackled by university academics, and the long- and short-term consequences of intercultural and transnational exchange experiences for professional life as a university academic (see also Fabricius 2014).

This chapter therefore presents a close analysis of a one-to-one interview with a Danish-born-and-educated researcher who has a personal history as an exchange student in an English-speaking country during adolescence. Methodologically, the research project takes its point of departure in an anthropological interest in observing language use in its cultural setting, seeing 'language as deeply constitutive of reality' (Riessman 1993: 4), in common with many traditions within the humanities. It specifically draws methodologically on the identification of surprising 'rich points' (inspired by Agar 1996) in the emergent flow of conversation. The present author has been employed within Danish higher education since 1997, and also draws on that ethnographic knowledge in interpretation and analysis of the material collected and presented here. Inspired also by a sociolinguistic gaze that pays attention to forms of language operating on several indexical levels (see also Fabricius 2014; Johnstone 2000), this chapter employs, first, a close linguistic analysis of a range of multilingual code-switched forms, and, second, an informal discourse analysis approach that identifies significant rich points emerging in the flow of discourse (for the methodological approach, see also Cameron 2001). Using this methodological gaze, as well as a close focus on multilingual linguistic form, it emerged that this particular interview seemed to constitute a constant counterpoint of the need to perform in international professional contexts and the need to negotiate local Danish and regional Scandinavian identities and contexts. The analyses presented here will exemplify these micro-linguistic and thematic moves to illustrate this precise negotiation of self-presentation and construction at work (Angouri and Marra 2011). These examples of reflective workplace talk illustrate this individual's response to the local–global spaces of the international yet simultaneously locally anchored workplace, and exemplify the range of linguistic resources available to such an individual. In that way, the chapter shows that multilingual practice can become intrinsically linked with lived 'internationalisation', and can in effect symbolically manage the hybridity of working in an internationalised context.

The present research was conducted as a component of the CALPIU project at Roskilde University.[2] CALPIU stands for 'Cultural and Linguistic Practices at the International University' and seeks to document the practices of the university 'going about its business', through interactions such as teaching, supervision and administration (Mortensen 2014; Mortensen and Fabricius 2014; Fabricius et al. 2016; Haberland 2011; Hazel and Mortensen 2013; Haberland et al. 2013). The project's aim was to document a Danish university during its conscious process of transformation from a nationally focused higher education institution, teaching mainly through the medium of Danish, to a hybrid institution admitting transnationally mobile students and teaching them through the medium of English. Governmental pressure to attract and retain international students at all levels of their education increased substantially during the decade from 2001,[3] and this had ramifications for university quality assurance (Andersen and Jacobsen 2012), especially for staff members (Tange 2010; Tange and Kastberg 2013; Tange and Lauring 2009; Singh 2011). This process has had winners as well as losers, those who enthusiastically adopt the process and celebrate its opportunities, as well as those who resent the challenges it presents. This chapter examines one example of a professional academic who has taken on teaching in English in a positive spirit, engaged with it, and is willing to reflect on it in an experiential interview.[4] This research therefore adds to an existing body of work on the international experience and its shaping of the individual, with the specific focus here on linguistic resources of several kinds. As Cushner (2007: 29) points out, this shaping 'occurs twice – once during entry into the host culture and then again upon re-entry into the home culture'; albeit the 'culture' any individual faces will be a fragmentary rather than a unitary phenomenon. Thus, this project was shaped by a hypothesis that an individual who has had an exchange experience and lived and worked academically in another cultural setting will potentially handle international academic contact in a different way to an academic who has only worked within the domestic scene, and the research interview which is discussed here was framed to explore that possibility. The experiences of globally mobile university academics, understood as a particular case of transnational mobility and boundary crossing, are presently under-researched from a sociolinguistic perspective, and this chapter contributes to filling that gap.

2. Internationalisation and the university teacher

The recently emergent discourse of the internationalisation of higher education in Europe has been a market-based and economically rationalised discourse that has framed universities as operating in a global 'market', promoting a flow of the best talent to the most competitive parts of the world (Wright 2012). The challenge for any one university is to position itself as 'most attractive' in this market. Universities have always been internationally competitive (and cooperative) research workplaces, but national universities have also been at the core of nation-building activities since the nineteenth century (Clark 1993). The neo-liberal wave of internationalisation rhetoric in Denmark came about after the ratification of the Bologna Declaration in 1999 (Andersen and Jacobsen 2012), ushering in an era of accelerated internationalisation of the student body, with the quantity of international students at any one institution becoming a measurable parameter, and deemed to be a mark of quality. This has led to an increased emphasis on teaching through the medium of English, in order to attract and accommodate this new student population. As Haberland (2009) explains, this particular realisation of the internationalisation agenda resulted from a hegemonic interpretation of internationalisation as 'Englishisation' whereby other languages of instruction, which previously played a greater role, become downplayed or even excluded. English-medium teaching made its entry into what was previously a wider multilingual space, with many consequences for research and teaching (Mortensen et al. 2012; Fabricius et al. 2016; see also Gunnarsson 2001 on the Swedish case).

A key part of this process – teachers accommodating to multilingual and multicultural classrooms – has only recently begun to be addressed widely (for example in Tange 2010; Tange and Kastberg 2013; House and Lévy-Tödter 2010). When this process began, the initial presumption on the part of university administrations, at least in Denmark, seemed to be that those who now had to teach in English would do so willingly and unproblematically (and without needing extra economic resources in the form of tutoring or mentoring, which were in any case not provided). This stance came under pressure from negative student evaluations of teachers' English language competence, which meant that quality of language in teaching became a public issue in Denmark around the year 2005. Testing regimes have since then gradually been put in place at university level, so that universities can document the certification of their English-medium teachers as competent for this task. Roskilde and Copenhagen Universities are examples where this certification process has taken hold within the last five to six years; at Roskilde University, certification is now a requirement for being allowed to teach in English-medium programmes at BA level. Other things being equal, professional academics with previous experience of using English in their professional or personal lives can bring positive linguistic capital to the teaching task, while those who lack such experience either do not participate at all in English-medium teaching, or have to work intensely to achieve satisfactory certification.

3. The Danish context

Questions of scale and societal language ideologies also come into play in this discussion. Danish is a first language spoken by approximately five and a half million people within an overall European Union population of over 500 million, amounting to under 1 per cent of the EU population. Some 120 immigrant languages are also spoken in Denmark, but the country's ideological landscape often renders this diversity invisible (Risager 2012). Denmark tends to represent itself as a small and relatively homogeneous nation, speaking its own 'difficult language', at times tinged with an attitude of 'why should anyone bother to learn Danish?' Alongside this, however, there is also an expressed need for foreigners beyond a certain limited period of grace to learn the language, so as to be accepted as 'good' immigrants (for a description of this complex set of social expectations, see Lønsmann 2011: 235–69). Daryai-Hansen (2010) observes that Danish and English are often presented ideologically as languages of parallel use in Denmark, and that English has an ambiguous role as not only an international necessity, and the most relevant foreign language in Denmark, but also a threat if it competes too strongly with Danish as the conventional language of contexts such as business, science or education (Harder 2009; Davidsen-Nielsen, Hansen and Jarvad 1999). In 2014, Denmark lowered the age for instruction in English as a foreign language for children in Denmark to age seven, as a result of the recommendations of a governmental working group from 2011.

These observations are also relevant to the domain of higher education. The internationalisation process becomes more analytically complex, because we are constantly dealing with a situation of counterpoint between the local and the global, with other levels to consider as well, as we shall see below. The role of the local in internationalisation histories cannot be ignored, since the global does not make the local disappear (Nielsen and Simonsen 2003).

4. Data and methods

As noted above, this chapter provides a detailed analysis of a one-to-one interview conducted in June 2011 between the present author (INT in the transcriptions below), and an interviewee (INE), where the matrix language of the interview was Danish. The two participants were previously known to each other. INE is a tenured researcher at associate professor level, and of Danish nationality. He was initially asked if he would be willing to be interviewed about his experiences of teaching in two languages at university level. INT (of Australian background) has been a resident of Denmark since 1993, and an employee at Roskilde University since 2000.

The interview was recorded using multiple cameras and a sound recorder in the interviewee's office, and consisted of one hour and six minutes of a semi-structured interview. This began with questions about experiences of teaching in both languages and then widened to include related topics suggested by the interviewee, including language in everyday life. The interview was transcribed completely by student assistants using CLAN transcription-linking software (MacWhinney 2000a, 2000b), allowing pinning of transcriptions to precise moments so that individual utterances could be reviewed multiple times.

The transcript was initially reviewed to isolate both details of language use as well as longer passages developing wider language themes of sociolinguistic interest. The result of scrutinising the research interview in full was the identification of what we will call a series of language-form and sociolinguistic-thematic *boundary crossings*, places where forms of non-Danish and Danish language practice, as well as Danish and non-Danish contexts, meanings and interpretations, were brought into counterpoint. This was done by examining the interview to identify places where speech diverged from the matrix language Danish, or places where the topic of conversation simply turned to events and places outside Denmark. In this way, the author was able to observe multiple layers of meaning-making in language alternation, as well as in the topics raised and their discursive presuppositions, by looking at language form and language meaning, from the micro to the macro, as it were, as examples of hybridities (Otsuji and Pennycook 2010). Since the aim of the research interview was to see the linguistic and conceptual effects in the interview of the speaker recalling and reflecting on these actual historical transitions, it was important to identify these crossings as articulated not only through propositional content but also symbolically, through micro-linguistic strategies such as code-switches. In keeping with this multilayered analytical aim, the transcripts below reproduce utterances with interactional detail, including pauses and back-channel responses. The extracts presented below are comprehensively translated from Danish to English, and cases of English-in-Danish are presented in bold type.

We turn now to looking in detail at two types of data, which have been divided between examples of 'language data', where I will illustrate three different sub-types, and 'meta-commentary on language in Scandinavia', where I also analyse three separate extracts. These extracts were selected as interesting, marked and unexpected points requiring deeper analysis after the whole interview was examined multiple times, as explained above. These particular sequences were selected because they resonated as relevant to the ethnographic situation of the Danish university in line with my own long-term observation of the context. After presentation of the concrete examples, I will synthesise these findings and their implications for the coherence between multi-lingual practice and 'lived internationalisation' in the concluding section.

5. Data type 1: Language data

English loanwords and examples of English in Danish are often noted as features of present-day spoken (and to some extent written) Danish (Jarvad 2001; Andersen 2003; Lønsmann 2009, 2011; Rathje 2010), and these were also evident in the research interview. One view of such multilingual linguistic practice sees language choices in multilingual settings as 'inseparable from political arrangements, relations of power, language ideologies, and interlocutors' views of their own and others' identities' (Pavlenko and Blackledge 2004: 1). That is also the stance taken here: that the use of English in Danish discourse is becoming mainstreamed in many contexts in Denmark, such that several different ways of incorporating English into Danish are available to speakers, and that speakers thereby invest in a form of symbolic capital which is par-ticularly relevant to professional contexts such as academia. The following discussion presents three specific examples of different types of English-in-Danish usage and discusses their differences vis-à-vis the matrix language. On formal and functional grounds, the present analysis distinguishes between the use of well-established and officially codified English loanwords in Danish, interactional code-switching practices and, finally, a third phenomenon observed in the data, labelled code-switch mirroring. The following discussion will show how these types of language use constitute sym-bolic language encounters between Danish and the non-Danish. We take the theoreti-cal stance that identification of patterns of code-switching must pay attention to local circumstances in speech events (Auer 1998: 3), that the interactional context, as well as macro-sociolinguistic aspects, can play a role in language choice. We also take Auer's analytical stance on board: 'the interactional analysis of conversational code-switching is not independent of the structural analysis of language contact phenomena, and vice-versa' (Auer 1998: 15). We here unite several linguistic codeshifts under a boundary-crossing mantle, and see them in the light of a larger ethnographic picture of Danish higher education and Danish society.

5.1 Loanwords

We begin with an example of the first type of phenomenon in extract 1, an example of an English loanword into Danish.

    Extract 1 Transcript part 2, lines 80–3
    80   INE: og jeg tror egentlig måske også at de studerende oplevede at (0.2)
                 and I think really perhaps also the students experienced that

81	jeg ikke var så committed
	i wasn't as committed
82	(0.8) på dem
	to them
83	(0.5) som de gerne ville have ikke (.) ⌈altså⌉
	as they would have liked, yeah?

Extract 1 shows the usage of an English loanword *committed* in a matrix Danish sentence. *Committed* comes from an English loan, *committe (sig)*, documented in print usage for the first time in 1991 ('Committed' n.d.). Its assimilated status is also demonstrated here by the fact that its final segment approximates Danish pronunciation, with the dental fricative word-finally in this token in the interview.

There is a short pause of 0.8 seconds after the speaker utters the English word 'committed' here, and the speaker's gaze is fixed on the middle distance during the pause (possibly indicating a thinking pause). The speaker does not have eye contact with the interviewer at this moment, nor during the utterance of lines 81 and 82, but resumes eye contact at the end of line 83. There is no clear signal in the multimodal performance that this is to be understood as anything but matrix Danish usage with a word which happens to be a loanword historically. *Comitte sig* ('commit' plus reflexive pronoun) is listed in *Den Danske Ordbog* as an established idiom, 'to commit oneself', where the final orthographic *-e*, pronounced as a close rounded front central vowel, shows that this particular verb has assimilated to a Danish morphophonological system in which this vowel is a regular verbal infinitive ending.

Extract 2 presents a second extract from the interview transcript, using the item *mainstream*. *Mainstream* as an English loan has been documented in Danish since 1982 ('Mainstream' n.d.a), and it is also an assimilated loan which takes for example, the regular *-e* ending for an adjective when inflected for plural. It can be noted that in one official dictionary, *Den Danske Ordbog*, it is listed only as a noun, but adjectival uses are also documented in the printed citations listed in KorpusDK ('Mainstream' n.d.b), a written Danish corpus collection dating from the 2000s, available online. As in the first example with *committed*, the speaker does not establish special eye contact during the utterance of *mainstream*, or make any special physical gesture to draw attention to it as a special usage.

Extract 2   Transcript part 1, lines 698–700

698	INE:	(0.8) øhm altså det vi kalder s- amerikansk
		um what we call american
699		men men klassiske mainstream socialpsykologi med eksperimenter og
		but but classic mainstream social psychology with experiments and
700		øhm
		um

Note, that *Den Danske Ordbog* presents *mainstream* with a citation form containing an English alveolar central approximant, rather than a Danish uvular fricative in

-stream, which sets *mainstream* apart from Danish phonology, for example with the uvular [R] in Danish *strøm* (stream, current). The speaker here also uses an alveolar [ɹ] pronunciation, in line with the citation form in the dictionary.

The third example of English loanwords in Danish is the use of two officially recognised Danish loanwords from English, *basketball*, *basket* (the latter also meaning 'basketball'). These occur in extract 3, where the interviewee talks about his own and his friends' motivations for going to the US on student exchange at the age of seventeen.

Extract 3 Transcript part 2, lines 782–7

782	INE:	og en øh i- æh en af vores ideer var at (0.2) vi vil- ville over og
		and um one of our ideas was that we would go over and
783		spille **basketball** vi spillede **basketball** i danmark
		play basketball, we played basketball in denmark
784		(0.5) og ⌈så havde jeg faktisk en⌉ en tredje kammerat også
		and then in fact i have a third friend also
785	INT:	⌊mmm⌋
786	INE:	(0.8) som jeg også spillede **basket** med
		that i also played basketball with
787		(0.4) som (0.4) tog derover samtidig med mig
		who also went over there at the same time as me

Basketball is first attested in print in 1951. The game was introduced to Denmark in the period following the Second World War, at first under the name *kurvbold*, which is a loan translation of 'basketball'. In recent years, *basket* as an abbreviation of *basketball* has come to be used as a common name for the game in Danish, but is in fact attested with this meaning as early as 1951. Informal investigations by the author seem to point to present-day younger speakers preferring *basket* as the most common Danish name of the game, but this would need to be investigated further.

These three examples then are examples of recent loanwords from English into Danish that have assimilated to the Danish syntactic, morphological, and phonological system. Each one, however, has a unique history, differing in time depth and in degree of assimilation to a Danish linguistic system, both the phonological and the morphological systems. They exemplify a mainstreaming of English in Danish, one used daily by many educated Danes with a similar social profile as the speaker. These examples of linguistic form originating in English are embedded smoothly and seamlessly within the Danish language code. These examples contrast with the cases below, where boundary crossing of a different linguistic kind takes place.

5.2 Code-switching

As our second case, there are also examples in the interview which are more clearly cases of what has traditionally been described as code-switching. These examples differ from the loanword cases described above. In the first example, extract 4, there are potentially meaningful non-verbal signals present in the interaction, which I claim have the consequence of marking the utterance more conspicuously as a conscious code-switch from Danish to English. Thus, in extract 4, the speaker inserts 'native English speaker' in the complement position of the clause.

Extract 4 Transcript part 1, lines 623–6

623 INE: ⌊men⌋på ((study programme x)) (0.7) der varetager jeg sammen med †nn†
som
but on study programme x there i'm responsible for it ((a course) together with nn who

624 er native english speaker
is a native english speaker

625 ppp: (0.3)

626 INT: ⌈mmm⌉

Simultaneously with the beginning of the utterance segment 'native English speaker', the speaker gains and maintains eye contact with the interviewer and makes a novel gesture, departing from the sequence of gestures he has been making previously. He holds his right hand straight out over the desk in front of him with the palm downwards and fingers spread, and moves his hand horizontally in a waving movement, about 10 or 15cm from side to side three times, before ending with a small circle and lifting the forearm to vertical. At the same time, he raises his eyebrows. I would argue that in doing this he is signalling in some way the special status of his utterance as a code-switch, distinct from the language which surrounds it.

Not all such code-switches are marked out multi-modally, however. The sequence represented in extract 5 is produced without any change of posture, gesture or facial expression, being seamlessly embedded into the flow of talk.

Extract 5 Transcript part 2, lines 784–8

784 INE: (0.5) og⌈så havde jeg faktisk en⌉en tredje kammerat også
and then in fact i have a third friend also

785 INT: ⌊mmm⌋

786 INE: (0.8) som jeg også spillede basket med
that i also played basketball with

787 (0.4) som (0.4) tog derover samtidig med mig
who also went over there at the same time as me

788 (0.7) også gennem **american field service**
also through american field service

Note here that 'american field service' refers to a name and functions as modifier within a prepositional phrase adjunct (Preisler 1992), and so lower down in the syntactic structure, rather than functioning as subject complement, as is the case with 'native English speaker' in extract 4 above. With the very limited data at hand here, it is not yet possible to make any generalisations about the insertion of code-switches into Danish syntactic constructions, but the distinction between the two cases, one multi-modally marked and one not so, is an interesting one which should also be taken up in future work.

5.3 Code-switch mirroring

A third type of English-in-Danish practice that was observed in this data will be labelled code-switch mirroring. By this term, I refer to a practice which uses code-switched material from one language (in the cases presented below, the mirrored items, marked in bold type, are from German/Danish and English) and then 'mirrors' it by using exactly the same (usually phrasal) structure matrix with a translation in another language. The first two mirrored cases are marked in bold type in extract 6 and involve the carrier phrase *sådan lidt X* (a little bit X).

Extract 6 Transcript part 1, lines 391–401

391	INE:	⌈og det var ikke for⌉di at det der familieforskning det syntes jeg
		and it was not, because that family research, i thought
392		faktisk var **sådan lidt altmodisch**
		in fact it was like a bit old-fashioned
393	INT:	⌊haha ja⌋
394	ppp:	(0.4)
395	INT:	⌈aha⌉
396	INE:	⌊jeg syntes det⌋ der med familie var lidt
		i thought that thing with family was a bit
397	ppp:	(1.0)
398	INE:	altså (0.2) verden er jo blevet mere moderne end som så ikke ⌈og
		you know the world has become more modern than that, hasn't it and
399		studiet⌉
		the study
400	INT:	⌊aha⌋
401	INE:	af familier er måske **sådan lidt** (0.1) **outdated** ikke men
		of families is maybe like a bit outdated isn't it but

It is important to note here that *altmodisch* is actually a long-established Danish loanword from German: it is attested in a form inflected for definiteness according to Danish morphological rules from 1922 in *Ordbog over det danske sprog* ('Altmodisch' n.d.). Interactionally, then, by mirroring *altmodisch* with 'outdated', the two forms are contrasted, one of them Danish with a distinctly German texture to it, the other clearly, phonologically, an English word.

In the second episode of this kind in the interview, in extract 7, INE recalls how he once had to supervise a group of male students who wanted to work with a topic far removed from his own research, and who were not particularly willing to listen to the supervisor or take his advice. He reports his own mental reaction, again using a code-switch mirror, although in this instance it is a switch from English 'yikes' to Danish *hold da op*, whereas extract 6 represented a switch from German/Danish to English.

The carrier sentence here is *jeg tænkte bare* ('I just thought'), again, marked in bold type in the transcript in extract 7.

Extract 7 Transcript part 2, lines 138–40

138   INE: (.) og sådan nogle fik jeg og **jeg tænkte bare yikes** n- hvad nu
                  and i got some ((students)) like that and i just thought yikes what now
139   (0.3) og de ville skrive om religion og psykologi ikke
                  and they wanted to write about religion and psychology, you know
140   og **jeg tænkte bare** ⌈hold da op⌉ altså
                  and i just thought 'my goodness', so

Interestingly, the two examples presented in extracts 6 and 7 are both cases where INE is reporting on internal mental states, opinions or attitudinal reactions. Our final example, also to do with opinion or attitudinal reaction, in extract 8, is also a case of mirroring, but differs this time in being produced by both participants in concert. In response to the statement 'you hadn't ever expected they would do that' (line 212), the interviewee replies 'nope' (line 214), which the interviewer immediately echoes using Danish *nej*.

Extract 8 Transcript part 3, lines 201–15

201   INE: øhm (0.3) hvor de så simpelthen har boet et år dernede i afrika
                  um where they have simply lived for a year down there in africa
202   ppp: (0.2)
203   INT: ⌈mmm⌉
204   INE: ⌊hvilket også⌋
                  which also
205   ppp: (1.2)
206   INE: var har jo været en (0.2) fuldstændig verdens-
                  was has been you know a completely world-
207   ppp: (1.0)
208   INE: det har (0.2) det ⌈har vendt der⌉es verden op og ned ikke
                  it has it has turned their world upside down, you know
209   INT: ⌊ja⌋
210   ppp: (0.1)
211   INT: ja
212   (0.4) det havde du ikke forventet de ville gøre nogen⌈sinde (0.1) ne⌉j
                  you hadn't ever expected they would ever do that (0.1) no
213
214   INE: ⌊nope⌋
215   INT: (0.4) haha

'Nope' has a special emphatic meaning here which makes it stronger than simply *nej*. The fact that the mirroring is produced by two interlocutors makes it a case of a cooperative interaction, but it again shows a cross-code interactional strategy. 'Yes' can be used in a similar way in Danish, a contrast with the more neutral Danish *ja*.

If we accept the premise that all of the examples above, by moving between Danish, English and in one case, German, are performing boundary crossing symbolically as well as linguistically, we see a range of cases performed in different linguistic ways. These examples of English-in-Danish (or non-Danish and Danish) interaction have provided us with a range of types of ways of negotiating between two language systems and indeed synthesising a new hybrid system out of the two, in a range of ways that we have seen exemplified in sections 5.1–5.3. In these three types of strategies – using loanwords of differing time-depths and differing degrees of assimilation to the matrix code, performing multi-modally marked and unmarked code-switches, and using micro-interactional mirroring of multilingual structures – we see the range of resources the speaker can employ to cross boundaries between non-Danish language worlds and Danish language worlds.

In the following section, we move to a different level of analysis and a different type of data, but, as with the analysis of linguistic boundary crossings above, the intention of the data analysis is the same: to show how the internationalised university as professional context is negotiated by a speaker using boundary-defining and boundary-crossing language practices. The micro-practices we have seen above, located as they are in an interview between a Danish interviewee and a non-Danish interviewer, have had the effect of making the crossing between the two language worlds more explicit and obvious. In what follows, we examine some of the statements and presuppositions made on language by the interviewee, and discuss their sociolinguistic implications.

6. Data type 2: Commentary on language in Scandinavia

We turn now to look at our second set of data, a more macro-level thematic analysis where we consider how the speaker reflects on the sociolinguistic landscape surrounding his professional, academic work in Denmark. We see here signs that internationalisation of higher education must take local context into account if it is to be in any way an adequate opening up of real global possibilities for participants (see also Fabricius et al. 2016). We begin with extract 9 at about twenty minutes into the interview where the interviewee talks about a Scandinavian research network he has been part of since his PhD studies. The interviewer asks what language or languages are used at these meetings.

Extract 9 Transcript part 2, lines 381–410

381	INT:	øhm hv- hvilket sprog (0.1) eller hvilke ⌈sp⌉rog foregår ⌈de på⌉
		um what language or what languages do they take place in
382	INE:	⌊det⌋⌊det er fa⌋ktisk mest engelsk
		it is in fact mostly english
383	ppp:	(0.3)
384	INT:	⌈ja⌉
385	INE:	⌊og⌋ det (0.2) er fordi der er finnere med
		and that's because there are Finns there
386	ppp:	(0.5)
387	INT:	ja

388 ppp: (0.4)
389 INE: ⌈det er jo⌉ tit sådan at man formidler fra nordisk ministerråd
        it's often the case that the nordic council of ministers says
390 INT: ⌊ja⌋
391 INE: eller r- æh (0.2) NORFA
        or um NORFA
392 ppp: (0.4)
393 INT: ok⌈ay⌉
394 INE: ⌊så⌋ skal man så vil de helst have at man ligesom (0.2) dyrker de
        then one should, well, they prefer that people kind of cultivate the
395   skandinaviske sprog
        scandinavian languages
396 ppp: (0.3)
397 INT: ja (0.3) ⌈ja⌉
398 INE: ⌊men⌋ æhm
        but um
399   (0.7) altså
        well
400 ppp: (1.1)
401 INE: nå men finnerne n- (0.2) m- (.) de kan godt til nød (0.1) tale
        well, but the finns they can if need be speak
402   svensk
        swedish
403 ppp: (0.4)
404 INT: a⌈ha⌉
405 INE: ⌊men⌋ når be- man begynder at tale dansk (.) det (0.2) går slet ikke
        but when one begins to speak danish that doesn't work at all
407 ppp: (0.2)
408 INT: n⌈ej⌉
409 INE: ⌊det kan de⌋ det står de fuldstændigt af på≈
        they give up completely on that
410 INT: +≈ ja

Here the author explains the policies of official Scandinavian research funding bodies and the requirements they set regarding intra-Nordic research cooperation, with an overt policy of preferring the use of Scandinavian languages. One typical modelling of these practices would entail a passive receptive multilingual network, where speakers use their mother tongue and are mutually understood. This has been a well-established practice in Scandinavia for some generations (Zeevaert 2007). The interviewee, however, problematises this: from his own experience, while (some) Finns can use Swedish, their lack of ability to understand spoken Danish means that passive multilingualism quickly breaks down in a research meeting context, where fast online processing of spoken language is required. There are also reports that younger Scandinavians are increasingly reliant on English to communicate with peers or colleagues in other Nordic countries (see for example Louhiala-Salminen et al. 2005 reporting on a company merger context). Receptive multilingual competences are thus perhaps only partially being taken up by younger generations of Scandinavians, at least in the case of spoken interaction. This adds a layer of complexity to what we might understand as the problem of mutual intelligibility, which is of course always ideologically mediated, since linguistic mutual intelligibility can be complicated by beliefs and ideologies that break the Scandinavian area into separate non-mutually intelligible language areas. Scandinavian receptive multilingualism has long been recognised, as noted above, but may be coming under threat from the local consequences of wider political moves towards 'Englishisation' (Haberland 2009).

Extract 10 continues this theme of the special character of the Scandinavian area, where the interviewee reflects on his interpretations of the term 'international' in his research context. This comment is in fact a timely reminder that local and regional contexts can impinge on the conceptualisation of terms in unexpected ways. At the point where we enter this interaction, about forty minutes into the interview, the interviewee has been describing his research contacts in the US, gained while on exchange in the US during his PhD programme. We take up the analysis where the interviewer sums up this foregoing discourse by asking, 'so it's through that contact that your research comes to into its "international" own, so to speak?', implying: 'is this your most important international research context?'

Extract 10 Transcript part 3, lines 520–48

520	INT:	så det er primært gennem dén kontakt der at du
		so it's primarily through that contact that you
521	ppp:	(1.0)
522	INT:	at du vil sige dit (0.6) din forskning
		that you would say your research
523		(0.2) kommer til ret k- til sin rette til sin internationale rette
		comes to its own, comes to its 'international own'
524	INE:	((draws in air))
525	INT:	så at ⌈sige⌉
		so to speak
526	INE:	⌊ja⌋ altså det (0.1) ja altså så det er jo ja så er der også nogle
		yeah well yeah well there is yes then there are also some
527		relation- som altså p- h- via den (0.3) og så ad omveje er der også
		relation- which you know via that and then by a detour there's also
528		nogle steder i italien
		some places in italy
529		hvor de også har sådan et et ⌈et hverdagslivsper⌋spektiv og så er der
		where they also have this kind of an everyday life perspective and then there's
530		selvfølgelig hele den
		of course all the
531	INT:	⌊mmm⌋
532	INE:	(0.4) den skandinaviske æh nordiske kontekst≈
		the scandinavian um nordic context
533	INT:	+≈ m⌈mm⌉

534	INE:	⌊men den⌋ betragter jeg faktisk ikke sådan rigtigt som international
		but that i don't in fact really regard as international
535		(0.4) det er jo det der med at når man ⌈snakker om international⌉ så
		there's that thing with when one talks about international then
536		er det altid **syd for grænsen** ikke≈
		it's always south of the border, you know
537	INT:	⌊mmm⌋
538	INT:	+≈ mmm
539	ppp:	(0.2)
540	INE:	⌈men det er jo⌉ men det er jo klart det er vel også (0.1) i ⌈en eller
		but it is but clearly it is also in one
541		anden forstand⌉
		way or another
542	INT:	⌊mmm⌋
543	INT:	⌊mmm⌋
544	ppp:	(0.4)
545	INT:	mmm≈
546	INE:	+≈ internationalt
		international
547	ppp:	(0.3)
548	INT:	mmm

The interesting aspect of this extract is the interviewee's qualification of what the term 'international' means. While his contacts in the US and Italy are more straight-forwardly labelled 'international' in his mind, his Scandinavian research network is also strong and important to his work, as he has pointed out earlier in the interview, because of similar national welfare-state conditions. His hesitation and in-breath at line 524 presage the feeling that he then expresses: in his mind, at least, the Scandinavian network is something other than 'international', since the latter always refers to places 'south of the border'. He is referring here to the land border between Denmark and Germany, using the conventional Danish expression for this: *syd for grænsen* (line 536). This ideological stance is one that has a long history in Scandinavia, emphasis-ing the unification of Scandinavia rather than its division into separate nation states (a perspective that can emerge in other contexts, for example intra-Scandinavian sports rivalry). But here it is the unity of Scandinavia that is more important. The speaker concedes, however, on reflection, that Scandinavia is in some sense to be understood as international, although not prototypically. This interesting 'boundary drawing' that unites Scandinavia is a significant moment for the interviewee's discussion of 'internationalisation', and shows that interlocutors' perceptions and understandings of terms can vary in interesting ways; this may potentially have consequences for interna-tionalisation processes and policy decisions (see for example Saarinen 2008a, 2008b).

The final example in this section sheds light on the interviewee's own experiences of the relative importance of two named languages, English and German, for his work. While he is proficient in English and comfortable using it for many research activities, German plays a much more restricted role. The interviewee makes the point that his competence in German has been acquired through formal instruction, in contrast to his competence in English, which was substantially reinforced by living abroad as an exchange student.

Extract 11 Transcript part 3, lines 720–82

720	INE:	⌊og så⌋ tog j- jeg også øh tysk herude der var jo også dengang vi
		and then i also took um german out here that was also at that time we
721		startede på RUC
		started at RUC
722		der sk- (0.2) var der også krav om at vi skulle tage sprog- (0.2)
		there was there was a requirement that we take language
723		kurser
		courses
724	ppp:	(0.6)
725	INT:	aha
726	ppp:	(0.9)
727	INE:	så ⌈der⌉ (0.4) ej der tænkte jeg så ej
		so there ah there i thought oh (you know what)
728	INT:	⌊yes⌋
729	INE:	(0.4) engelsk det kan jeg altså godt nok så vil jeg hellere b-
		english i can do well enough so i would rather
730		(0.2) blive bedre til tysk
		get better at german
731		så havde jeg †nn†
		so i had (name of university teacher, known to both speakers)
732	ppp:	(0.3)
733	INT:	mmm≈
734	INE:	+≈ †nn† til tysk
		(name) in german
735	ppp:	(0.2)
736	INT:	mmm (0.3) mm (0.2) mmm
737	ppp:	(0.6)
738	INE:	ja≈
739	INT:	+≈ og bruger du det stadigvæk (0.2) tysk (0.4) altså
		and do you still use it, german, then?
740	ppp:	(0.1)
741	INE:	altså jeg s- jeg publicerer ikke på det og jeg prøver og
		well, i don't publish in it and i try and
742		(0.2) og øh (0.1) snakke med †nn† på tysk men jeg (0.2) giver
		and um speak with (name of colleague) in german but i give
743		altid fortabt
		up always
744	ppp:	(0.3)
745	INT:	mmm
746	ppp:	(0.1)

747	INE:	men jeg kan godt læse det
		but i can read it
748		(0.6) men jeg læser ⌈ikke æhm⌉ jeg læser ikke meget på tysk
		but i don't read, i don't read much in german
749	INT:	⌊mm hmm⌋
750	INE:	altså ⌈det er⌉ engelsk
		well it's english
751	INT:	⌊nej⌋
752	ppp:	(0.4)
753	INT:	okay (0.2) ⌈så øh⌉ de fleste tag- fag- (0.1) tidsskrifter er på øh
		okay so most journals are um
754	INE:	⌊ja⌋
755	ppp:	(1.0)
756	INT:	på engelsk≈
		in english?
757	INE:	+≈ ja
		yes
758	ppp:	(0.3)
759	INT:	som du læ⌈ser⌉
		that you read?
760	INE:	⌊ja⌋
		yes
761	ppp:	(0.3)
762	INT:	ja
763	ppp:	(0.1)
764	INE:	altså det ja (0.2) det er måske også sådan lidt den der dårlige
		well it yes, there's maybe also a bit of bad
765		samvittighed fordi
		conscience because
766		(0.8) jeg (0.3) hvis jeg satte mig for det så kunne jeg godt
		i if i sat down to do it then i would be able to
767		(0.2) gnave mig igennem det men det (.) kræver altså en indsats ikke
		chew my way through it but it needs effort, yeah?
768		((blank line in transcript))
769		(0.6) men for eks- altså jeg sad og læ-
		but for example, well i sat and read
770		(0.7) l- altså (0.2) læste noget †author† (0.2) igen på tysk og det
		well read some of ((academic author)) again in german and it
771		er altså sådan lidt småkompliceret tysk
		is, you know, sort of tricky / somewhat complicated german
772		(0.4) så jeg kan godt og så skal jeg selvfølgelig bruge ordbog og
		so i can and i have to use a dictionary of course
773		alt sådan noget
		and all that
774	ppp:	(0.6)

775	NT:	⌈hmm⌉
776	INE:	⌊men⌋ jeg kan godt ⌈øhm⌉
		but i can!
777	INT:	⌊mmm⌋
778	ppp:	(1.0)
779	INE:	ja (0.4) og og når man (0.4) når man kan tysk også og man tænker sig
		yes and when you when you know german and you think about it
780		lidt om
		a little bit
781		(0.4) og man er dansker så er det faktisk muligt at gnave sig
		and you're a dane then it is in fact possible to chew your way
782		igennem det
		through it

This extract fleshes out several aspects of the role of German for this speaker. He reports that academic reading is demonstrably possible but requires extra effort (described using the Danish metaphor *gnave sig igennem* ('chew one's way through', lines 767, 781–2). Publishing in German is not part of his daily research practice, and chatting informally with a German-born colleague is usually sporadic and temporary, until he has to 'give up' (lines 742–3, possibly also complicated by the formal institutional settings in which they meet). Yet, as the interviewer concludes, there is an element of 'bad conscience' to this limited practice (lines 764–5), since the language is in fact part of his repertoire, due to previous instruction in the language and the fact that many linguistic features of German are straightforwardly accessible to Danish speakers. While it is not possible here to report to what extent this experience is general for Danish nationals (having a passive but not active competence in written or spoken German), we see that publications in German presently originate from Danish universities at a much lower rate than publications in English, across all university disciplines (Mortensen and Haberland 2012: 189).

In summary, the interviewee sets up distinctions between the relationship of Denmark to Scandinavia, and of Denmark to non-Scandinavian contexts. He also draws distinctions between the roles of the English language and English proficiency and the roles of the German language and German proficiency in his own work and experience. These roles hinge on access to personal language competencies, which are differentiated for this speaker between English (a language he has self-confident mastery of) and German (which is more difficult but for which he still feels he 'should' make an effort). The German language has a role as a language one 'ought' to be able to use (partly because of national heritage and neighbourhood), and 'ought' to make the effort to use, so neglect of German becomes tinged with 'bad conscience'. English plays a very different role in the Scandinavian research contexts that the interviewee is familiar with, as we saw in extract 9, in spite of language-political stances from official Nordic research bodies that emphasise the use of Scandinavian languages in lingua franca settings (see also further Daryai-Hansen 2010).

7. Discussion and conclusion

Together, these qualitative and discursive analyses illustrate the complexities of the lived experience of multilingual practices as the present-day results of 'internationalisation' processes. Here we see internationalisation not as a global, market-driven pursuit of resources for the benefit of the economies of nation states, but as a personal process enacted and reflected upon by individuals. While there is no doubt that some academics in Denmark experience linguistic challenges in a global context (Tange 2010), it is important to remember that not all do so, and to leave room to examine what it might mean to work and live as an international academic. In future, perhaps, with English language instruction at school in Denmark beginning at age seven (as of September 2014), a Danish generation will emerge with even more access to global English. But the interaction of the global and the local is always one which defies simplistic either/or distinctions. The saturation of the local in the international experience is particularly acute in a profession which has traditionally been predicated on the universality of scholarship. This complicates our understanding of the long-term consequences of these larger-scale population movements, such as the student exchanges undertaken by the interviewee, and we need to constantly reflect on and tap into the working realities of the participants in this intense internationalisation process, for academics as well as students.

What individual experiences bring to the theoretical table can be challenging to generalise, but if we restrict our gaze for the moment to the Scandinavian regional context, there are clearly facets of the nature of internationalisation as process and product that emerge from the present findings and that need to be explored further. First of all, we find hybridity and boundary crossing on a micro-linguistic level. As was shown above, micro-parallel language practice/code-switch mirroring can evoke two experiential worlds at the same time as it blends them together. Second, the thematic observations in the second set of data have implications for our understanding of a changing Danish language ecology. The meetings of English, Danish, German and Scandinavian language praxis that are illustrated here point to a complex language ecology at a seminal point in its history. The employment of a range of linguistic resources in Danish and Scandinavian academia can bring inherent challenges and self-contradictions. Globalisation is not just the nebulous global, but also the regional, the local and the personal, flavoured by a range of language competences and language practices that can demonstrably be revealed in reflective talk.

Transcription conventions

⌈ ⌉   overlap between two or more speakers, upper brackets for the first speaker,
⌊ ⌋   lower brackets for the second speaker
+≈   latching, one speaker to another (no detectable pause between utterances)
(0.3)   pause, length measured in seconds
(.)   pause, less than 0.2 seconds
((text))   transcriber comments
ppp   a (timed) silence

bold bold type is used to highlight the particular data phenomena that are in focus in each analytical section

Notes

1. Thanks are due first, to my interviewee, who generously made this research possible, and second, to academic colleagues at the CALPIU Centre for feedback along the way (Janus Mortensen, Hartmut Haberland, Bent Preisler, Spencer Hazel and Kamilla Kraft) and to the CALPIU Lab for assistance with data collection and transcription work (Kamilla Kraft, Lise Lopez Nielsen, Steffen Haurholm-Larsen and Julie de Molade). I also thank Jo Angouri, Meredith Marra and Janet Holmes and an anonymous reviewer for their editorial work. Any remaining errors are my responsibility.
2. CALPIU was supported by the Danish Research Council for the Humanities from 2009 to 2013.
3. Recently, however (and especially during 2015), the societal mood on this seems to have subtly shifted. A terrorist attack in Copenhagen in February 2015 followed by the European refugee crisis of summer 2015, which came to prominence during August of that year, and economic challenges in general, seem to have led in public media discourse to a downplaying of internationalist agendas and a refocusing on local issues and local welfare. Only time will tell whether this is a sustained shift that has an impact on higher education generally.
4. The interview participants knew each other from a Danish-speaking context, so the interview was conducted in Danish.

References

Agar, M. (1996), *Language shock: understanding the culture of conversation*, New York: Morrow.

'Altmodisch' (n.d.), *Ordbog over det danske sprog (ODS) 1700–1950* [Dictionary of the Danish language 1700–1950], <http://ordnet.dk/ods/ordbog?query=altmodisch&tab=for> (last accessed 16 November 2016).

Andersen, H. L. and J. C. Jacobsen (eds) (2012), *Uddannelseskvalitet i en globaliseret verden: Vidensøkonomiens indtog i de videregående uddannelser*, Frederiksberg: Samfundslitteratur.

Andersen, M. H. (2003), 'Engelsk i dansk. Sprogholdninger i Danmark – helt vildt sjovt eller wannabeagtigt og ejendomsmæglerkækt?' [English in Danish. Language attitudes in Denmark – really fun, or 'wannabe' and real-estate-salesman – fresh?], Aarhus: MUDS, Aarhus University, pp. 34–42.

Angouri, J. and M. Marra (eds) (2011), *Constructing identities at work*, Basingstoke: Palgrave Macmillan.

Auer, P. (1998), *Code-switching in conversation: language, interaction and identity*, London: Routledge.

Cameron, D. (2001), *Working with spoken discourse*, London, Thousand Oaks, CA and New Delhi: Sage.

Clark, B. R. (ed.) (1993), *The research foundations of graduate education: Germany, Britain, France, United States, Japan*, Oakland, CA: University of California Press.

'Committed' (n.d.), *Den danske ordbog 1950 – (DDO)* [The Danish Dictionary 1950–], <http://ordnet.dk/ddo/ordbog?query=committe> (last accessed 23 November 2016).

Cushner, K. (2007), 'The role of experience in the making of internationally-minded teachers', *Teacher Education Quarterly*, Winter, pp. 27–39.

Daryai-Hansen, P. G. (2010), 'Begegnungen mit fremden Sprachen: Sprachliche Hierarchien im sprachenpolitischen Diskurs im Dänemark und Deutschland der Gegenwart' [Encounters with foreign languages: linguistic hierarchies present in language policy discourse in Denmark and Germany], PhD thesis, Roskilde University.

Davidsen-Nielsen, N., E. Hansen and P. Jarvad (eds) (1999), *Engelsk eller ikke engelsk? That is the question*, Dansk Sprognævns skrifter, 28, Copenhagen: Gyldendal.

Fabricius, A. (2014), 'The transnational and the individual: a life-history narrative in a Danish university context', *Journal of Education for Teaching*, 40: 3, pp. 284–99.

Fabricius, A. H., J. Mortensen and H. Haberland (2016), 'The lure of internationalization: paradoxical discourses of transnational student mobility, linguistic diversity and cross-cultural exchange', *Higher Education*, pp. 1–19, <http://doi.org/10.1007/s10734-015-9978-3> (last accessed 9 November 2016).

Gunnarsson, B. L. (2001), 'Swedish, English, French or German – the language situation at Swedish universities', in U. Ammon (ed.), *The dominance of English as a language of science: effects on other languages and language communities*, Berlin and New York: Mouton de Gruyter, pp. 229–316.

Haberland, H. (2009), 'English – the language of globalism?', *RASK: Internationalt tidsskrift for sprog og kommunikation*, 30, pp. 17–45.

Haberland, H. (2011), 'Ownership and maintenance of a language in transnational use: should we leave our lingua franca alone?', *Journal of Pragmatics*, 43: 4, pp. 937–49.

Haberland, H., D. Lønsmann and B. Preisler (eds) (2013), *Language alternation, language choice and language encounter in international tertiary education*, Dordrecht: Springer.

Harder, P. (2009), 'Parallel language use: a case for active social construction', in P. Harder (ed.), *English in Denmark: language policy, internationalisation and university teaching*, Special issue of *Angles on the English-Speaking World*, 9, pp. 109–28. Copenhagen: Museum Tusculanum Press.

Hazel, S. and J. Mortensen (2013), 'Kitchen talk – exploring linguistic practices in liminal institutional interactions in a multilingual university setting', in H. Haberland, D. Lønsmann and B. Preisler (eds), *Language alternation, language choice and language encounter in international tertiary education*, Dordrecht: Springer, pp. 3–30.

House, J. and M. Lévy-Tödter (2010), 'Linguistic competence and professional identity in English medium instruction', in B. Meyer and B. Apfelbaum (eds), *Multilingualism at work: from policies to practices in public, medical, and business settings*, Amsterdam and Philadelphia: John Benjamins, pp. 13–46.

Jarvad, P. (2001), *Det danske sprogs status med særligt henblik på domænetab* [The status of the Danish language with special consideration of domain loss], Dansk Sprognævns skrifter, 32, Copenhagen: Dansk Sprognævn.

Johnstone, B. (2000), *Qualitative methods in sociolinguistics*, New York: Oxford University Press.

Lønsmann, D. (2009), 'From subculture to mainstream: the spread of English in Denmark', *Journal of Pragmatics*, 41: 6, pp. 1139–51.

Lønsmann, D. (2011), 'English as a corporate language: language choice and language ideologies in an international company in Denmark', PhD thesis, Roskilde University.

Louhiala-Salminen, L., M. Charles and A. Kankaanranta (2005), 'English as a lingua franca in Nordic corporate mergers: two case companies', *English for Specific Purposes*, 24, pp. 401–21.

MacWhinney, B. (2000a), *The CHILDES Project: tools for analyzing talk, vol. 1: The format and programs*, Mahwah, NJ: Lawrence Erlbaum.

MacWhinney, B. (2000b), *The CHILDES Project: tools for analyzing talk, vol. 2: The database*, Mahwah, NJ: Lawrence Erlbaum.

'Mainstream' (n.d.a), *Den danske ordbog 1950 – (DDO)* [The Danish Dictionary 1950–], <http://ordnet.dk/ddo/ordbog?query=mainstream&tab=for> (last accessed 16 November 2016).

'Mainstream' (n.d.b), *KorpusDK 1990–2000 (KDK)* [CorpusDK 1990–2000], <http://ordnet.dk/korpusdk> (last accessed 16 November 2016).

Mortensen, J. (2014), 'Language policy from below: language choice in student project groups in a multilingual university setting', *Journal of Multilingual & Multicultural Development*, 35: 4, pp. 425–42.

Mortensen, J. and A. H. Fabricius (2014), 'Language ideologies in Danish higher education: exploring student perspectives', in A. K. Hultgren, F. Gregersen and J. Thøgersen (eds), *English in Nordic universities: ideologies and practices*, Amsterdam: John Benjamins, pp. 193–223.

Mortensen, J. and H. Haberland (2012), 'English – the new Latin of academia? Danish universities as a case', *International Journal of the Sociology of Language*, 216, pp. 175–97.

Mortensen, J., H. Haberland and A. H. Fabricius (2012), 'Uddannelse on the move: transnational studentermobilitet og uddannelseskvalitet', in H. L. Andersen and J. C. Jacobsen (eds), *Uddannelseskvalitet i en globaliseret verden: Vidensøkonomiens indtog i de videregående uddannelser*, Frederiksberg: Samfundslitteratur, pp. 191–205.

Nielsen, E. H. and K. Simonsen (2003), 'Scaling from below: practices, strategies and urban spaces', *European Planning Studies*, 11: 8, pp. 911–28.

Otsuji, E. and A. Pennycook (2010), 'Metrolingualism: fixity, fluidity and language in flux', *International Journal of Multilingualism*, 7: 3, pp. 240–54.

Pavlenko, A. and A. Blackledge (2004), 'Introduction: new theoretical approaches to the study of negotiation of identities in multilingual contexts', in A. Pavlenko and A. Blackledge (eds), *Negotiation of identities in multilingual contexts*, Clevedon: Multilingual Matters.

Preisler, B. (1992), *A handbook of English grammar on functional principles*, Aarhus: Aarhus Universitetsforlag.

Rathje, M. (2010), *Generationssprog* [Generational language], Copenhagen: Dansk Sprognævns skrifter.

Riessman, C. (1993), *Narrative analysis*, London: Sage.

Risager, K. (2012), 'Language hierarchies at the international university', *International Journal of the Sociology of Language*, 216, pp. 111–30.

Saarinen, T. (2008a), 'Persuasive presuppositions in OECD and EU higher education policy documents', *Discourse Studies*, 10: 3, pp. 341–59.

Saarinen, T. (2008b), 'Whose quality? Social actors in the interface of transnational and national higher education policy', *Discourse: Studies in the Cultural Politics of Education*, 29: 2, pp. 179–93.

Singh, M. (2011), 'Multicultural international mindedness: pedagogies of intellectual e/quality for Australian engagement with Indian and Chinese theorising', in L. Harborn and L. Woodrow (eds), *Multiculturalism: perspectives from Australia, Canada and China*, Sydney: Faculty of Education and Social Work, University of Sydney.

Tange, H. (2010), 'Caught in the Tower of Babel: university lecturers' experiences with internationalisation', *Language and Intercultural Communication*, 10: 2, pp. 137–49.

Tange, H. and P. Kastberg (2013), 'Coming to terms with "double knowing": an inclusive approach to international education', *International Journal of Inclusive Education*, 17: 1, pp. 1–14.

Tange, H. and J. Lauring (2009), 'Language management and social interaction within the multilingual workplace', *Journal of Communication Management*, 13: 3, pp. 218–32.

Wright, S. (2012), 'Ranking universities within a globalised world of competition states: to what purpose, and with what implications for students?', in H. L. Andersen and J. C. Jacobsen (eds), *Uddannelseskvalitet i en globaliseret verden: Vidensøkonomiens indtog i de videregående uddannelser*, Frederiksberg: Samfundslitteratur, pp. 81–102.

Zeevaert, L. (2007), 'Receptive multilingualism and inter-Scandinavian semi-communication', in J. D. T. Thije and L. Zeevaert (eds), *Receptive multilingualism: linguistic analyses, language policies, and didactic concepts*, Amsterdam: John Benjamins.

9

'Have You Still Not Learnt Luxembourgish?': Negotiating Language Boundaries in a Distribution Company in Luxembourg

Anne Franziskus

1. Introduction

In today's globalised economy, people frequently move between jobs, crossing national, professional and linguistic boundaries in order to optimise their career opportunities. In turn, the increased mobility of workers results in the emergence of more dynamic workplace communities, in which people of diverse national, ethnic and linguistic backgrounds get together and interact. Because people spend a large amount of time in their workplaces, these constitute promising social and interactional contexts for investigating how language ideologies, group norms and various identities are negotiated, constructed and challenged through talk (Holmes et al. 2011; Marra and Angouri 2011). When moving between linguistic, national and professional spaces, workers are faced with the need to socialise into new groups and, therefore, to engage in a process of learning and adapting to different norms and expectations (Roberts 2010). Speaker's language resources, as well as their ability to conform to new norms for language use, can be crucial for successfully navigating their way into the community. Given that such norms exist at different societal, community and interactional levels (Holmes et al. 2011), the transition is a multilayered process for newcomers and 'old-timers' alike.

Where newcomers are expected to adapt to shared ways of doing and speaking, existing group members may also be faced with changes to their established practices. They might show resistance to this change, if they perceive it as threatening power structures. Recent research into multilingualism at work provides evidence that established groups can feel threatened by the internationalisation processes of their company. In a case study involving multinational companies (MNCs) in the Czech Republic, Nekvapil and Sherman (2009, 2013) demonstrate that the local Czech staff members, who were predominantly blue-collar workers and less educated than international staff, expressed ambivalent feelings towards the expatriates. Similarly, in a study of a Danish company that had recently adopted English as its corporate language, Lønsman (2011) found that low-skilled Danish staff members showed resistance to the need to use English and created boundaries with international expatriates who did not learn the local language. They drew on an essentialist language ideology, arguing for a norm of 'Danish because we are in Denmark'. The ability to speak Danish thus promoted the inclusion of newcomers into the social life of the company. These studies suggest that language resources and an accompanying effort to engage in language learning may play a crucial role in the extent to which staff of multilingual companies can successfully negotiate their way into a new workplace. In this sense, language resources contribute to the dynamics of exclusion and to the construction of linguistic boundaries in the workplace.

This chapter proposes to further explore the links between the presence of newcomers, multilingualism, the negotiation of group norms and the construction of boundaries at work through the investigation of a company in Luxembourg.

2. Luxembourg context

The small Grand Duchy of Luxembourg presents an intriguing case for studying multilingual workplace communication and the ways in which language resources influence the construction of boundaries at work, because of both the longstanding community multilingualism and the growing linguistic diversity, which has resulted from more recent demographic and economic developments.

Due to very favourable economic development, particularly in the financial sector, Luxembourg has experienced high levels of immigration in terms of residents and cross-border workers. It has the highest migration rates in the Organization for Economic Cooperation and Development (OECD), with the non-national population reaching 45.9 per cent in 2013 (STATEC 2015). The majority are European residents employed across different sectors of the economy. The term 'cross-border workers' refers to a growing group of people (over 150,000) who live in neighbouring countries (France, Belgium and Germany) but commute to Luxembourg for work. The largest number are from France (50 per cent), followed by more or less equal numbers from Belgium and Germany. Today, they represent around 43 per cent of the Luxembourg workforce. Taken together with the non-national residents, 'foreign' workers thus make up two thirds of the workforce. As a result, Luxembourg's workplaces are highly diverse social contexts where people with different national, linguistic and cultural backgrounds interact with each other.

Adding to this complexity is the fact that Luxembourg is traditionally a trilingual country. The 1984 language law (*Loi du 24 février 1984 sur le régime des langues*), states that Luxembourgish, a Germanic language belonging to the Franco-Mosellian dialect area, is the national language; French, the language of the law, and Luxembourgish, German and French are all languages of administration. Luxembourgish was traditionally used for informal and spoken domains, with French and German used in formal and written domains. All three languages, in addition to English, are taught in the national school system. Luxembourg's multilingualism is thus not territorially based, but reflected in different patterns of language use in spoken and written domains. In practice, the use of these languages depends on people's national and linguistic background (Horner and Weber 2008). Multilingualism, be it at home, in public, or at work, is everyday business for everyone living and working in Luxembourg (see Horner and Weber 2008 for a comprehensive overview of the Luxembourgish language situation). The established trilingual situation has, however, recently undergone important changes, which are mainly attributable to the demographic developments described above. Most importantly, French has become the spoken lingua franca among the different language groups who live and work in Luxembourg (particularly in the workplace) and so has partially lost its status as the prestige language. Luxembourgish, on the other hand, increasingly serves as a marker of group identity among the autochthonous population, most noted in the fact that it is used in a growing number of (written) domains, such as the new media (de Bres and Franziskus 2014; Belling and de Bres 2014).

The increased presence of newcomers in public life and in the economy is also paralleled by a growing resentment of those migrants who do not appear to make an effort to learn Luxembourgish. Some public discourses present the increased presence of other languages as a threat to the vitality of Luxembourgish. The (Francophone) cross-border workers are often constructed as constituting the biggest 'problem' in this regard. For example, in a recent survey, 73 per cent of the respondents expressed the view that cross-border workers do not make enough efforts to learn the local language and 59 per cent described them as invading the country (CEFIS 2011). Similar results emerged from another research project, in which 57 per cent of those interviewed believed that cross-border workers constitute a threat to the national language and culture (Baltes-Löhr et al. 2011). At the same time, people are aware of the value of these workers for the national economy. Indeed, 87 per cent of the respondents of the same study also recognised their necessity for the Luxembourgish labour market (Baltes-Löhr et al. 2011). There is thus an ambivalent view on the presence of cross-border workers, to say the least. These public discourses are of particular relevance for the organisation described in this chapter, given that the language issues observed in the company primarily relate to the tension between Luxembourgish-speaking and Francophone employees.

3. Language norms, ideologies and the negotiation of linguistic boundaries at work

As mentioned in the introduction, this chapter aims to investigate the relationship between language resources, the negotiation of language norms and the construction of boundaries at work. I define language norms as norms for socially appropriate language use. This approach reflects a realist perspective on the relationship between social structure and agency, which holds that social behaviour is always constrained by societal norms and structures that manifest themselves at different levels of generality (Coupland 2001; Holmes et al. 2011). These range from the broad societal level down through the specific level of a community of practice (CofP) (Wenger 1998) or workplace team (Holmes et al. 2011). At the broadest level, language norms are shaped by language ideologies, that is, the shared systems of belief about the relationship between language and society, or, to put it in Woolard's terms, 'representations, whether explicit or implicit, that construe the intersection of language and human beings in a social world' (Woolard 1998: 3). Language ideologies have attracted increased attention in recent sociolinguistic research (Woolard 1998; Gal 2006; Cameron 2003; Duchêne and Heller 2007), including the workplace context (Lønsman 2011; de Bres 2014; Nekvapil and Sherman 2013).

Language ideologies provide 'normative orientations' for appropriate communicative behaviour (Nekvapil and Sherman 2013). They constitute overarching sets of beliefs that people hold about language and its relationship to the social world, while language norms are the 'concrete plan[s] of action' (Franziskus 2013) that emerge from them. In multilingual contexts, language norms can, for example, include what is seen as the appropriate language for a specific context, expectations about the range of languages one should speak or the degree of tolerance exhibited towards multilingual practices. An important feature of language norms is that they are rarely explicitly formulated. They are 'taken-for-granted background expectancies' (Garfinkel 1967), which may make it difficult for newcomers to recognise them. It is when norms are violated that they surface, so that deviations from them 'reflexively' reveal the norm (Gafaranga 2001). Interactions in which speakers metalinguistically comment on each other's 'failures' to adhere to the norm allow us to access and describe them.

Reflecting on language ideologies and national identity construction in Luxembourg, Horner and Weber (2008) distinguish between two prevailing identification strategies: identification with the trilingual ideal on the one hand and monolingual identification with Luxembourgish language on the other. The rhetoric of 'trilingual Luxembourg' is used in official discourses to convey an image of Luxembourg as a harmonious multilingual place in which multiple languages coexist side by side (Horner and Weber 2008: 85–6). The second ideology – the nationalist language ideology – posits Luxembourgish as the only true language of Luxembourg. This view is more prevalent in media representations and lay opinions and is based on the idea that Luxembourgish is under threat from other languages and the growing presence of non-nationals in the country. Given the inherently contradictory and conflicting nature of language ideologies (Kroskrity 2004), individuals may adhere to these two identification strategies at different times.

Building on the distinction operated by these authors, I suggest elsewhere (Franziskus 2013: 196) that the 'two-pronged' language ideology can be viewed as being associated with two different sets of language norms: 'use Luxembourgish because we are in Luxembourg' and 'use the trilingual repertoire as required'. As I will show in my analysis, CofPs are often characterised by an orientation to one of these two overarching sets of norms in particular, by a particularly dominant language norm so to speak. For example, the 'speak Luxembourgish because we are in Luxembourg' norm is most influential at Thommes & Schneider, the company under investigation in this chapter. When participants fail or refuse to conform to this overall CofP language norm, they run the risk of getting reprimanded or even excluded. In this sense, a failure to conform to the norm – whether this is due to a lack of language resources or a rejection of the dominant workplace norm – can contribute to the construction of boundaries at work. The subsequent analysis will demonstrate to what extent these language norms influence the construction of boundaries in the specific workplace under investigation.

4. Data collection

The data analysed are part of a larger linguistic ethnographic study that investigates the multilingual practices of cross-border workers in Luxembourg in both white-collar and blue-collar workplaces. Linguistic ethnography focuses on 'the ways in which language practices are socially and politically situated' (Blackledge and Creese 2010: 58). It advocates a critical engagement with multilingual practices, taking into account the language ideologies and norms that govern language practices (Agar 2009; Blommaert and Jie 2010). Its main methods are participant observation, recording of face-to-face interactions, sociolinguistic interviews and the collection of other sources of information. All these methods were used in the study, which was conducted in a supermarket (Fresh and Fruity), an IT company (InfoTech) and a retailing company (Thommes & Schneider).[1] A number of employees were asked to record their daily interactions with colleagues. The main participants were French, (Francophone) Belgian and German cross-border workers. Some had worked in Luxembourg for as little as a year while others had been commuting into Luxembourg for over ten years. They also had diverse language repertoires[2] depending on their national origin and their language learning experiences in school and later life. The data collection took place consecutively in each workplace from April 2009 to July 2011. Interviews were conducted with key participants and management. Sixty hours of recorded spontaneous interactions were transcribed.

The focus of this chapter is the distribution company Thommes & Schneider, which sells office materials. At the time of the study, the company employed around ninety people, of whom around half were Luxembourgish and 12 per cent were Portuguese residents of Luxembourg. The remaining staff members were French and Belgian cross-border workers. The company has both blue- and white-collar jobs. Blue-collar jobs include employees in the depot and lorry drivers. The white-collar jobs include the company's administration and the commercial or sales department. The cross-border workers are represented equally in both blue- and white-collar jobs, whereas Luxembourgers predominantly occupy white-collar positions. The demographic prevalence of Luxembourgers, along with a significant number of Francophone cross-border workers and Portuguese employees, is reflected in the overall linguistic profile of the company. For interactions between colleagues, Luxembourgish is the dominant language of interaction between Luxembourgers, and French is the dominant language between Francophone employees. French is used in all official written communication and it also functions as the lingua franca between the different linguistic groups. For interactions with clients and other outsiders to the workplace, Luxembourgish, French and German are used most frequently. The main participants in this study are all French, or Francophone Belgian cross-border workers whose first language is French. They have language resources in other languages, mostly German and English, but their skills in Luxembourgish are low. This is of crucial importance for the subsequent analysis of language practices and dynamics of boundary negotiating in the company. This company can be considered a constellation of practice (Wenger 1998), wherein some teams and departments constitute smaller-scale communities of practice.

5. Language policies in the company: Luxembourgish vs. French

Before moving to the analysis of face-to-face interactions between workers in the company, I will briefly consider the language policy in this company. Language policy, defined as attempts to influence or change the language practices of a speech community (Spolsky 2004), is an area that has gained increased attention in workplace discourse research (Gunnarsson 2010; Thomas 2008; Angouri 2013). Multinational companies operating in different countries across the globe often decide to adopt one, or more, corporate language(s) with English being most prominent in the globalised economy. The decision to choose a common working language reflects the overall language ideologies and norms that the company's top management orients to but often does not reflect language practices in face-to-face interactions, as has been frequently shown (Kingsley 2009; Lønsman 2011). Language policy can provide insights into language norms that operate in a company. Many workplaces do not have an explicit official policy, but this does not mean that they do not have a language policy. At Thommes & Schneider, for example, no document called a 'language policy' could be found. Nevertheless, Catherine, the head of the HR department, expressed clear views on language policy in an interview.

Interview quote 1 Catherine (Head of Human Resources)[3]
We don't have a linguistic policy.
It's true that the language of the house is Luxembourgish because it's a Luxembourgish company with Luxembourgish management, eh.
And so we have the cross-border workers who speak French.
There's no problem that management and the other people speak French.
The language here eh that's administrative, everything is written in French.
Mails are written in French between us because we respect the people who don't understand.
But there's no problem to speak with management in Luxembourgish.
On the other hand if we have meetings, even top management meetings or meetings between departmental managers,
there's only one who's not Luxembourgish, we speak French.
We respect people like that.

In this interview excerpt, the HR manager first argues that the company does not have a language policy, but then contradicts this by positing Luxembourgish as the house language, 'because it is a Luxembourgish company'. In that, she constructs the link between Luxembourgish as the language of the company and its Luxembourgish origins as 'natural'. At the same time, she refers to French as the lingua franca between Luxembourgers and Francophone cross-border workers and as the language of written communication. She thereby projects an image of the company as respectful of linguistic differences and of those staff who do not speak the local language: 'we respect people like that'. In later parts of the interview, Catherine further emphasises the company's will to promote multilingualism – (e.g. by proposing a multilingual website to its clients). On the other hand, Catherine nevertheless projects group boundaries by contrasting the Luxembourgish management and other Luxembourgish employees with the 'the cross-border workers'. Her comment 'and so we have the cross-border workers who speak French' reflects that she operates the group distinction on the basis of language resources. The implicit meaning of this statement is in fact that cross-border workers do not speak Luxembourgish.

In sum, the above quote highlights the importance of two languages in the company: Luxembourgish and French. In her answer, Catherine suggests equal status for the two languages. In doing so, she projects two language norms: Luxembourgish is the 'symbolic' and the interactional language between those who speak it; and, French is the language of written communication and the lingua franca with Francophones. I shall now illustrate how this position relates to the reality of everyday practices.

6. Constructing the language boundary: Luxembourgish is the default language

Statements by Catherine project an image of Thommes & Schneider as a tolerant workplace; where divergent language resources are looked upon benevolently, where the local language is positively valued, and where staff members do not mind accommodating to those who have not mastered the local language, that is, the cross-border workers; however, this official view does not correspond to the realities faced by non-locals in everyday interactions at work. These daily interactions testify to tensions and the existence of a language boundary between linguistic groups. The data provides numerous examples of metalinguistic discourse, i.e. interactions in which issues relating to language are explicitly raised. Excerpt 1 illustrates this practice. It is an interaction between a white-collar worker Luxembourgish employee, Pit, and Christophe (CHR), a French cross-border worker from the depot. Pit enters the depot and greets Christophe. The interaction is in French.

Excerpt 1
1 PIT: salut
            hi
2   //ça va\
            you're fine
3 CHR: /ça va\\
            you're fine
4   //travaille (travaille beaucoup)\
            you work (you work a lot)
5 PIT: /très bien très bien merci\\ oui //(c'est bon merci)\
            very well very well thanks yes it's good thanks
6 CHR: /très bea- t'as beaucoup\\ de boulot aujourd'hui\\
            very we- you have a lot of work today
7 PIT: ouais
            yes
8   beaucoup //beaucoup\
            a lot a lot

9	CHR:	/ouais\\ beaucoup=hein
		yes a lot=eh
10	PIT:	+ ouais
		yes
11		(1.3)
12		t'as encore appris encore à parler luxembourgeois non
		have you learnt to speak Luxembourgish yet no
13	CHR:	+ un peu
		a little
14		//(um) pouc (um)\ pouco
		a little a little
15	PIT:	/(xxx xxx)\\
16		ouais il //il faut quand-même=hein\
		yeah you have to though eh
17	CHR:	/ [laughs] \\
18	PIT:	c'est temps
		it's time
19	CHR:	+ [uses a smiling voice] um pouco
		a little
20	PIT:	parce qu'à partir de 2011 on parle que luxembourgeois ici hein
		because from 2011 on we are only speaking Luxembourgish here eh
21		(3.0)
22	CHR:	ouais mais//eh\
		yeah but er
23	EST:	/merci\\merci
		/thanks\\thanks
24	CHR:	de rien de rien de rien
		you're welcome you're welcome you're welcome
25	EST:	[laughs]

This interaction starts in a very casual way. Pit greets Christophe and asks about his well-being (lines 1–2). Christophe returns the greeting and asks if Pit has a lot of work to do (lines 3, 4, 6); a suggestion that Pit confirms positively (lines 7, 8, 10). Such small talk (Holmes 2000; J. Coupland 2001) is common between these staff members and is part of how they engage in constructing positive relationships in the most fleeting of encounters. The silence of 1.3 seconds following Pit's last minimal answer suggests this interaction is over, and both men move on – they are literally moving through the building; however, when Pit takes the floor again, the tone of the interaction has changed abruptly. His direct question 'have you learnt to speak Luxembourgish yet=no' (line 12) indexes a change of frame to a more serious topic, namely, Christophe's efforts in acquiring skills in the local language. His latched use of the adverb *non* suggests he infers the answer to his own question. Christophe reacts by claiming that he has a little (lines 13, 14, 19) – in fact, Christophe had not engaged in any formal language learning at the time. Pit continues to emphasise the need to learn the language, by claiming that from 2011 onwards, Luxembourgish will be the only language spoken in the company: '*ouais il il faut quand-même=hein, c'est temps, parce qu'à partir de 2011 on parle que luxembourgeois ici=hein*' (lines 16, 18, 20). The urgency of the matter is notably achieved through his use of the modal verb 'have to' (line 16), his insistence that 'it's time' and by adding a deadline (the year 2011). In fact, no such language policy was actually planned but was made up by Pit in the course of this interaction. By urging Christophe to learn Luxembourgish, Pit is criticising his colleague for his lack of efforts to acquire the local language. His actions not only threaten Christophe's positive face but also draw a clear linguistic boundary between them.

Throughout the interaction, Pit's tone of voice is serious, which makes the nature of his comment ambiguous. Is this a real criticism or rather a sarcastic joke? Either way, the use of humour has been described as a particularly salient strategy to draw boundaries between social groups in a socially acceptable way (Marra and Holmes 2007; de Bres et al. 2010). In his responses, Christophe attempts to frame the discussion as a humorous sequence by adopting a jovial tone and by laughing hesitantly (lines 17, 19). His switch to Portuguese in self-repeating 'a little' (*um pouco*, lines 14, 19) can be further interpreted as an attempt to perhaps 'ridicule' the interaction. Christophe is indeed not an actual speaker of Portuguese, but this language is spoken by many of his colleagues from the depot and so he has picked up some elements. This strategy to mobilise Portuguese resources could be seen as an attempt by Christophe to distance himself from Pit's criticism. Nevertheless, his colleague does not respond to the invitation to frame this as a good-natured joke. Pit's last comment is followed by a silence of 3 seconds, which we can interpret as an indication of a conversation breakdown. Christophe then self-selects by uttering the contrastive discourse marker *but* (Fraser 1998), which could be read as an attempt to engage in a further defence strategy. He is, however, interrupted by a staff member Estelle (EST) who is passing by (line 23), after which the interaction remains unresolved.

This interaction highlights one of the dominant language norms that govern this workplace, namely that Luxembourgish is the 'normal' language of the company. Pit thereby reproduces the monolingual ideological stance, 'Luxembourgish because we are in Luxembourg'. In particular, the comment that only Luxembourgish will be spoken in the company in future reinforces this boundary and suggests that Christophe will inevitably be excluded if he does not make greater efforts to learn the local language. In the interview, Christophe mentioned that this kind of teasing or jocular abuse occurred frequently and, in his view, had a dark and offensive side. Christophe characterised the teasing practices that he is exposed to as 'mean' and even related them to racist discourses.

The emphasis on Luxembourgish as the default language at Thommes & Schneider became further evident when the idea that my project was about 'testing' the Luxembourgish skills of cross-border workers circulated among some staff. In one interaction, for example, Alberto, a Portuguese employee, explicitly asked Christophe whether he needed to record himself to test his Luxembourgish skills. Christophe responded to this by emphasising that the project was about 'testing' languages more generally, thus taking the focus away from Luxembourgish – it is important to note that this was not at all how I had framed the research.

The following excerpt between Francophone cross-border worker Sandrine (SAN) and her Luxembourgish manager Pierre (PIE) also illustrates the strong focus on Luxembourgish among some members of the company.

Excerpt 2

1	PIE:	[enters the office] ah: vous avez eu de l'aide
		ah: did you get some help
2	SAN:	oui
		yes
3	PIE:	ouais ça c'est bien //[laughs]\
		yes that's good
4	SAN:	/c'est bien hein\\
		that's good=eh
5		(1.5) y a des gens qui sont qui compatissent
		there are people who sympathise
6	PIE:	[laughs] (2.2)
7	SAN:	tu veux aussi venir,
		do you want to come as well
8	PIE:	(1.4) voir si je parles luxembourgeois [laughs]
		see whether I speak Luxembourgish
9		je crois un petit peu [laughs]
		I think a little
10	SAN:	c'est pas la question qu'ils posaient
		that was not the question they were asking
11	PIE:	hein [smiles]
		huh

Pierre enters Sandrine's office and notices my presence in the corner of the room, during a period of observation and recording. He wittily asks whether Sandrine and her colleagues have been given additional staff (line 1). After she confirms this, she asks Pierre if he would also like to join the team: 'do you want to come as well' (line 7). In a way, this is risky, given that Pierre is her boss. Instead of answering her question, Pierre replies with a rhetorical counter-question: 'to see whether I speak Luxembourgish' (line 8), and the (self-evident) answer to this question 'I think a little' (line 9). Given that he is a native speaker of Luxembourgish, the claim that he speaks the language a little bit is an ironic understatement, matched by his tone. He frames this as a humorous sequence, as is further evidenced by his repeated laughter (lines 8, 9, 11). This laughter indicates how ridiculous he finds the idea that his Luxembourgish should be tested. Pierre is arguably enacting reinforcing humour (Holmes and Marra 2002), which emphasises the boundary between himself, a native speaker of Luxembourgish who is beyond all language testing, and Sandrine, as a cross-border worker whose language skills should be assessed. This excerpt thus illustrates that from the perspective of staff, if not the researcher, the most important focus for a research project is the cross-border workers' skills in Luxembourgish.

As in excerpt 1, Pierre uses bald strategies in highlighting Sandrine's failure to speak Luxembourgish, and therefore probably failing the test. In doing so, he reinforces the language boundary. Sandrine's scope of action, like Christophe's, is limited. She reacts by taking a defensive stance with her comment 'that was not the question they were asking' (line 10). This can be seen as an intention to divert the focus away from the Luxembourgish language. The boundary is further emphasised by the fact that the issue raised in this interaction remains unresolved – Pierre reacts to Sandrine's comment with a minimal feedback token 'huh' and then appears to move away.

While the previous excerpts illustrate different ways in which cross-border workers are targeted for failing to adhere to the Luxembourgish workplace norm, the data shows that the language boundary can also be constructed and reinforced at times where the Francophone participants attempt to use the local language. This is illustrated in the following excerpt, an interaction between Pedro (PED), a Luxembourgish-speaking staff member with Portuguese origins, and Christophe (CHR, from excerpt 1). The interaction is in Luxembourgish.

Excerpt 3

1	PED:	moien
		hello
2	CHR:	moien wéi ass //et \
		hello how are you
3	PED:	/wéi\\ ass et
		how are you
4	CHR:	gutt an du
		well and you
5		(1.3)
6	PED:	geet dech näischt un
		that's none of your business
7	CHR:	jo
		yes
8		((10.3))

Pedro enters the depot and greets Christophe with *moien* (line 1), the standard routine for greeting in Luxembourgish. Christophe returns the greeting in Luxembourgish and follows with the expected how-are-you sequence (Coupland et al. 1992) in the same language (line 2). In an overlapping move, Pedro returns the question to Christophe (line 3) and the latter again answers in Luxembourgish (line 4). In accommodating to Pedro's use of Luxembourgish, Christophe not only displays his knowledge of greeting routines in the local language but also indexes his adherence to the workplace norm of greeting in this language. At this point, however, the interaction takes an unforeseen turn. After a remarkable silence of 1.3 seconds, which could indicate a closure to this phatic exchange, Pedro takes the floor again but answers 'that's none of your business' (line 6). Christophe's positive minimal feedback *yes* (line 7) can be seen as an inappropriate answer to this blunt and powerful move. Pedro is perhaps working on the assumption that his colleague does not understand the meaning of his utterance. Pedro's comment is, to say the least, an unexpected reply to a how-are-you sequence. The role of phatic communication, that is, 'talk with relatively little referential content or information load' (Holmes 2000: 37), is usually described as functioning to establish good interpersonal relationships between partici- pants (Jaworski 2009). Pedro is flouting one of the most mundane interactional rules, which arguably results in a strong power move. This power move then also causes an interaction breakdown given that Christophe has little leeway to counteract. We might also interpret Pedro's act as ridiculing Christophe, who is at pains to draw on what little Luxembourgish resources he has. This highlights the power imbalance that exists between them. Pedro has the linguistic ability both to make Christophe use the Luxembourgish routines and to play out his Luxembourgish competence in a way that makes Christophe look silly.

A similar act of boundary construction was found in other interactions. In one example, the Luxembourger François apes his Francophone colleague Fred because the latter uses a Luxembourgish routine '*t ass gutt*' ('that's fine') while talking to someone on the phone. After he hangs up, François imitates him by saying 'nothing's fine' and recreates Fred's non-standard pronunciation of *ass gutt* in a mocking tone. Like excerpt 3, this interaction also remains 'unresolved' (like all the others); the Luxembourger does not make the effort to explain his comment. In such instances, the boundary marking effect is reinforced through the breakdown that ends the inter- action. These breakdowns are reminiscent of Garfinkel's (1967) breaching experi- ments, in which he asked students to behave inappropriately in ordinary interactional situations to demonstrate the power of social and interactional norms in everyday communication.

The mocking of cross-border workers when they attempt to use Luxembourgish stands in apparent contradiction to the more explicit expectation that they should learn the language. This duality can, however, be explained in terms of the identity value of the local language for the Luxembourgish group. Because Francophones do not speak the local language, the nationals can rely on it as a marker of group iden- tity, which confers some privileges on them in their workplace context. All in all, the Luxembourgish-speaking group at this workplace thus adopts a rather monolingual point of view and can be said to adhere to the previously mentioned monolingual identification strategy with Luxembourgish (Horner and Weber 2008).

7. Counteracting the linguistic boundary: retreating into a French-only approach

The previous section illustrated how language competence in Luxembourgish serves as a strategy to construct group boundaries at Thommes & Schneider. The excerpts presented suggest that this company is a challenging workplace for cross-border workers. But how do they react to this? What strategies do they adopt to counter- act this monolingually Luxembourgish-focused language norm and to challenge the boundary construction? These questions are explored in the final section.

The ethnographic study showed that the cross-border participants respond by adopting an equally monolingual point of view through foregrounding the importance of French in the company. This is first reflected in the expectation that colleagues accommodate to them in French. The argument most commonly put forward is that, insofar as everyone speaks French, it is 'normal' to be accommodated to. This attitude is expressed in the following interview quote in which Joel acknowledges that it is a matter of convenience for cross-border workers that everyone speaks French.

> Interview quote 2 Joel (worker at the depot)
> well insofar as everyone speaks French
> I mean that for us it's [. . .] a solution of comfort for us

The normative expectation that cross-border workers are spoken to in French is further expressed when Joel argues it is a 'reflex' for him to speak in French when someone addresses him in Luxembourgish. His phrase 'it comes out like that' in the quotation below reflects the discourse of normalcy to speak and to be spoken to in French.

> Interview quote 3 Joel (worker at the depot)
> in fact as a reflex I speak French
> so someone speaks to me someone tells me yes er in Luxembourgish
> I answer in French,
> er well I don't know if that shocks or hurts people but well for me that's
> (—-) it comes out like that

A second reaction emanating from the participants' discourses is to display resentment at some Luxembourgish colleagues for speaking Luxembourgish in their presence, both in workplace interactions and in moments of small talk or social events. Karolina describes the displeasure she feels when a colleague enters the office and circulates work-related information in Luxembourgish, which she does not understand, thus compelling her to ask for a translation.

> Interview quote 4 Karolina (employee in the purchasing department)
> somebody comes to our office says something, an information about work but
> it was said in Luxembourgish, so I had to ask after the person left
> 'what did he say, what did she say?'
> yes
> I didn't think this was normal, even though I agree that could just learn it
> yes
> but still I thought that they could have made the effort well or otherwise for
> example at lunch at the . . .
> at the cafeteria
> at the cafeteria well everything happens in Luxembourgish they make . . . the
> did not make the effort eh

Karolina's resentment is expressed in her statement 'I didn't think this was normal' and her affirmation 'I still thought that they could have made the effort'. Sometimes, the feeling of exclusion caused by the fact that Luxembourgish is spoken in their presence means Francophones do not attend a particular social function. Such a scenario was reported by Karolina at a different point in her interview. Finally, feeling excluded due to language practices can create a mistrust of colleagues who speak a different language. This is shown in excerpt 4, in which Christophe (CHR) narrates a conflictual interaction he had with Paul, a Luxembourger, to his French colleague Manu.

Excerpt 4
1   CHR: le (paul) là
            the paul there
2   là je lui ai demandé un truc
            I asked him something
3   puis il me parlait en luxembourgeois (t'sais)=
            then he talked to me in Luxembourgish (you know)=
4   =je ne comprenais pas t'sais
            =i didn't understand you know
5   + il avait pas vu (brian ça) t'sais
            he hadn't seen this brian you know
6   puis il parlait (LËTZ) il a sûrement dû m'insulter
            then he spoke (in lux) he certainly insulted me

Christophe had asked Paul a question (line 2), whereupon the latter responded in Luxembourgish: 'then he talked to me in Luxembourgish (you know)' (line 3). Christophe did not understand what he said (line 4), and, from there, he concludes that his colleague must have been insulting him (line 6). Such feelings of exclusion and mistrust point to intolerance towards the presence of languages in the workplace that one does not understand, and thereby reflect a monolingual perspective, respectively an adherence to the ideological view of 'multilingualism as a problem' (de Bres 2013).

Finally, a further way in which the cross-border workers express their monolingual point of view is in showing surprise at their colleagues' low competence in French.

Interview quote 5 Karolina (employee in the purchasing department)
oh, when they explained my work to me (--) oh they (--)
explained but I was at pains to understand sometimes because they were searching for
words they invented words, they turned their sentences
oh . . . I expected that they nevertheless speak better French
because I was always told in Luxembourg they speak all the languages eh

Karolina explains how at the beginning of her time at the company she struggled to understand her Luxembourgish colleagues when they explained work-related tasks to her. She depicts them as hesitant and lacking in proficiency. She concludes that 'I expected that they nevertheless speak better French', based on her pre-existing perceptions that in Luxembourg people speak all languages.

In sum, this section has illustrated how cross-border workers respond to the 'Luxembourgish because we are in Luxembourg' norm projected by their colleagues. The excerpts illustrate that both language groups adopt a similarly monolingual perspective. Rather than attempting to deconstruct the group boundaries, they in fact reinforce them with their own discursive practices. This appraisal suggests that the construction of group boundaries is always a dynamic process, in which both sides are equally involved.

8. Conclusion

In this chapter, I have argued that language resources can contribute to the creation of linguistic boundaries through an investigation of one particular Luxembourgish workplace. The analysis has shown that in this workplace, the linguistic boundaries both contribute to and arise as a result of the tension created by the perception that cross-border workers do not make enough efforts to learn and speak the local language. Although top management projects an image of the company as tolerant towards linguistic difference and as having an openness to accommodate to non-speakers of Luxembourgish, this attitude is not (always) reflected in language practices and metalinguistic discourse. The data provided numerous examples in which Luxembourgish-speaking staff members either criticise Francophones for not speaking the language (excerpt 1), sometimes in rather covert ways (excerpt 2), or where they mock them when they attempt to use the local language (excerpt 3). Through their linguistic practices, they adhere to a view of Luxembourgish as the default language and thus to the essentialist language ideology, 'Luxembourgish because we are in Luxembourg'. Cross-border workers, on the other hand, react to this boundary marking. They sometimes attempt to use humour as an interactional strategy to defuse the face-threat (excerpt 1). Most of the time, however, they express similarly monolingual views to counteract the boundary, which reflect a 'French-only position'. This position involves them expecting colleagues to accommodate to them in French since Luxembourgers are expected to have skills in their first language, being suspicious of Luxembourgish colleagues and constructing themselves as excluded and left out when others speak Luxembourgish among themselves. Both groups contribute equally to the construction and the maintaining of the linguistic boundary, which appears to be rather fixed in this case. We could thus conclude that there is potential for serious tension in the company that appears to be ignored or not recognised by the management.

On a more global scale, the language tensions observed at Thommes & Schneider reflect current developments in the sociolinguistic landscape of Luxembourg, described at the beginning of this chapter. Cross-border workers are often attacked for their (perceived) lack of efforts towards learning the local language, and public discourses request that more emphasis is put on Luxembourgish. One strategy used by cross-border workers to react to these face-threatening discourses is to insist on the historical presence of French and the excellent language skills of residents of Luxembourg in this language. These arguments legitimate their own lack of language skills. Furthermore, data from this workplace also illustrate an ambiguous attitude of Luxembourgers: if there is a strong expectation of 'foreigners' to learn the local language, the fact that more and more actually speak it also constitutes a potential threat to the value of it as a marker of in-group identity. What the analysis suggests, thus, is that the linguistic boundary observed in this workplace is co-constructed by the two groups simultaneously, who each contribute to the maintaining and reinforcement of the conflicting opposition through their respective metalinguistic practice. In that, my work confirms previous research on the co-constructed nature of social identities and group boundaries. Finally, my analysis also confirms the supposition made in the introduction that the globalised economy presents challenges for newcomers and established groups alike – both need to engage in a repositioning process.

Transcription conventions

[ ]	paralinguistic features and editorial information in square brackets
+	pause up to one second
(1.3)	pauses in seconds
//yes\	overlapping speech, double slashes indicate beginning and ending
/oh\\	
(xxxx)	unclear utterances
(oh)	transcriber's best guess at an unclear utterance
=	turn continuation
-	utterance cut off
um pouco	Portuguese is underlined

Notes

1. The names of the companies are pseudonyms, as are those of the participants.
2. Throughout this chapter and in line with recent theoretical advances in multilingualism research (Blommaert and Backus 2012; Jørgensen et al. 2011), I prefer the term 'language resources' or 'repertoires' to 'language competence'.
3. The original interviews were conducted in French; my own translation.

References

Agar, M. (2009), 'Ethnography', in G. Senft, J.-O. Östman and J. Verschueren (eds), *Culture and language use*, Amsterdam and Philadelphia: John Benjamins, pp. 110–20.

Angouri, J. (2013), 'The multilingual reality of the multinational workplace: language policy and language use', *Journal of Multilingual and Multicultural Development*, 34: 6, pp. 564–81.

Baltes-Löhr, C., A. Prüm, R. Reckinger and C. Wille (2011), 'Everyday cultures and identities', in IPSE (ed.), *Doing identity in Luxembourg: subjective appropriations – institutional attributions – socio-cultural milieus*, Bielefeld: Transcript Verlag, pp. 233–84.

Belling, L. and J. de Bres (2014), 'Digital super-diversity in Luxembourg: language and communication practices in a multilingual Facebook group', *Discourse, Context and Media*, 4–5, pp. 74–86.

Blackledge, A. and A. Creese (2010), *Multilingualism: a critical perspective*, London and New York: Continuum.

Blommaert, J. and A. Backus (2012), 'Superdiverse repertoires and the individual', *Tilburg Papers in Culture Studies*, 24, pp. 1–32.

Blommaert, J. and D. Jie (2010), *Ethnographic fieldwork: a beginner's guide*, Bristol: Multilingual Matters.

Cameron, D. (2003), 'Gender and language ideologies', in J. Holmes and M. Meyerhoff (eds), *The handbook of language and gender*, Malden, MA and Oxford: Blackwell, pp. 447–67.

CEFIS (2011), *L'intégration au Luxembourg. Focus sur les réseaux sociaux, la confiance et les stéréotypes sur les frontaliers*, Luxembourg: CEFIS.

Coupland, J. (ed.) (2001), *Small talk*, Harlow: Pearson.

Coupland, J., N. Coupland and J. D. Robinson (1992), '"How are you?": negotiating phatic communication', *Language in Society*, 21, pp. 207–30.

Coupland, N. (2001), 'Introduction: sociolinguistic theory and social theory', in N. Coupland, S. Sarangi and C. N. Candlin (eds), *Sociolinguistics and social theory*, Harlow: Pearson, pp. 1–26.

de Bres, J. (2013), 'Language ideologies for constructing inclusion and exclusion: identity and interest in the metalinguistic discourse of cross-border workers in Luxembourg', in E. Barát, P. Studer and J. Nekvapil (eds), *Ideological conceptualisations of language: discourse of linguistic diversity*, Frankfurt am Main: Peter Lang, pp. 57–83.

de Bres, J. (2014), 'Competing language ideologies about societal multilingualism among cross-border workers in Luxembourg', *International Journal of the Sociology of Language*, 227, pp. 119–37.

de Bres, J. and A. Franziskus (2014), 'Multilingual practices of university students and changing forms of multilingualism in Luxembourg', *International Journal of Multilingualism*, 11: 1, pp. 62–75.

de Bres, J., J. Holmes, M. Marra and B. Vine (2010), 'Kia ora matua: humour and the Maori language in the workplace', *Journal of Asian Pacific Communication*, 20: 1, pp. 46–68.

Duchêne, A. and M. Heller (eds) (2007), *Discourses of endangerment: interest and ideology in the defense of languages*, London: Continuum.

Franziskus, A. (2013), 'Getting by in a multilingual workplace: language practices, ideologies and norms of cross-border workers in Luxembourg', unpublished PhD thesis, University of Luxembourg.

Fraser, B. (1998), 'Contrastive discourse markers in English', in A. Jucker and Y. Ziv (eds), *Discourse markers: descriptions and theory*, Amsterdam and Philadelphia: John Benjamins, pp. 301–26.

Gal, S. (2006), 'Contradictions of standard language in Europe: implications for the study of practices and publics', *Social Anthropology*, 14: 2, pp. 163–81.

Gafaranga, J. (2001), 'Linguistic identities in talk-in-interaction: order in bilingual conversation', *Journal of Pragmatics*, 33, pp. 1901–25.

Garfinkel, H. (1967), *Studies in ethnomethodology*, Englewood Cliffs, NJ: Prentice Hall.

Gunnarsson, B.-L. (2010), 'Multilingualism within transnational companies: an analysis of company policy and practice in a diversity perspective', in H. Kelly-Holmes and G. Mautner (eds), *Language and the market*, Basingstoke: Palgrave Macmillan, pp. 171–84.

Holmes, J. (2000), 'Doing collegiality and keeping control at work: small talk in government departments', in J. Coupland (ed.), *Small talk*, London: Longman, pp. 32–61.

Holmes, J. and M. Marra (2002), 'Humour as a discursive boundary marker in social interaction', in A. Duszak (ed.), *Us and others: social identities across languages, discourses and cultures*, Amsterdam: John Benjamins, pp. 377–400.

Holmes, J., M. Marra and B. Vine (2011), *Leadership, discourse, and ethnicity*, Oxford: Oxford University Press.

Horner, K. and J.-J. Weber (2008), 'The language situation in Luxembourg', *Current Issues in Language Planning*, 9: 1, pp. 69–128.

Jaworski, A. (2009), 'Greetings in tourist–host encounters', in N. Coupland and A. Jaworski (eds), *The new sociolinguistics reader*, Basingstoke: Palgrave Macmillan, pp. 662–79.

Jørgensen, N. J., M. Karrebaek, L. M. Madsen and J. S. Møller (2011), 'Polylanguaging in superdiversity', *Diversities*, 13: 2, pp. 23–37.

Kingsley, L. (2009), 'Explicit and implicit dimensions of language policy in multilingual banks in Luxembourg: an analysis of top-down and bottom-up pressures on practices', *Language Problems & Language Planning*, 33: 2, pp. 153–73.

Kroskrity, P. V. (2004), 'Language ideologies', in A. Duranti (ed.), *A companion to linguistic anthropology*, Malden, MA: Blackwell, pp. 496–517.

Lønsman, D. (2011), 'English as a corporate language', unpublished PhD thesis, Roskilde University.

Marra, M. and J. Angouri (2011), 'Investigating the negotiation of identity: a view from the field of workplace discourse', in J. Angouri and M. Marra (eds), *Constructing identities at work*, New York: Palgrave Macmillan, pp. 1–14.

Marra, M. and J. Holmes (2007), 'Humour across cultures', in H. Kotthoff and H. Spencer-Oatey (eds), *Handbook of intercultural communication*, Berlin: Walter de Gruyter, pp. 153–72.

Nekvapil, J. and T. Sherman (2009), 'Czech, German and English: finding their place in multinational companies in the Czech Republic', in P. Stevenson and J. Carl (eds), *Language, discourse and identity in Central Europe*, Basingstoke: Palgrave Macmillan, pp. 122–46.

Nekvapil, J. and T. Sherman (2013), 'Language ideologies and linguistic practices: the case of multinational companies in Central Europe', in E. Barát, P. Studer and J. Nekvapil (eds), *Ideological conceptualizations of language: discourses of linguistic diversity*, Frankfurt am Main: Peter Lang, pp. 85–118.

Roberts, C. (2010), 'Language socialisation in the workplace', *Annual Review of Applied Linguistics*, 30, pp. 211–27.

Spolsky, B. (2004), *Language policy*, Cambridge: Cambridge University Press.

STATEC (2015), *Le Luxembourg en chiffres*, Luxembourg: STATEC.

Thomas, C. A. (2008), 'Bridging the gap between theory and practice: language policy in multilingual organisations', *Language Awareness*, 17: 4, pp. 307–25.

Wenger, E. (1998), *Communities of practice: learning, meaning, and identity*, Cambridge: Cambridge University Press.

Woolard, K. A. (1998), 'Introduction: language ideology as a field of inquiry', in B. Schieffelin, K. A. Woolard and P. V. Kroskrity (eds), *Language ideologies: practice and theory*, Oxford: Oxford University Press, pp. 3–47.

10

Working and Learning in a New Niche: Ecological Interpretations of Work-Related Migration

Minna Suni

1. Background

Finland is a Western welfare state which has been receiving an increasing amount of migrants since the early 1990s and the number is steadily growing.[1] Situated up in the north and having two national languages, Finnish and Swedish, which are not widely spoken around the globe, Finland faces challenges when competing with other nations in the globalised labour market. Language is one such challenge. Particularly in the health care sector, which is the focus here, internationally educated professionals may find it more practical and appealing to look for jobs in English-speaking countries in which their prior language knowledge is valuable and sufficient. Also, migrants studying in international nursing programmes in Finland tend to consider English-speaking countries the most attractive option for employment, because they perceive it as too challenging to quickly develop sufficient Finnish language skills (see Virtanen 2013). This language barrier confronts anyone planning to enter the Finnish labour market and thus acts as an effective pre-selection mechanism in recruitment processes.

At the same time, over the last twenty years, Finland has been attracting numerous international health care professionals, and more than 600 medical professionals educated abroad become licensed to work in Finland each year (Ministry of Education and Culture 2014). Despite the language barrier, the good reputation of the Nordic model of organising and managing health care, as well as that of the Finnish social security system, education system and general living conditions have been noted as adequate reasons to migrate (Magnussen et al. 2009). Finland is also known as a high-tech society which provides smooth access to up-to-date medical equipment, creditable working time legislation and progressive, research-oriented working practices appreciated by many international specialists perhaps lacking the corresponding resources in their countries of origin (Haukilahti et al. 2012; see also Stilwell et al. 2004: 595–7). This chapter addresses the significance of language in international recruitment and work-related migration processes of health care professionals from an ecological perspective. 'Ecology' refers here to the deep interrelatedness between an individual and the surrounding social and physical environment in which he or she lives and acts (van Lier 2000). In this framework, the concept of 'niche' will be introduced and applied in the analysis of interview data to draw attention to the often limited roles, positions and operating ranges provided for newcomers in work communities.

The globalising labour market and economy, as well as societal language policies, are obvious environmental factors influencing the general dynamics of migration, but local work communities are those sites in which individual migrants primarily operate in their daily lives. The global and local tendencies thus intersect in the choices made by migrating individuals and in the spaces (un)available to them. In the globalising world, these people are crossing state borders more or less smoothly, but are they also able to cross the less visible boundaries between language communities and to broaden the often very tight niches provided for them in workplaces, if they are successful in finding an international job at all?

In this chapter, experiences of fear, frustration and success narrated by migrated professionals with full-time health care jobs are analysed from the point of view of niches and boundary crossings. The main goal is to find out (1) how language policies are seen to affect the niches available for an individual, and (2) how existing or experienced niche boundaries can be crossed.

In a biological sense, a niche provides the optimal conditions for each species and its individual representatives – a sheltered area in which to live, develop and employ the available resources necessary for that particular species to develop (see for example Brown and Wilson 1956). Adapted to the language ecology of workplaces, a niche[2] can be seen as the operating space provided for or taken by an individual, allowing certain freedoms and containing resources for target-oriented activities, but being simultaneously restricted by different, surrounding niches governed by others and their policies and practices. It is one's individual place or area with existing but (in)visible boundaries.

Finding optimal conditions is a challenge for anyone entering working life, but for a migrant with limited language skills it is a major one; such themes will be discussed by introducing two migrants who have entered the Finnish labour market with limited Finnish language skills. As boundary crossers they are also seen as potential 'new speakers' of Finnish, facing and crossing the rather fixed categorisations of language users, typical of the idea of a homogenous nation-state (see Walsh and O'Rourke 2014). These case studies from the Finnish health care sector are thus presented to discuss the specific properties of the linguistic 'breeding ground' available for newcomers in these and corresponding settings.

2. New speakers in a workplace ecology

An ecological approach suggested by van Lier (2000), Kramsch (2002), Kramsch and Whiteside (2008) and Steffensen and Fill (2014) forms a starting point for the analysis of the case study data. In this framework, each language user or learner is seen as a part of a larger social (eco)system, which continuously reacts to various changes in the environment and affects the options and opportunities available for the individual. The holistic and situated perspectives of the language ecology approach bring together the social and cognitive dimension of language use and learning, and highlight the interplay between an active, agentive individual and the environment in which he or she is acting, for example, learning and working. The roots of this approach are in Gibsonian perceptual psychology; Gibson (1977) launched the concept of affordance, referring to the tight, reciprocal relation between an organism and its environment – in this case the individual and his or her new work environment. As Kramsch puts it, language ecology is a

> convenient metaphor for a post-structuralist conceptualization of language learning as a nonlinear, relational human activity, co-constructed between humans and their environment, contingent upon their position in space and history, and a site of struggle for the control of social power and cultural memory. (Kramsch 2002: 5)

What makes this approach relevant for working life research is that the focus is on relationships and not isolated individuals, on sharedness and not private ownership, and on learning opportunities and not outcomes. Kramsch (2002: 5) refers to both positions and struggles, and these two themes are essential in analysing workplace ecology, too.

At the level of language ecology, the 'breeding ground' of transnational health care professionals in Finland is partially shaped by the official EU and national level language policies regulating the minimum level of working language skills – in this case, proficiency in Finnish (see Ministry of Education and Culture 2014). It is also shaped by the expectations set and evaluations made by the local level stakeholders such as recruiters, health care managers and directors. The attitudinal climate of the work community (open, supportive, collaborative vs. closed, competitive, etc.), the leadership and management models represented (authoritarian, collegial, etc.), and the flexibility vs. permanency of roles shape the general conditions for each employee to practise their profession and to develop their own role and professional identity (Sias 2009).

When the work is changing in context and content, employees are actually forced to reconstruct their professional identities and reconfigure their shared work communities (Angouri 2014). This is done in interpersonal encounters and communication processes. The ecological perspective offers a means to examine these changes from a holistic perspective. However, especially in institutional contexts like health care, there may exist highly resistant practices, which lean on, for example, professional hierarchies. These and linguistic boundaries may be quite hard to cross, as will be shown.

The new speaker perspective suggested by Walsh and O'Rourke (2014) and Pujolar and Puigdevall (2015) opens up yet another view on the phenomena in question. It has been shown by the latter that in autobiographical interviews, specific biographic junctures such as entering university, getting employed or creating a family may be quite meaningful as they bring with them an attachment to specific languages and the construction of identities in which the new, developing language skills are a characteristic feature (Pujolar and Puigdevall 2015: 168). In migration contexts, workplaces may form junctures similar to those reported by Pujolar and Puigdevall (2015) in bilingual Catalonia: there is a strong need to display second language skills, and typi-cally a desire to gain membership in the language and work community at the same time. The question of legitimacy (Bourdieu 1977; Heller 1996; Lave and Wenger 1991) is essential here: who are actually regarded as legitimate new speakers or users of a language and, thus, allowed to enter the core of a community by crossing invisible boundaries? The new speaker perspective also questions the well-established native/non-native speaker distinction and adds a socially based, time-sensitive approach to the overlapping developments of belonging, identity construction and language skills.

It is obvious that migrants may also have trouble gaining agency in the workplace. From an ecological point of view (van Lier 2008), agency is not simply an individual phenomenon but a social event involving initiative. Lantolf and Thorne (2006) point out that agency can be exercised by both individuals and communities, and it entails the ability to assign relevance and significance to events. It also includes an aware-ness of the responsibility for one's own action in relation to the environment and others (van Lier 2008). Agency thus develops with the help of others, and supporting participation and agency is crucial in order to help individuals to notice affordances (Pavlenko and Lantolf 2000) and to find their own niches in a changing ecosystem such as the workplace.

3. Data and methods

The narrative interview data to be analysed consist of two sets of case study data, gathered as a part of a much broader database collected for the research project 'Finnish as a work language: socio-cognitive perspectives to the work-related lan-guage skills of immigrants' (University of Jyväskylä, Finland). The total amount of data serving as the basis for the analysis consists of four separate interviews, two with each participant who both have migrated to Finland to work in the health care sector. The main focus area of the biographical interviews was the interface between language and working life. Lived experiences and observations concerning one's own pathway as a migrated employee and a developing Finnish language user and learner were collected by open, conversation-like questions and prompts. The examples analysed in more detail in this chapter are selected to illustrate the junctures named by the participants (see Pujolar and Puigdevall 2015) and the interplay between them and their new environments (van Lier 2000). The latter covers recurring themes such as language policies, workplace practices, observations made and felt emotions expressed by the research participants.

The key participants are referred to by the pseudonyms Nóra (N) and Sergei (S), and the interviewers are marked in the transcriptions by the letter I. Nóra has migrated from Hungary through a tailored recruitment project. She was interviewed for the first time just before moving from Hungary to Finland and again when she had two years' experience of Finnish working life. She speaks Hungarian as her mother tongue and Finnish as her second language at an advanced level; according to the National Certificates language test result, she has achieved the level C1 in all skill areas except writing. Nóra uses Finnish actively in her work as a dentist and elsewhere outside the family context. She also learned English during her studies in Hungary, and her first interview was in English while the second one was in Finnish at her request. She spoke Finnish in a remarkably fluent and accurate way.

Sergei is medical doctor. He was also interviewed twice, but with shorter intervals when he had worked for almost four years in Finnish hospitals. He has moved to Finland with his family. Before that, he had finished his studies and worked for several years as a medical doctor in his home country outside of the EU/EEA area. He worked as an amanuensis but was in the middle of the authorisation process throughout the data collection phase. He still had to pass one exam and receive the results of another to obtain the full right to work as a medical doctor in Finland. Sergei speaks Russian as his mother tongue and also English at an advanced level. His own choice was to be interviewed in Finnish about his working life instead of using an interpreter or English.

In this chapter, only English translations are presented. The translations are not idiomatic but they convey the content and style of the two interviewees. This inevitably eliminates some characteristic linguistic features, such as the lack of accuracy in complex morphology and prosody of Finnish, but makes the content of their speech more accessible for readers than an interlinear glossed translation would. This serves the goals of the speakers' narrative methods, which are more content-oriented than form-focused, and capture the different voices and positions present in the stories told (see Vitanova 2010).

Both research participants have moved to Finland with their families. They both also knew the basics of Finnish in advance: Nóra had attended an intensive Finnish A2 level language course for three months before moving to Finland. The course was financed by her future employer in Finland and organised by a private language school in collaboration with a recruitment company. For reasons of economic efficiency, this model has become more and more popular in international recruitment programmes. In Finland, Nóra received some more instruction and consultancy paid by her employer but ended up financing some further studies herself. Sergei's first Finnish language course had lasted half a year, but there were only two lessons per week. He participated in it before moving to Finland and took part in some language classes in Finland, too. From the very beginning, Sergei has been active in note-taking at work, and he employs multilingual lexicons and professional journals in appropriating Finnish equivalents for the medical terminology that he knows in Latin and English.[3]

While Nóra was head-hunted in Hungary and according to EU regulations was allowed to start working in another EU country directly without any specific authorisation, Sergei has had a longer pathway as a specialist educated outside of the EU/EEA area. He was actively looking for various opportunities on the Internet before starting to negotiate on training opportunities in Finnish hospital districts. Within a couple of years of his arrival in Finland, he passed the B1 level language test required of those who intend to apply for the multi-phase authorisation process. As noted above, he has mainly worked as an amanuensis, which is a position combining training and closely mentored, non-independent medical work in a hospital environment.

The analysis is mainly based on the methodological model suggested by Vitanova (2010) who works in a socio-cultural and dialogical framework quite closely related to the ecological approach (see Dufva et al. 2014). Vitanova (2010) has analysed the ways in which adult East European migrants in the US construct their voices through second language discourse. For her, narratives are a dialogical genre in which a close interplay between different authors and voices is present. Narratives told in interviews thus carry with them voices from significant others and the surrounding environment affecting one's lived experiences, instead of being constructed in isolation and expressed as solely individually produced outcomes. Narrating may contain seeds of empowerment, too. As Vitanova puts it,

> we are analysing someone else's experiences not only because we want to understand our own, but to give these specific others a voice, to allow a certain group or population to claim a position on the map of social discourses. In this view, research can become an expression of subjectivity and an authoring act itself. (Vitanova 2010: 36)

Through narrating experiences, new positions can also thus be claimed.

Following Vitanova's model (2010: 44), the small stories approach introduced by Bamberg (2004; see also De Fina and Georgakopoulou 2012) will be applied. In this framework, the construction of self and other(s) through narrating is seen as even more essential than the story told as such. In this study, the focus will first be on the briefly narrated lived experiences connected to language policies and (self-)assessments, and then on the struggle and means of expanding one's niche or crossing the existing niche boundaries at work. In the examples selected for a closer analysis, meaningful turning points or everyday occurrences are told about or different emotional states are expressed in connection with working life.

The main focus area of the analysis is the fears and frustrations experienced at work when attempting to regain one's professional autonomy when working in a gradually developing second language. The others present in the surrounding community will be shown to play a central role – not only in narrowing down the operational space available, but also in providing linguistic support and adequate means for communication. The findings will be discussed in relation to legitimacy and 'new speakerness', in particular.

4. Lived experiences of language policies and assessments

The increasing international mobility of health care professionals has been analysed in several studies (e.g. Stilwell et al. 2004), and at the individual level, finding a suitable niche abroad is a common desire. It is also rather commonly acknowledged by authorities, the general public and even trade unions in Finland that, particularly in the health sector, an international workforce is needed both now and in the future. Promotion of labour migration has also been mentioned in some recent government platforms and other key documents directing societal decision-making (e.g. Ministry of Interior 2013). This means that officially, at the policy level, there is space for internationally educated professionals in the Finnish health care system. Therefore, since the first recruitment process of Philippine nurses in 2008, there have been several projects aiming at the effective recruitment and smooth integration of foreign-born health care specialists into Finnish working life. Nóra is a representative of this trend. Even more numerous specialists – such as Sergei – have also come on their own from neighbouring countries to look for better jobs and benefits in Finland.

As a result, Finland already has a relatively high percentage of international professionals working in the health care sector compared with many other EU countries: in 2012, 8.4 per cent of medical doctors and 5.7 per cent of dentists were foreign-born (Ailasmaa 2015). Among the most common countries of origin were Russia, Estonia, Sweden, Romania and Hungary. The participants introduced above are thus typical representatives of this kind of migration.

The following two examples from Sergei's and Nóra's interviews reveal some of their key motives in looking for working opportunities in Finland. Comparative reasoning is strongly present in their small stories focusing on what is possible and what is not in each work environment.

Example 1
S: I am interested in what medicine is like in another European country – I want to know if there is any difference, if there is a difference also in this country, in another country, and what is it like and if it is possible, and if it is possible, if I can help at work for example. Yeah, it is also interesting whether it is sufficient, what the salary for work is in another European country.

Example 2
N: I knew already that living in Hungary will not be possible, not with such a wallet.

Having a fatter wallet is an obvious motivating factor, but not the only one, as Sergei points out. When listing other factors such as international comparisons of work practices, he personalises the content by speaking in the first person singular, but he also echoes the generally accepted, ethical ideas of professional development and opportunities to provide help. Both Sergei and Nóra mention better salaries, but they use more generic expressions and choose wordings that suggest the salary levels were not sufficient in the country of origin. Such background information might make money sound like a more acceptable motive, at least for the general public. It is obvious, however, that labour migration is often a rather privileged form of global mobility, and medical professionals are in an even more privileged position. In their case, migration is mostly based on free choice and conscious calculation. It can even be seen as some kind of shopping: looking for the most suitable alternative and paying a certain price for it.

Language has a specific value in all this: learning a language is expected to be worthwhile in an economic sense, too. Economic reasons are thus overtly present when arguing for such migration, and late modern logics can be seen as the guiding force behind it: getting a sufficient salary is the profit one orients towards, and learning a new language is a necessary investment facilitating that (see Heller and Duchêne 2012; Darvin and Norton 2015). This is basically how the context has been understood in Finnish migration policy, too: if one is not a refugee or an unemployed person looking for a job, it is one's own business to look for suitable language courses and to pay for them, while those in a weaker position get their basic language education for free (Pöyhönen et al. 2010). Those who are employed upon arrival are thus expected to pay for their choice to migrate and for their language education.

Nóra's contract originally included an intensive language course in Hungary and some language classes and linguistic consultation in Finland, too. This combination was expected to ensure a sufficient command of Finnish and smooth access to the new work environment. Nevertheless, Nóra ended up investing some money in private online lessons. Sergei, in turn, invested considerable time in self-study. From an early stage, both participants had fulfilled the primary language requirements set by the authorities or their employers. They had also made good progress since then, but they were not yet satisfied with their current Finnish language proficiency. Their own 'inner' language policy was strict in comparison with the official one, but their descriptions are well in line with the official and public 'sufficiency discourse', analysed in detail by Virtanen (2011), and with commonly repeated comments on the importance of speaking skills, in particular. Sergei observed that speaking was his weakest skill set, and he experienced pressure to learn more and develop this skill, and he mainly talks about this as his own problem (example 3).

Example 3
S: well for example, in my opinion, I think that in my case for example, it is not sufficient
       yet, one should still learn, certainly learn more language.
S: I think reading and comprehension are better but I should certainly develop speaking,
       this is, in this area I think I have more problems.

Nóra, in turn, had reached an advanced proficiency level in a couple of years, but her goal was still higher. She still felt uncertain, particularly in regard to situational and stylistic features of oral language use. In addition, she found speaking and thinking as deeply interconnected and explained that her problems were partially rooted in the observation that one should also learn to figure out how people think in another language. She felt that she had made some progress in this respect, but although she tried hard, she was not yet able to follow the style in which her native speaker colleagues talked to their patients. Some crucial components of the resources available to the native speakers of Finnish simply remained unattainable, which made her hesitant in relation to her own Finnish language speaking performance (example 4).

Example 4
N: He simply speaks in a marvellous way to the patients, exactly in such a style that the
       patient can understand more about reasons and solutions, but it is difficult for me
       to remember that style in, let's say that when you speak another language then you
       think differently, although now at some points I feel how Finnish people think. I
       can't speak that way, and that irritates me, that irritates me terribly much. Although I
       want, and I try, I plan, I try, but there is no success. I would like to do that way, and
       this is how I wanted to do. My language proficiency is not exactly at the level I want
       it to be.

Nóra's story shows how intensively she observes the ways in which her Finnish colleagues work and interact, and the description of her own trials and failures is loaded with frustration and irritation. She thus seems to construct and question her identity as a professional by actively comparing her performance against that of her local colleagues. As a result, she sets the goal for herself at a native-like level, trying to adhere to the best model available in her current work environment. The most intensive and emotional part of the story is focused on Nóra herself as a person: 'I want, and I try, I plan, I try.' In spite of the serious efforts to strengthen her agency as a new Finnish language speaker, the conclusion is that it does not lead anywhere and that the proficiency level is still insufficient and unsatisfactory, at least in her own eyes. These inferences, which question Nóra's competence, are not made in a vacuum, but in relation to significant others and their language use as a part of professional practice. There are authoritative voices on the native speaker ideal and social and cultural acceptability present in her highly emotional expressions (see for example Dufva et al. 2011: 111–13).

The question of sufficient language skills is currently highly debated in Finland (e.g. Kela and Komppa 2011). In order to ensure patient safety and to update authorisation processes, some rather extensive assessment and education reforms have been suggested (Ministry of Education and Culture 2014). Tightening of language requirements is one of the core areas of the suggested reform, facilitated by the changes recently made in the EU directive on professional qualifications.

According to current regulations, Finnish or Swedish language proficiency level B1 is required of professionals educated outside of the EU/EEA area, and they must have documentation to demonstrate this before applying for authorisation. In addition, medical doctors belonging to this group must pass three professional competence examinations (in Finnish/Swedish) before they can work independently (Valvira 2016). This authorisation process tends to take several years, and after four years in Finland, Sergei is thus in the middle of this process. In example 5, Sergei describes the lengthy process and the delays within it in an interview.

Example 5
S: Now I'm having these three exams. The first exam is a clinical exam, it got passed
    already, and the second one. There are three parts, a prescription, forensic medicine,
    social medicine. The prescription and forensic medicine are passed now, and the last
    part is waiting for the results. In Finland it takes a rather long time. One should wait
    for six weeks ((laughing)). Yeah, and after that there is one exam more at a general
    practice in a health centre.
I: Well and how about the training period then? Is the one that you are doing now just
    that, or isn't there a half-year training? Before?
S: Yeah before one goes to exams there should be a half-year period as an amanuensis.
    Well I have been an amanuensis for almost two years, yeah, having a post as an
    amanuensis, and I'm also learning language, medical language.

Sergei describes his multiphase authorisation process in a rather generic, declaratory manner, but he clearly explicates the stages he has passed so far. Instead of overtly complaining about the long wait times and the entire process, he just laughs and lists the different phases and, finally, as requested, clarifies his current status. In Sergei's case, the minimum six-month training period has lasted almost four times longer, which could feel like being stuck, but again, instead of complaining he highlights the relevance of the language learning opportunities: he has received many affordances while constantly being surrounded by medical language. He might be both echoing some surrounding authoritative voices on the opportunities to learn at work, and expressing his own lived experience at the same time. In Sergei's spoken narrative, this serves at least as a legitimate excuse for the current setting where he remains at the periphery of the professional community (see Lave and Wenger 1991), not being allowed to work independently yet. It is to be noted that he has actually lost his prior autonomy as a professional when moving to Finland: in his country of origin, he had been a qualified professional with a rather flexible sphere of operations, but he gave up that status when moving to Finland. As an amanuensis, he seems to have found a relatively satisfactory niche for now but not permanently. He has a clear goal of getting full authorisation and expanding his niche in Finland to regain his responsibilities in the current work environment, but this is taking a lot of time and effort.

Nóra, in turn, who is qualified within the EU/EEA area, can basically work freely in any EU/EEA country, given that her language skills are assessed to be sufficient for the work tasks to be performed (see Valvira 2016). In the future, people like her may face higher barriers in entering the Finnish labour market. As a part of the suggested reform (Ministry of Education and Culture 2014), both tightening the language requirements from level B1 to level B2 and investigating opportunities to start testing professional language skills in the health care sector have been suggested, and such new practices are meant to include EU/EEA professionals, too. In comparison with the suggested model, Nóra has thus had easy access to Finnish working life – and very much easier than Sergei who arrived from outside of the EU/EEA area, took a B1 level language test first and then needs some years to pass all three exams required for full authorisation as a medical doctor.

5. Struggling for a broader niche

At a first glance, Nóra thus seems to have had a well-paved route to working life in Finland: there was a ready-made, tailored niche for a trial period of six months waiting for her. Indeed, the only thing expected from her was to learn enough Finnish before arrival.

Hungarian and Finnish are distantly related Finno-Ugric languages, and Hungarian language speakers tend to pick up the pronunciation, prosody and certain grammatical features of Finnish rather smoothly (and vice versa), due to the underlying grammatical similarities between these two languages. This might imply a relatively fast and unproblematic learning process in comparison with many others. In addition, as noted by Straszer (2014), Hungarian speakers are treated differently in Finland than in Sweden, for example, due to the well-known linguistic connection between Hungarian and Finnish languages. Such a promising starting point and optimistic expectations did not save Nóra from disappointment, however.

The next example illustrates the first shock caused by the deeply heteroglossic (see Bakhtin 1986) nature of Finnish that Nóra and other newly recruited Hungarians faced soon after arrival: the standard Finnish introduced on the language course in Hungary did not help much when encountering the commonly used colloquial Finnish dominating spoken interaction. Nóra commented on this with a kind of disbelief (example 6).

Example 6
N: I think it all was mixed up then – when we came to Finland, spoken Finnish was
     something quite different. Everyone was just sitting there and listening that what is
     the language you are speaking for real.

The standard-like register Nóra had familiarised herself with on the language course created a linguistically tight niche from the very beginning; she felt as if she knew a totally inappropriate variety of Finnish without any access to the variety everyone spoke. Her agency and legitimacy as a language user and speaker were questioned due to lacking resources in interaction. Not only professional language and communication practices but also colloquial Finnish thus had to be learnt in order to cope with the daily practices at work. Such a sociolinguistic reality was the first thing that Nóra was not prepared for when entering the new workplace.

In the first interview, just before leaving for Finland, Nóra had described a twofold imagined self. Her positive imagined self was portraying a successful language user who feels safe with the new language within some months (example 7).

Example 7
N: I think that when I spend a lot of time in that area, in that country, and use that
     language and live in that language for a long time, it is easier to get used to it, and in
     some months I will be safe in Finnish.

Instead of some months, it took a couple of years before confidence replaced her fears and disappointments. 'Living in a language' did not open the doors into the inner circles of the language community as fast and easily as she had expected. Still, after more than two years she says – in quite fluent, advanced level Finnish – that she does not yet feel safe and satisfied with her language proficiency (example 8).

Example 8
I: I remember when we met for the first time and you said that it takes some months and
     I will have a safe feeling.
N: And that has not happened yet ((laughing)).

Entering the language and work community has thus been challenging for Nóra: her niche has remained constricted, because she has not been able to cross the remaining sociolinguistic boundaries and start talking with her patients in the same way as her Finnish colleagues do. She has a strong desire to engage with the Finnish worldview and to interact with Finns. Thus, when starting to work in Finland, Nóra faced a difficult reality – more difficult than she could have ever imagined in advance. Although she anticipated feeling like an outsider in Finland before she even left Hungary, she did not imagine how extreme it could be at first. She described her fears in the first interview, and this more negative side of her imagined self as a Finnish language speaker really came true during the six-month trial period after her arrival (example 9).

Example 9
N: I have a lot of [fears]. I will feel lonely in that community, because I'm new, I'm a foreigner, I can't speak Finnish like all, if I can say so. I know some words only.

For the first months, Nóra had a tutoring colleague, a Finnish dentist, but her collaboration and communication with the tutor did not work at all. In example 10, Nóra recounts how she was panicking to such an extent that she felt that she was not able to acquire new skills or to remember what she already knew.

Example 10
N: I had huge expectations and then, well it failed while I was given a tutor who caused me a panic disorder, because s/he[4] didn't accept anything, my style was not OK at all for her/him, and I was panicking all day long. Well the first day it was OK, but due to stress my brain didn't work at all, I had forgotten everything, just everything, I couldn't even learn anything.

Nóra made several attempts to solve the communication problems. She opened a discussion on the expectations set by the tutor, but without any positive outcome. Figuring out the educational roots of the professional practices might have been helpful perhaps, but there was no sign of finding a shared footing. Nóra was simply advised to work like the Finns do (example 11).

Example 11
N: I asked the tutor, what your expectations are like and how I should do, but the answer simply was that 'like the Finns'. But listen, how can I know what you have at the university, what you study there. I came from Hungary. But s/he could not respond, s/he didn't say a word, OK, so then I tried again but with no success.

From the point of view of language and workplace ecology, this narrated event is interesting. The Finnish way of working was given to Nóra as a simple and strong norm, quite obviously encompassing the Finnish way of communicating at work, too. As a newly migrated employee, Nóra had no agency over the local linguistic and professional practices and she received no support for gaining that either. She was left in a peripheral position where she felt as if she was losing her ability to work and losing her voice with which to interact and defend herself. The core of the community was experienced as reserved for the Finns or like-the-Finns only. There was no niche available for someone like Nóra who did not fit into the norms set.

Even the EU/EEA professionals who basically have it easy may thus face real difficulties with their niches. Although Nóra officially had full authorisation to practise her occupation as a dentist, she ended up in an extremely tight niche where she was not allowed to work alone. In the example 12, taken from a lengthy narrative, she talks about a month when her tutoring colleague was absent and she got positioned as an assistant only.

Example 12
N: then there was a month when that tutor was absent, and I was forbidden to do the work of dentist. I was a dental nurse.
I: so when s/he was away, you were not allowed to do anything?
N: I was a dental nurse working with a candidate. And then with a dental hygienist, with the help of the dental hygienist working just opposite to me, I was allowed to remove dental calculus.

Nóra tells this story with an emotional tone, which can be read as astonishment, frustration and irritation. As a professional with a university degree and previous work experience in Hungary, she was suddenly positioned as a dental nurse assisting someone who was still studying dental medicine, and only under the supervision of a dental hygienist was she allowed to perform a few tasks that represented lower degree duties.

All the excerpts above are clear examples of emotion discourses (Vitanova 2010). At the same time, they are representative cases of stories told by individuals working in a second language, at least in our database: continuous balancing between a learner identity and a professional identity is fairly common. Both Sergei and Nóra took up the frustrating slowness of the process of regaining autonomy at work, and when constructing their views on success or lack of it they were clearly surrounded by the native speaker ideals and expectations. The niches provided may be really constricted sometimes, and extending them is not possible without support received from those who have more power and agency and who collectively are the 'owners' of the linguistic resources needed at work. It was finally an enormous relief for Nóra to get a new job elsewhere very soon after the problematic trial period. It was also a great surprise that she was not given any tutor there any more although she had learnt to think that she definitely needed one. This helped her to regain her agency as a professional (example 13).

Example 13
N: And I said that I want a tutor, and it was a big surprise that they said 'why do you want a tutor, you are a dentist, a licensed dentist, and you just do the work of dentist, that's all'.

By leaving behind the constricted niche of the previous organisation she attained one where she immediately received full responsibility and was treated as a full professional. As example 14 shows, Nóra sees a tight interconnectedness between the general atmosphere at the workplace and the development of her language skills; the language ecology of the workplace either hinders or facilitates learning.

Example 14
N: There was quite a nice working atmosphere there, and in half a year I learned more
     Finnish than in eight months before that.

By changing job, Nóra finally found helpful colleagues, too, in particular one who
was willing and able to provide assistance and feedback in social encounters. As a
whole, the process became a highly empowering one: Nóra got her voice back and
saw that the struggle she experienced actually helped her to find her own place – her
extended niche in which she is quite satisfied. She locates herself clearly in time and
space: she is 'here now' as a result of a lengthy, painful struggle for agency and participation (example 15).

Example 15
N: but it was really good, well not in the beginning, but if that didn't happen, I wouldn't
     be here now. It had to happen to bring me here where I am now.

Nóra is not yet satisfied with her language skills: there is always something to learn,
and due to the processual nature of language learning the goal is quite unattainable.
She seems to accept the native speaker norms without calling them into question,
which is a sign of an extensive exposure to those norms and the authoritative voices
attached to them. As the last example from her interviews shows, she is a little envious
of the native speakers who acquired their Finnish language so easily, but she adds that
something else would be missing if she were born in Finland. The surrounding native
speakers thus remain as a relevant point of comparison and reference; however, they
are not only setting norms but also supporting her development. On the whole, she is
grateful for having found a niche like the present one (example 16).

Example 16
N: Day after day I notice that I should still learn this and that and something like that
     and still something, and there is always something little missing and still something.
     If I were born here, but I don't know what all I were lacking in that case. I am quite
     thankful.

Nóra's case on the whole clearly shows that shame and fear as a language user are
signs or even the result of a lack of power and agency (see also Vitanova 2010). At
first, Nóra was not rated nor treated as a legitimate member of the work community,
and her Finnish language speakerness was questioned as a part of the process, too,
although not quite overtly perhaps by others as by herself. The reactions of others
made her question it in many ways, however. It is noteworthy, that, still after four
years, Sergei also reports something slightly similar, although mainly in relation to his
written language skills (example 17).

Example 17
S: If I have to write something, I always have a stress and I can write wrong – I have a
     fear all the time.

Experiencing fear and stress in some linguistically demanding situations is not a dominating feature of Sergei's working life narratives any more, however. Although he has remained for many years in a relatively low position as an amanuensis, he mainly reports positive experiences of Finnish working life. On numerous occasions, he refers to the concrete linguistic support received from his work community members and the scaffolding practices adopted by the whole community. His narratives are full of comments on the support received from nurses, doctors and even patients, and descriptions of moments which he has found to be relevant for language learning, as illustrated in example 18.

Example 18

S: Well, sure, all the time learning in the beginning. It was when I entered the operating theatre with her/him, and they first discuss and I listen to what they ask the patient, what the patient says and in this situation. After that I discuss if there is something unclear with the patient. Then I also read the documents of the patient if there is something unclear I ask a doctor, another doctor, what it is all about.

S: There are nurses. S/he is all the time close to me and can help, but in the beginning I just follow. Then I try, but I ask the doctor to stay close in first, and after that I do on my own.

S: Well, from the patients one can learn for example responses not heard before ((laughs)), I can for example find that phrase out, and then, in such a case it may be that one also learns it.

Sergei's niche as a language user and a professional has obviously been expanding through such practices, although his officially set niche as an amanuensis has remained the same. He has a rather smooth access to the linguistic resources available in the work environment, and he is well prepared for the next step as a fully authorised medical doctor. His skills are shaped by the continuous interaction with colleagues and patients, and also by the gradual shift of responsibility described in the examples above: his mentors have allowed him more freedom and independence little by little. Asking for peer support in daily practices and having potential help available from colleagues seems to be the key to such successful development. By providing new tasks and linguistic resources, working life quite obviously serves for him as a forum for constructing a new kind of speakerness and expertise which are closely intertwined (see also Pujolar and Puigdevall 2015).

6. Conclusions

In language studies, time, space, scales and sites are gaining a lot of attention nowadays. This analysis has illustrated how an ecological approach suggested by, for example, Kramsch (2002) and van Lier (2000, 2008) could be adopted in an analysis of narratives focusing on working life experiences. In the rather emotional small stories told in interviews, the research participants Sergei and Nóra highlight the role of other people in the progress they have made as Finnish language learners and speakers, and the everyday work environment is strongly present in these stories on the whole. They also outline clear turning points or junctures (see Pujolar and Puigdevall 2015) that have affected their agency as language speakers and the size and type of their niches as well. Moving to a new country to work had first brought with it a much more constricted niche than they had had before, but the opportunities to stretch or cross its boundaries improved as their professional language skills gradually developed. The local language policies applied within work communities seem to have a crucial effect on the agency and independency of newcomers: the more they receive tailored scaffolding from others, the better chance they have of developing their professional language skills and of expanding their niches or settling down in new ones.

The niches get shaped and reshaped partially by the official language policies as well: people are positioned in different niches according to their migration status, and there may be different policy-driven linguistic criteria one has to fulfil before a wider niche can be attained. This should be seen as a central environmental factor as such. The participants in this study were treated differently by the Finnish language policies: Sergei had to provide proof of his B1 level knowledge in Finnish and pass several exams before the official authorisation, which kept him in a relatively constricted niche for many years, while Nóra was free to work as a licensed dentist upon arrival, but still ended up in an extremely constricted niche at first. In fact, the grassroots level norms and expectations concerning the sufficiency of language skills seem to be even more influential than official policies, however, since they regulate migrants' access to work and language communities and shape their identities as language speakers. As the analysis revealed, the participants set their own criteria for sufficient language skills very high. In part, this may be a reflection of the expectations set by the general public (e.g. in media discourse; see Virtanen 2011) and the authoritative voices that clearly regard native speakers as a norm (Dufva et al. 2014). This was a predominant feature of Nóra, whose language skills were at an advanced level but who rather desperately compared her skills with those of her native speaker colleagues. There is thus a highly controversial position provided for potential new speakers in work and language communities: they may get officially accepted but still partially rejected due to not fulfilling some subconscious, collectively set criteria of true speakerness.

As a whole, language skills and profiles are either restricting or facilitating factors: a narrow skill profile tends to result in a constricted niche, and it is mainly through developing language proficiency that one can then cross the less visible but existing boundaries separating the legitimate speakers from those who are only potential new speakers. Working life typically serves as a meaningful juncture where new language identities get constructed (Pujolar and Puigdevall 2015) and participation, agency and new skills develop (Suni 2011). This happens with the help of others, however; participation is something that the community must allow and support, and only in this way can new opportunities for learning and action be received (van Lier 2008; Pavlenko and Lantolf 2000; Lave and Wenger 1991). As the cases of Nóra and Sergei show, a suitable niche is not something that one can simply select alone. It must be allowed, negotiated or even fought for.

Transcription convention

((laughs))   non-verbal communication

Notes

1. Research leading to this chapter has benefited from ongoing discussions on the 'new speaker' theme as part of the EU COST Action IS1306 network entitled 'New Speakers in a Multilingual Europe: Opportunities and Challenges'.
2. In applied language studies, Block (2011) has previously employed the concept of niche in connection to languages used in intercultural working life contexts: by 'niche lingua francas', he refers to lingua francas other than the majority language that may act as group membership markers in the workplace.
3. A more detailed analysis of Sergei's case is available in Elina Mähönen's MA thesis (2015) reported in Finnish (accepted in 2014).
4. The data gathered in Finnish do not reveal whether the tutor was male or female.

References

Ailasmaa, R. (2015), *Terveys- ja hyvinvointipalvelujen henkilöstö 2012* [Health care and social welfare personnel 2012], Tilastoraportti 8/2015, Helsinki: National Institute of Health and Welfare.

Angouri, J. (2014), 'Multilingualism in the workplace: language practices in multilingual contexts', *Multilingua*, 33: 1–2, pp. 1–9.

Bakhtin, M. M. (1986), *Speech genres and other late essays*, trans. V. W. McGee, Austin, TX: University of Texas Press.

Bamberg, M. (2004), 'Talk, small stories, and adolescent identities', *Human Development*, 47, pp. 366–9.

Block, D. (2011), 'Niche lingua francas: an ignored phenomenon', *TESOL Quarterly*, 41: 3, pp. 561–6.

Bourdieu, P. (1977), *Outline of a theory of practice*, Cambridge: Cambridge University Press.

Brown, W. L. and E. O. Wilson (1956), 'Character displacement', *Systematic Zoology*, 5, pp. 49–65.

Darvin, R. and B. Norton (2015), 'Identity and the model of investment in applied linguistics', *Annual Review of Applied Linguistics*, 34, pp. 36–56.

De Fina, A. and A. Georgakopoulou (2012), *Analyzing narrative: discourse and sociolinguistic perspectives*, Cambridge: Cambridge University Press.

Dufva, H., M. Suni, M. Aro and O.-P. Salo (2011), 'Languages as objects of learning: language learning as a case of multilingualism', *Apples – Journal of Applied Language Studies*, 5: 1, pp. 109–24.

Dufva, H., M. Aro and M. Suni (2014), 'Language learning as appropriation: how linguistic resources are recycled and regenerated?', in P. Lintunen, M. S. Peltola and M.-L. Varila (eds), *AFinLA-e Soveltavan kielitieteen tutkimuksia*, 6, Jyväskylä: AFinLA, pp. 20–31.

Gibson, J. (1977), 'The theory of affordances', in R. Shaw and J. Bransford (eds), *Perceiving, acting, and knowing: toward an ecological psychology*, Hillsdale, NJ: Lawrence Erlbaum, pp. 67–82.

Haukilahti, R. L., I. Virjo and K. Mattila (2012), 'ETA-alueen ulkopuolella perustutkintonsa suorittaneiden lääkärien Suomeen tulon syyt, työllistyminen ja jatkosuunnitelmat', *Sosiaalilääketieteellinen aikakauskirja*, 40, pp. 13–30.

Heller, M. (1996), 'Legitimate language in a multilingual school', *Linguistics and Education*, 8: 2, pp. 139–57.

Heller, M. and A. Duchêne (2012), 'Pride and profit: changing discourses of language, capital and nation state', in M. Heller and A. Duchêne (eds), *Language in late capitalism: pride and profit*, London: Routledge, pp. 1–21.

Kela, M. and J. Komppa (2011), 'Sairaanhoitajan työkieli – yleiskieltä vai ammattikieltä? Funktionaalinen näkökulma ammattikielen oppimiseen toisella kielellä', *Puhe ja kieli*, 31: 4, pp. 173–92.

Kramsch, C. (2002), *Language acquisition and language socialization: ecological perspectives*, London: Continuum.

Kramsch, C. and A. Whiteside (2008), 'Language ecology in multilingual settings: towards a theory of symbolic competence', *Applied Linguistics*, 29: 4, pp. 645–71.

Lantolf, J. and S. Thorne (2006), *Sociocultural theory and the genesis of second language development*, Oxford: Oxford University Press.

Lave, J. and E. Wenger (1991), *Situated learning: legitimate peripheral participation*, New York: Cambridge University Press.

Magnussen, J., K. Vrangbaek, R. B. Saltman and P. E. Martinussen (2009), 'Introduction: the Nordic model of health care', in J. Magnussen, K. Vrangbaek and R. B. Saltman (eds), *Nordic health care systems: recent reforms and current policy challenges*, Maidenhead: Open University Press, pp. 3–20.

Mähönen, E. (2014), 'Maahanmuuttajalääkärin kokemuksia ammatillisen kielitaidon kehittymisestä: "no se mun kurssi oli töissä"', MA thesis, Department of Languages, University of Jyväskylä.

Ministry of Education and Culture (2014), 'Kielitaidon määrittäminen sekä kielitaidon ja EU/ETA-alueen ulkopuolella hankitun koulutuksen täydentäminen terveys-alal-la' [Evaluating and complementing language proficiency and qualifications in the health care sector], *Reports 2014: 5*, Helsinki: Ministry of Education and Culture.

Ministry of Interior (2013), *Maahanmuuton tulevaisuus 2020 -strategia* [The future of immigration 2020 strategy], <http://www.intermin.fi/maahanmuutto2020> (last accessed 15 November 2016).

Pavlenko, A. and J. P. Lantolf (2000), 'Second language learning as participation and the (re)construction of selves', in J. P. Lantolf (ed.), *Sociocultural theory and second language learning*, Oxford: Oxford University Press, pp. 155–77.

Pöyhönen, S., M. Tarnanen, E.-M. Vehviläinen, A. Virtanen and L. Pihlaja (2010), *Osallisena Suomessa. Kehittämissuunnitelma maahanmuuttajien kotoutumisen edistämiseksi*, Jyväskylä: University of Jyväskylä, Centre for Applied Language Studies and Finnish Cultural Foundation.

Pujolar, J. and M. Puigdevall (2015), 'Linguistic mudes: how to become a new speaker in Catalonia?', *International Journal of Sociology of Language*, 231, pp. 167–87.

Sias, P. M. (2009), *Organizing relationships: traditional and emerging perspectives on workplace relationships*, Thousand Oaks, CA: Sage.

Steffensen, S. V. and A. Fill (2014), 'Ecolinguistics: state of the art and future horizons', *Language Sciences*, 41, pp. 6–27.

Stilwell, B., K. Diallo, P. Zurn, M. Vujicic, O. Adams and M. Dal Poz (2004), 'Migration of health-care workers from developing countries: strategic approaches to its management', *Bulletin of the World Health Organization*, 82: 8, pp. 595–600.

Straszer, B. (2014), 'Maahanmuuttajien kielitaito – yhteiskunnan resurssi vai yksilön kätköissä oleva pääoma? Esimerkkinä toisen polven suomenunkarilaiset', in M. Mutta, P. Lintunen, I. Ivaska and P. Peltonen (eds), *Tulevaisuuden kielenkäyttäjä – Language users of tomorrow*, AFinLA Yearbook 72, Jyväskylä: AFinLA, pp. 109–32.

Suni, M. (2011), 'Missä ja miten maahanmuuttajat kehittävät ammatillista kielitaitoaan?', *Ammattikasvatuksen aikakauskirja*, 2, pp. 8–22.

Valvira (2016), 'Language requirements', National Supervisory Authority for Welfare and Health, <http://www.valvira.fi/web/en/healthcare/professional_practice_rights/language_requirements> (last accessed 15 November 2016).

van Lier, L. (2000), 'From input to affordance: social-interactive learning from an ecological perspective', in J. Lantolf (ed.), *Sociocultural theory and second language learning*, Oxford: Oxford University Press, pp. 245–60.

van Lier, L. (2008), 'Agency in the classroom', in J. P. Lantolf and M. E. Poehner (eds), *Sociocultural theory and the teaching of second languages*, London: Equinox, pp. 163–88.

Virtanen, A. (2011), 'Käsityksiä kansainvälisesti rekrytoitujen hoitajien ammatillisesta kielitaidosta ja sen riittävyydestä. Mediakeskusteluiden ja asiantuntijan haastattelun analyysia', *Puhe ja kieli*, 31: 4, pp. 153–72.

Virtanen, A. (2013), 'Minä sairaanhoitajana: tulevaisuuden minuudet motivaatiota muokkaamassa', *Lähivõrdlusi–Lähivertailuja*, 23, pp. 403–27.

Vitanova, G. (2010), *Authoring the dialogical self: gender, agency and language practices*, Amsterdam: John Benjamins.

Walsh, J. and B. O'Rourke (2014), 'Becoming a new speaker of Irish: linguistic mudes throughout the life cycle', *DIGITHUM: The Humanities in the Digital Era*, 16, pp. 67–74.

11

Collaborating beyond Disciplinary Boundaries

Seongsook Choi

1. Introduction

This chapter reports on the impact of one of the many transitions currently reconfiguring the academic landscape, namely, interdisciplinary approaches to research. Due to financial constraints, most universities and major funding agencies in the UK (and beyond) encourage, and increasingly expect, collaborations across disciplinary boundaries, simultaneously breaking down existing disciplinary silos; however, the impact of these changes remains largely unexplored (Choi and Schnurr 2014).

I draw on an ongoing large-scale research study that follows several interdisciplinary teams over the life cycle of a research project. To date, more than 400 hours of authentic interactions have been recorded, including large team meetings, as well as smaller (interdisciplinary) PhD supervision meetings. The overall aim of the project is to explore the ways in which interdisciplinary engagement is reflected at the micro-level of interaction: how do team members from different disciplines work together successfully by drawing on their expert knowledge? Using a subsection of the larger corpus, this chapter aims to identify and describe some of the discursive processes used by team members including the ways in which opposing viewpoints and approaches are negotiated within the group.

Preliminary analyses suggest that in these interdisciplinary teams hierarchical ranking has less relevance than subject expertise. As a consequence, knowledge exchange and generation takes place dynamically, involving senior as well as relatively junior team members. Nevertheless, disciplinary orientations also feature. This boundary crossing has been described by Repko (2008: 22) as 'the process of moving across knowledge formations for the purpose of achieving an enlarged understanding'. Here, I show how this is only one aspect of a more complex phenomenon with important relational implications.

2. (Inter)disciplinarity

The literature on interdisciplinarity has yet to settle on a definition or on core terminology. Common terms such as multidisciplinary, interdisciplinary and transdisciplinary (Klein 2008; Stokols et al. 2003) shed little light on the theory and practice of interdisciplinarity, and all assume an underlying disciplinary structure. As Aldrich notes:

> one cannot build an interdisciplinary approach except on the basis of disciplines, because there is nothing to be 'inter' about without disciplines coming first. But more than that academy [sic] is itself built on disciplines, and the academy's values are grounded in the values of a discipline. (Aldrich 2014: 1–2)

Thus, interdisciplinarity essentially means crossing disciplinary boundaries (Klein 1996; Salter and Hearn 1996); however, in order to be able to cross boundaries, one needs to know where these boundaries actually are (Hunt 1994).

One of the main problems with the notion of interdisciplinarity is that those involved in it typically lack clarity about what falls within a discipline or when/how boundaries are crossed. Although disciplinary distinctions have been used to differentiate forms of academic organisation – differences in knowledge construction and dissemination, mores and practices (Brew 2008) – there have always been certain ambiguities in the concept of a 'discipline' itself. Aram (2004), for example, defines disciplines as thought domains consisting of problems, theories and methods of investigation that are continually subject to the opening of new or revised ways of framing problems, theorising and investigating. Disciplines may also be tied together by a pattern of thought (Finkenthal 2001) or seen in terms of cultures and practices (Pickering 1992). Becher (1989) develops the metaphor of 'tribes' of people inhabiting intellectual 'territories' with 'their own traditions and categories of thought which provides the members of the field with shared concepts of theories, methods, techniques and problems' (Ylijoki 2000: 339).

As the academy has grown, disciplinary distinctions have become more robust and their members more isolated from one another (Price 1963; Wagner et al. 2011). These isolated modes of work can prevent academics from seeing the close connections between different phenomena (Klein 2004). Moreover, the tendency in most disciplines towards increasingly narrow and deep specialisation not only makes research less relevant to outsiders but also hinders the exchange of ideas across disciplines, which has the potential to enhance growth (Hollingsworth 1986). This realisation has led to a general recognition that interdisciplinarity is necessary for dealing with complex issues that are increasingly beyond the capacity of a single discipline; however, the practice of interdisciplinarity is notoriously fraught (Gray 1989, 1996; Huxham 1996). As Klein (1996: 381) acknowledges, 'Interdisciplinarity is on everyone's agenda; actually implementing it in institutional settings is a more difficult proposition.'

2.1 Systems biology as an interdiscipline

While some interdisciplinary teams come together for the duration of a particular project, others are associated with more stable academic fields. Boundaries between disciplines and subdisciplines are to some extent arbitrarily defined and agreed upon by communities of academics (Kuhn 1970; Klein 1990). This creates a space within which academic interdisciplines can develop. Systems biology (or computational biology), the focus of the analysis within this chapter, is one such example. Although widely recognised, its place within the academy has yet to stabilise, with the result that it is referred to sometimes as an approach, sometimes a field and occasionally as a discipline (Aderem 2005; Boogerd et al. 2007; Katze 2013). Interdiscipline represents a less contentious alternative and one that is widely recognised within interdisciplinary studies.

As an interdiscipline, systems biology has huge potential but faces a number of serious challenges. In a paper highlighting these challenges, Aderem (2005) points out that in order to succeed, systems biologists need to work in interdisciplinary teams of experts from mathematics, statistics, bioinformatics and computer science. Exploring how members of these teams interact (by crossing boundaries, by undergoing a composite intellectual and practical adventure, and by finding themselves in a new interdiscipline) has the potential to make a valuable contribution to our understanding of effective boundary-crossing interaction.

3. Context and method

3.1 Context

The data in this study are drawn from interactions between researchers in systems biology (and the related bioinformatics). Projects typically comprise two teams: a 'wet' team and a 'dry' team. The former refers to biologists who conduct laboratory experiments, and the latter covers theoreticians (statisticians, mathematicians and bioinformaticians) who analyse biological data with statistical models and computer-generated simulations. Differences between the two groups, which are at the heart of the analysis here, have been identified as lending systems biology a distinctive interactional quality:

> interdisciplinary interactions are often accompanied by lively discussions about the epistemic aspirations of systems biology, because some systems biologists aim to make biology as quantitative and predictive as physics and engineering. But others argue that this aspiration is misplaced, and instead stress the multiplicity, contingency and unruliness of biology. (Calvert and Fujimura 2011: 155)

While such discussions are not evident in the data here, the assumptions underlying the differences that Calvert and Fujimura identify account for much of the interaction around boundary issues considered in this chapter.

Table 11.1 Research project information

Project	Participant number	Project duration	Project nature
ALPHA	6	3 years	Research – funded
BETA	6–8	3 years	Research – funded
DELTA	Up to 26	5 years	Research – funded
GAMMA	4	6 months	Paper writing – unfunded
KAPPA	4	1 year	Grant proposal writing – unfunded

3.2 Data and method

The wider dataset comprises audio-recorded interdisciplinary scientific research project meetings ranging from large collaborative funded projects with at least six participants in each meeting to interdisciplinary PhD supervision meetings consisting of two supervisors and a student. The length of meetings varies from one to eight hours and the disciplines represented consist of physiology, medicine, mathematics, statistics, biology and bioinformatics. Since March 2011, I have collected over 400 hours of audio recordings in an ongoing recording process.

In this chapter, I make use of a smaller set of twenty hours of transcribed meeting interactions representing over 330,000 words of text. The analysis draws on data from several interdisciplinary research project meetings (essentially exploratory in nature and designed for sharing progress and decision making) and some writing meetings (focused on representing results) (Table 11.1).

Alongside the transcripts, my analysis makes use of visualisation charts. These have been generated using the Interactional Discourse Lab (IDLab), developed by the author, a free visualisation tool that captures the interactional dynamics of talk-in-action using both qualitative and quantitative methods (Choi 2016). The tool automatically generates interactive visualisations from an input transcript that has been tagged by an analyst. The IDLab processes the tags using R, a statistical programming language (R Core Team 2014). The visuals are then displayed in three separate panels: speakers and tags, interactions and timeline, each panel updating the relevant statistics and graphs according to the tags selected by the analyst. This provides a synaptic view of the dynamics of spoken engagement, highlighting frequent exchanges and important contributors. Tools such as these offer an opportunity to map patterns of talk within specific domains and are particularly valuable where the focus is on groups that have worked together over time and where distinctive interactional contours have developed.

4. Analysis

4.1 The group – systems biology

I begin with three brief extracts revealing how the members see and negotiate their identities as group insiders as set against outsiders' views and expectations of them. Despite the wide recognition of the name 'systems biology', the group members are still struggling with the ways in which they are referred to by outsiders, including funding bodies. This struggle and negotiation is illustrated by an extract from the second team meeting of a group working on a bid for a major systems biology project involving three UK institutions. The topic of their disciplinary identity has emerged in their interaction.

```
Extract 1  KAPPA 15 Apr 001
1    MRK:   ='snot call' the:=you don't call
2           it °>systems biology any
3           mo ⌐re<° you call it new ways of⌐ =
4    GRY:      └new ways of wo:rk. (.) yea:h┘
5    MRK:   =working. Yeah kh!hah ⌐ahah
6    PUL:                         └or new
7           directions ⌐becaus:e ⌐
8    MRK:              └'s >'at rh┘ ight<=
9    PUL:   's use ⌐ful.
10   MRK:          └>i'll have to-< we'll
11          have to remember that.=

[22 turns omitted]

34   GRY:   =wu- yeah > ⌐'s does ⌐ n't mention=
35   MRK:               └°bizarre°┘
36   GRY:   =systems >biology j's say they
37          want< mathematical 'n
38          computational.
```

Mark's (MRK) laughter in line 5 of extract 1 shows that he finds the alternative name of systems biology offered by funding bodies, 'new ways of working' (lines 3–5), deserving of ridicule. Gary (GRY) draws attention to the fact that the new name that they have been assigned involves listing the disciplinary approaches typically associated with systems biology: mathematical and computational (lines 37–8). Paul (PUL), however, seems to just accept the new name as a useful label for their interdisciplinary research. The exchange in extract 1 reveals the challenge of appeasing outsiders. For Mark and Gary at least, it seems that 'systems biology' has a single boundary.

The negotiation of their interdisciplinary identity and its boundary means members have some knowledge of other disciplines within the group. As the following comments show, there are limits to the extent of this knowledge and occasionally members make this explicit by recognising the disciplinary boundaries within which they work: 'well so I'm fuzzy on the biological interpretation myself but . . .' (Alex, GAMMA-22Mar: 1798–9). Nevertheless, it is necessary for the members to have a 'rounded' or 'hybrid' quality to achieve the shared objectives of a research project.

This challenge is illustrated in extract 2. The topic of 'roundedness' has arisen near the end of an exploratory project meeting. Mark, a biologist, seeks help from a collaborator from a different institution on behalf of his dry postdoc who is about to have a job interview.

Extract 2 BETA 15 Apr 002

1	MRK:	but if you can <u>find</u> a sort of
2		random if there is a random
3		biologist who would be willing to
4		talk to him at the same time then
5		that would be very good as well if
6		there is somebody (0.2)
7	GRY:	erm yeah we could try to sort
8		someone out like Jim
9		Smith ⌐who's our BBSRC person ⌐
10	MRK:	∟yeah Jim would be actually⌐
11		Jim would be absolutely <u>excellent</u>
12		if he'd do it yeah

This is an indicative example of what is expected of a member of systems biology. Having a distinct disciplinary background is not in itself adequate to meet the inter-disciplinary demands. A member with a dry background who works with biological data needs to have some experience in wet experiments or, as is the case here, some wet input is needed to gain the hybrid approach. All members of systems biology consequently need to gain extra knowledge about other disciplines. This is not only necessary for working together but also important for publishing research outcomes. The typical outputs are journal articles in either or both dry and wet areas. The former includes aspects of modelling or new tools, and the latter focuses on aspects of biological phenomena; however, when it comes to writing such papers, both the dry and wet input are necessary even though all members have some relevant knowledge across disciplines.

Extract 3 demonstrates not only the members' recognition of the disciplinary boundaries to be negotiated in the process of writing but also the interdisciplinary needs of the readers of the paper.

Extract 3 DELTA 26 May 005

1	JOA:	exactly I mean certainly if a biologist reads
2		it they won't even think about it. But if a
3		<u>statistician</u> reads it.
4	DUG:	if a statistician reads it they'll tell you
5		it's wrong to (xxx) times theory (xxx)
6	JOA:	well (xxx)
7	DUG:	it assumes that the time points are <u>independent</u>.
8	TNA:	well yeah it's not well you could you know
9		it could be interesting but it's yeah there's
10		an assumption violated there (xxx) much with (xxx).

Extract 3 is from an interdisciplinary research project meeting that is at the end of the fourth year of their five-year project. Given that this is a large project involving multiple institutions and close to fifty members, there are numerous papers written simultaneously by small groups. The extract comes from one such group. Joan (JOA), a biologist, points out that the statistical aspect of the paper under discussion will be unlikely to be challenged if the reader is a biologist. On the other hand, this will not be the case if a statistician is the reader (lines 2–3), as is confirmed by statisticians Doug (DUG) and Tina (TNA) (line 7–10).

What the extracts in this section show is the way members explicitly recognise and refer to their own disciplinary boundaries within the context of planning, analysis and representation while at the same time resisting attempts to represent the group in terms of these boundaries (as extract 1 illustrates).

4.2 Wet/dry engagement

Before moving onto the ways in which wet and dry relationships are negotiated, it is worth pausing to consider the balance of their contributions. The IDLab plots show the level and distribution of the contributions of the two groups in exploratory research project meetings. The relative contributions are computed in the context of interaction (whether the subject of the meeting is wet or dry). For the purpose of illustration, the plots are generated from one research project comprising five consecutive fortnightly meetings. This particular project, ALPHA, has six members: two biologists (wet) and four theoreticians (dry). Despite the fact that the dry team has more members, their contributions seem to be relatively equal. Even though the data size is small, it nevertheless gives us an indicative picture. Figure 11.1 shows the relative

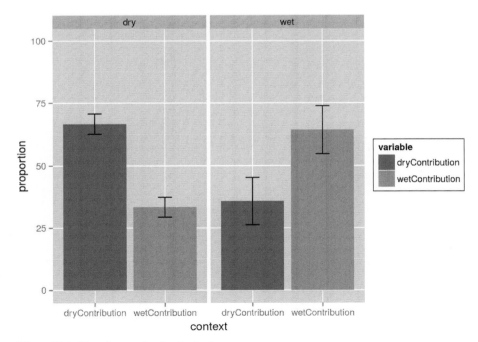

Figure 11.1 Team's contribution in dry/wet context

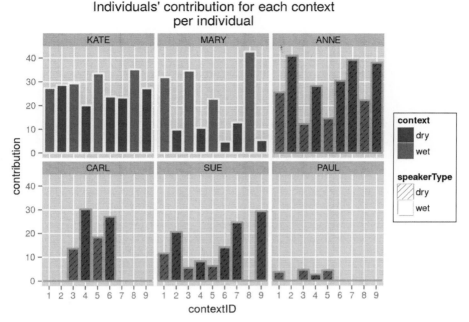

Figure 11.2 Individual's contribution for each context per individual

contributions of wet people in dry contexts and dry members in wet contexts. They look very similar; members with cross-group expertise participate around one third of the time.

In order to see how much each member contributes to each context, we plot the number of their contributions, normalised to each context (i.e. total turns of all members is 100 per cent for each context). In Figure 11.2, we see that the members of each team contribute more in their own contexts.[1] Mary, a biology postdoc, clearly participates more in wet contexts and dry members (Anne, Paul, Sue and Carl) match this behaviour. Kate, the PI (Principal Investigator) and a biologist, on the other hand, participates relatively equally in both contexts. This reflects her role as the PI of the project, which seems to be a more important determinant of participation than her biology background.

The only clear anomaly is Paul, who seems to contribute much more in wet contexts than in dry contexts despite the fact that he is a dry member (Figure 11.3). What this seems to suggest is that it is not necessarily the relevant knowledge of the subject that determines the nature of contribution of the members; it is possible that unfamiliarity of wet experimental procedures and the interpretation of the results also trigger contributions from dry participants through seeking and checking understanding (Choi and Richards 2014).

This division of labour and the disciplinary boundaries of the wets and dries are also evident in various stages of the projects. For example, at the level of planning a

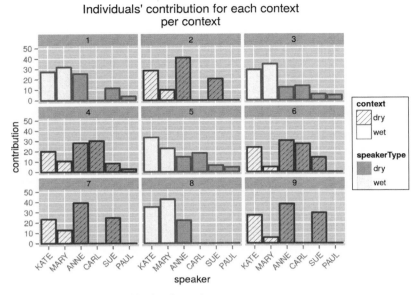

Figure 11.3 Individual's contribution for each context per context

project, the relevant expertise of wet and try teams dictates specific tasks at different stages. In extract 4 below, Bob and John (JHN) exchange the 'level of resource' needed for the various tasks. They not only explicitly recognise the disciplinary boundaries of the project members, but also expect the wets and dries to be flexible by saying 'the freedom to stagger the wet and the dry' (lines 2–3), reflecting an interdisciplinarity perhaps unique to systems biology projects.

Extract 4 KAPPA 15 Apr 001

```
 1   BOB:   yeah I think it would be a good
 2          idea to have the freedom to stagger the
 3          wet and the dry a little bit because I
 4          don't think in the first year the project
 5          that dry person would have a lot of work
 6          there's a lot to set up on the cell lines
 7          and getting the experiments to work so I
 8          think the first year of the project should
 9          probably just be wet work but then I don't
10          think we want to have a theoretician just
11          for a year two I think maybe four year
12          project
13   JHN:   that's what I ⌐was thinking⌐
14   BOB:         ⌐then we can ⌐ focus on wet
15          work on the first three year the dry
```

16   person from year two to year four
17   something like that would be.

As the project develops, the understanding of disciplinary boundaries also grows. While the extract above suggests keeping teams separate by 'staggering' them, extract 5 shows not only their complementary relationship but also how they come together.

Extract 5 DELTA 28 Apr 001

1   LCY: without having to go and <u>do</u> take each one
2   and show that mimics the endogenous gene
3   expression. So using theoretical stuff just
4   to show ┌(xxx)   ┐
5   AMY: └yeah completely dry┘ there's no(xxx)
6   experimental data in it erm.
7   DVE: but do you <u>need</u> erm erm wet insight well you
8   know biological <u>insight</u> into that or.
9   AMY: erm I think for this paper well we definitely
10   need
11 LCY: well Charlie's working on it
12 AMY: <u>yeah</u> I mean we've got but not actually in terms
13   of data I think the analysis on its own stands
14 LCY: ┌I think that the   ┐
15 AMY: └sort of bioinformatics┘ stuff
16 LCY: but I think it would be good to erm what we
17   should when we've got <u>this</u> draft done we've
18   done several drafts and we've got this draft
19   done it would be good to get it up on (xxx)
20   again and get everyone's
21 AMY: yeah have a look ┌have a read about it┐
22 LCY: └input into it   ┘ because
23   people have different ideas about the same <u>data</u>
24   how it can be interpreted to a better conclusion
25 AMY: yeah

Amy's agreement with Lucy's (LCY) point about the theoretical aspect of the paper (line 3), that is, it is 'completely dry there's no . . . experimental data in it' (lines 5–6), clearly recognises the boundaries. Dave (DVE) then asks the team whether there is the need for 'biological insight' (line 8) for the dry analysis of the paper, which reflects the complementary relationship of the two teams. Amy's confirmation, and the support of a biologist, Lucy (line 11), shows that while the boundaries of the two teams are respected in academic terms, in representational terms they are crossed. This is further reinforced when the team agrees to upload the draft paper for comments from all members (lines 19–25).

Extract 6 is also a discussion about writing a paper. The issue is the presentation of the dry analysis of biology experimental results in their paper. The exchanges show the boundaries of their disciplinary 'norms' and diverse understandings.

Extract 6 ALPHA 15 Sep 001

1	CRL:	WHAT'S WRONG with just working out the
2		probability that there are noise? And
3		just rank them according to that? (4.0)
4	ANN:	That's er-
5	CRL:	It's a meaningful thing.
6	ANN:	Yeah going back to your previous erm
7		likelihood test or something.
8	KTE:	I think what it comes down to is how
9		much time you want ANNE to spend on it.
10	CRL:	Oh this no time at all.
11	KTE:	Yeah (4.0)
12	CRL:	I mean (.) she's done the probability
13		distribution already.
14	KTE:	Mmm
15	CRL:	And that- it is quite well
16		characterised right? Anne?
17	ANN:	Huh? Err Yeah it's kind of er- er I
18		can put it into erm (.) (xxx) makes
19		normal kind of ⌜thing but er
20	SUE:	⌞Mm
21	KTE:	And the other thing (.)
22	SUE:	How ⌜do you fit into (xxx)
23	KTE:	⌞is >you know< does it speak to a
24		biologist
25	ANN:	⌜Yes (xxx) hhh
26	KTE:	⌞I mean if it speaks to a biologist so
27		that when I look at it I can
28		understand immediately >you know< you
29		might have your probability
30		distribution (xxx) well >you know< it
31		may or may not be (.) something that
32		you convey (information) to a biologist.
33	CRL:	Well I thought you wanted to rank
34		them? (2.0)
35	KTE:	Yeah ranking them <would be (.) nice>
36		but then (xxx)-
37	CRL:	Yeah that's what I am suggesting how
38		to rank them. (.) It's something
39		that's meaningful
40	KTE:	Mmm

Carl's (CRL) suggestion of a way to 'rank' the data using the probability (lines 1–3) is not immediately welcomed by the team, as shown by the four-second pause following his suggestion (indicating a dispreferred response) and Anne's (ANN) hesitation (line 4). Kate's (KTE) reaction in lines 8–9, as well as those by Carl and Kate (lines 10–14), also implies that his approach needs further thought. Anne's laughter in line 25 following Kate's rather explicit question 'does it speak to a biologist?' (lines 23–4) suggests that she also shares Kate's view. Although Kate defends Anne, who needs to spend more time on the probability distribution if the team decides to choose this option, Kate also extends the argument that the probability distribution is not necessary by pointing out what appears to be also an established view by outside readers. That is, ranking the data based on probability may appeal more to dry members as it represents the sort of precise calculation and argument that they strive for within the boundary of their own discipline (Gardiner 1993). Responses from Anne and Sue indicate that, while they understand the reasoning behind Carl's point, they are aware that the issue of what constitutes an appropriate level of precision is normally a matter for negotiation within the dry community. Biologists do not seem concerned about such a disciplinary-specific method for representing data if there are other ways of providing the same information (hence Kate's further elaboration that it may not be as meaningful for biologists: 'may or may not speak to a biologist', lines 26–32). All members are aware of the attraction and usefulness of ranking the data; however, given the time pressure they are under, presenting the information in another relevant way could also suffice. The disparity of the fundamental nature and practices of the two disciplines is challenged in this team discussion, and the team members need to negotiate which disciplinary approach they should adopt.

As the team works together in the context of planning, analysis and representation of a project, sometimes they also make the limits of their understanding and knowledge explicit, as when Alex acknowledges his limited knowledge of biology by saying 'I'm fuzzy on the biological interpretation' (Alex – GAMMA-22Mar: 1798–9) while showing his confidence in the statistical point of the paper. Despite such recognition, members inevitably find themselves crossing these boundaries. It is a challenge to recognise and respect boundaries that at times may not be entirely clear. As in the extracts above, there are situations where members stay within their own disciplinary boundaries, but, in what follows, I present two different forms of boundary crossing.

4.3 Forms of engagement across wet and dry boundaries

Across wet and dry boundaries in the data, we observe three forms of engagement: crossing boundaries, transgressing boundaries and interdisciplinary interaction demonstrating science at work.

4.3.1 Crossing

Extract 7, taken from a team meeting, illustrates crossing the disciplinary boundary with humour when Amy, a wet, reports back to the team about a conference that she attended alone. The extract starts at the end of her report on a conference presentation about a dry analysis of biological data.

Extract 7 DELTA 28 Apr 002

```
1    AMY:    so: I thought it w- (.) quite
2            good, I don't wanna do it. (0.4)
3            °so°
4    GRY:    do the:y=
5    AMY:    =khHUhha!
6            (1.0)
7    GRY:    do ⌈they try:⌉
8    AMY:        ⌊so tha-  ⌋ that's basically it
9            really.
10           (1.2)
11   AMY:    yeah
12           (0.6)
13   TIM:    So: so y:::ou now sid'n the e::m
14           the theoretician camp right.
15           (1.0)
16   AMY:    hh ⌈Huh!
17   TIM:       ⌊It sounds really good but I
18           don't wanna do i:t.
19   AMY:    Ye ⌈a:h
20   ???:       ⌊(xxxx ⌈xxx)hhehheh
21   AMY:             ⌊KhhHAHHAHhah·hh heh
```

In line 1, Amy expresses her evaluation of the dry analysis, which to an outsider appears to be the voice of a dry researcher. Her subsequent comment 'I don't wanna do it' (line 2) also gives the impression that as a dry she could do it if she wanted; however, her real identity is given away by her laughter (line 5) and hinted at in the abrupt way in which she puts an end to her report (lines 8–9). Gary's attempt to pursue his question related to the dry analysis is blocked by her closing statement: 'that's basically it really'. By way of breaking the awkward silence created by her sudden topic closing, Tim makes a humorous comment on Amy's 'passing' (Garfinkel 1967) as a dry, making a humorous disparagement by accusing her of crossing the boundary ('you are now siding the theoretician camp, right', lines 13–14). The academic discipline is being referred to as a camp that one could easily move across to. Tim's mimicking of Amy's 'passing off as a dry' in lines 17–18 following her brief but emphatic laugh (line 16) serves to mock the unusual situation of a wet presenting a dry topic. By using double-voicing (Bakhtin 1994; Baxter 2011), Tim raises not only the issue of what the boundaries are and where they lie but also the right of participants to cross these boundaries in an interdisciplinary context.

Extract 8 provides a further instance of the humour associated with boundary crossing between wet and dry, this time of the members making a joke of a dry 'becoming' a wet.

Extract 8 BETA 15 Apr 002

```
1    ROY:    oka:y another option:
2            (0.6)
3    ROY:    or suggestion
4    GRY:    That's if Paul does the experiment
5            is it.
6    ROY:    Ghh ┌eheh
7    EMA:        └Hh ┌hehhe┐ he ┌heh
8    PUL:             └Yeah ┘  |
9    MRK:                     └NHHEHEHEHH!
10   EMA:    hhh!
11   PUL:    that would be the safe option.
12           (1.6)
13   GRY:    a:::r
14           (3.0)
15   MRK:    Well Manuel's an experimentalist
16           >now s' he<=
17   GRY:    =oh is he yeah he's been trained
18           u: ┌p,
19   MRK:       └he's- (.) Manuel's been seen
20           re ┌peatedly ┐ walking round with
21   GRY:       └>hahaha <┘
22           (0.6)
23   MRK:    gloves on.
24   EMA:    mHHm=
25   PUL:    =°oh ┌my ┐ god°=
26   GRY:         └mm┘
27   MRK:    's incr- 's really=
28   ROY:    =yea:h=
29   MRK:    HONestly it's- it's qui- it's a
30           remarkable=
31   GRY:    but has he actually been seen
32           u:sing them for anything
33           (0.2)
34   MRK:    ↓Yea: ┌:h!
35   GRY:          └signific(h)ant.
36           H ┌eh!
37   MRK:      └int'resting but he has hasn't=
38   EMA:    =yeh! Yeh!
39           (0.8)
40   MRK:    it's really quite
41           (1.6)
42   PUL:    (xxxxxxxx)
43           (0.5)
44   GRY:    hehheheheheh=
```

45   EMA: °huh°
46   (10.0)
47   GRY: Maybe he'll go <u>na</u>tive.

Paul has just presented an argument relating to the problems of adopting a particular
approach. After a six-second pause immediately before the extract begins, Roy invites
other ways forward. Gary immediately suggests: 'That's if Paul does the experiment'
(line 4), which generates laughter because of Paul's status as a dry. After waiting for
the laughter to die down, Paul responds in a rather droll manner: 'That would be the
safe option' (line 11), implicitly claiming that he, a dry, would be a safer pair of hands
than the wet alternative. Mark extends this banter by calling a dry person, Manuel, an
experimentalist (line 15). The group is aware that Manuel, who is not present at the
meeting, has been training to do biological experiments. The comments the members
make describe what they perceive as a marker of a wet identity: wearing gloves. Gary's
(syntactically) rhetorical question, 'has he actually been seen using them for anything
significant' (lines 31–5), invites a response from the other group members. The two
wets, Mark and Emma (EMA), align emphatically with Gary's position (lines 34–8)
and its implication that the wearing of gloves is a matter of display rather than sub-
stance. The banter, mocking a colleague crossing over the boundary between dry and
wet, ends with Gary's final comment, 'Maybe he'll go native' (line 47), humorously
implying that a dry may never become an 'authentic' wet however much they may
imitate wet behaviour; however, making humorous references to a wet crossing into
a rival camp or a dry imitating the behaviour of a wet by wearing gloves and hanging
around as an experimenter not only bonds the whole group in a shared joke (Hay 1994;
Holmes 2000, 2006; Holmes and Marra 2002; Choi and Schnurr 2016) but also implicitly reinforces the boundaries of dry and wet. It underlines the assumption that such
boundary crossings are not in practice possible, as implied by Gary's comments about
whether Manuel's gloves have been used for anything significant and his reference
to going native. Again, the idea of crossing boundaries touches on Garfinkel's idea of
'passing' in the sense of 'being someone else'. Through this joking frame (Goffman
1981), the members paradoxically serve to reinforce the different disciplinary status
of dry and wet.

   This humour does not transgress the relevant disciplinary boundary by exceeding
epistemic limits. Where such limits are perceived to be exceeded, boundary crossing
is treated as illegitimate and, as the extracts in the next section show, has more serious
interactional consequences.

4.3.2 Transgressing

Members are expected to recognise the boundaries of dry and wet, but there is a
danger that they might immerse themselves in their own field at the expense of com-
prehensibility. When a dry or a wet member is explaining something to those from
another discipline, the member needs to respect the fact that others do not have the
same epistemic range or depth as they do. In extract 9, Lucy goes beyond the limits
of what is acceptable (lines 1–7) in explaining what she plans to do. This generates

general laughter followed by Gary's humorously ironic assessment, 'no jargon there then' (lines 14–15).

Extract 9 DELTA 28 Apr 002

```
 1   LCY:   so in terms of the dee ee effs
 2          I was gonna- (.) do an ee cee
 3          dee,
 4          (0.8)
 5   LCY:   but- then I think I could do an ee
 6          cee dee on the:: (0.4) three cee
 7          thing.
 8          (2.0)
 9   LCY:   e:: ⌈:m chromatin
10   JOA:        ⌊mhh!hhe ⌈hEHH
11   GRY:                 ⌊HEHEHEHAHA=
12          =HAH° ⌈hahah°!
13   TIM?:        ⌊°chromatin ⌈(xxxx)°
14   GRY:                     ⌊no jargon
15          there ‹then.
16          ((General laughter))
```

In extract 10, Sue steps over the boundary of relevant expertise and is forced to retreat. The extract is from a regular fortnightly research project meeting.

Extract 10 ALPHA 13 May 004

```
 1   SUE:   Why are the blue ones not (.) the sa:me
 2          across
 3          (2.0)
 4   SUE:   across the experiment.
 5   MRY:   eh just because of the variability of
 6          the ↓chip.
 7          (1.5)
 8   MRY:   'cuz: as much as I trie::d (.) like y'r
 9          gonna have a biological effect 'cuz each
10          sample's different.
11   SUE:   Oka:y.
12   MRY:   So=
13   SUE:   =So ⌈so if the- if THEIR if their⌉ =
14   MRY:       ⌊I don't think there's e- o-  ⌋
15   SUE:   =variability wasn't there (.) you would
16          have
17          (0.4)
18   SUE:   they- they'd be all the same.
19          (0.8)
20   KTE?:  °HHehuh°
```

21 MRY: I mea:n: w' ⌜try an' ⌝ get them as:=
22 KTE?:   └Heheh! ┘
23 MRY: =as (.) They're not that bad. Heh!hehheh!
24 ???:   ((Very short guttural sound.))
25 MRY: I've had them worse than ⌜that.
26 SUE: └No I w's jus-
27   trying to understand.

Sue, a dry, asks a question (lines 1–4) to Mary (MRY), a wet, who provides an explanation in a way that marks the boundary of her field. She describes a biological effect in a context where the term 'biological' is rarely used. There are in fact only three other uses of 'biological' in the meeting, each of them an essential constituent in technical expressions. Mary's initial response to Sue is followed by a silence, and, when Sue shows no sign of understanding or accepting the explanation, Mary is obliged to elaborate further. At this point, Mary becomes defensive by saying 'as much as I tried' (line 8) and also points out what is expected in such an experiment in her field (lines 9–10). In doing so, Mary marks where the disciplinary boundary lies and justifies her claim in terms of her specialist knowledge. Sue acknowledges this, but, when Mary attempts further explanation (line 12), she interrupts Mary and makes a claim (line 18) based on a hypothetical situation, in doing so stepping into the biology territory. This is followed by Kate's laughter and Mary's further defensive explanations (lines 20–5). Sue backtracks by making explicit the pragmatic force of her claim (Thomas 1984), recasting it as an attempt to understand (lines 26–7) and not a suggestion.

5. Discussion

Maza (2006: 17) has made the claim that 'Interdisciplinary work involves creativity, transgression, conformity, power and endless misunderstanding.' In this chapter, I have focused on the way a number of different team members interact in boundary-crossing research. Interdisciplinary research requires that team members import and export relevant knowledge/information across disciplinary boundaries in order to conduct integrative research. This requires members to have a clear understanding of where the limits of boundaries lie and when to cross or respect them as they work together in analysing biological data, integrating them in their hypothesis-driven science and representing their research to the wider academic community.

The analysis revealed two types of disciplinary relations: extra-group and intra-group. The former refers to the relations between systems biology and the academic community as a whole; the latter relates to doing interdisciplinary work within a team. The extra-group relations highlight the disciplinary boundaries that they have to negotiate in continuing their interdisciplinary endeavour. As pointed out in section 2.1, systems biology is not yet recognised as a new interdiscipline by the academy despite its wider practice. Although this interdisciplinary approach to biological science has brought success and resulted in the establishment of many systems biology institutes in universities around the world, systems biologists face challenges in representing themselves as a discipline to funding bodies in particular. As shown in extracts

1–3, the group needed to overcome rejection from a funding body that views systems biology as a collection disciplines (multidiscipline), not as a single interdiscipline ('a new way of working'). The exchanges between the members reveal that unlike crossing disciplinary boundaries internally within the team, external boundaries are obstacles to be overcome.

While the team represent themselves to outsiders as a single bounded entity, internally, they recognise and respect their disciplinary boundaries. The intra-group relations displayed by the team members show interdisciplinarity in practice. This involves recognising and respecting boundaries and when they encounter a disparity in the fundamental nature and practice of the two disciplines as shown in extract 6, the team must negotiate a solution. The challenge is to recognise and appreciate different ways of showing their respect for and understanding of the differences between them. Leitch (2003) made the point, as did Hunt (1994) a decade earlier, that interdisciplinarity predicates internal and external differences rather than seeking to unify or totalise these differences. The exchanges between the members of team in systems biology suggest that there may be as much to be gained from exposure to another discipline through a sharp appreciation of differences as seeking a synthesis in the pursuit of a single unified method.

While the members respect and appreciate the boundary differences that create conditions for creativity (as noted by Maza 2006 above), they are also subject to conditions for potential conflict. The analysis shows that team members sometimes need to cross these boundaries, either legitimately or illegitimately. The legitimate boundary crossing in the data serves as a resource to bind the team together; humour signals the crossing but supports it. Jacobs and Frickel (2009: 47) note that 'Epistemic barriers involve incompatible styles of thought, research traditions, techniques, and language that are difficult to translate across disciplinary domains' but it is this very incompatibility which makes possible the humorous reframing of potentially transgressive acts of boundary violation. When Amy passes herself off as a theoretician in extract 7, for example, this is quickly seized on by Tim as an opportunity for friendly banter, just as Manuel's wearing of gloves and involvement in biological experiments in extract 8 becomes a target of mockery by wets. Even potentially transgressive acts such as Lucy's in extract 9 can be defused by humorous reference to disciplinary divisions ('no jargon there then'). These crossings are not seen as illegitimate because (1) team members are not claiming epistemic rights falling outside their own disciplinary boundary; and (2) they do not change a member's fundamental disciplinary status. Rather, the humour they provoke indirectly reinforces the different disciplinary status of dry and wet.

The illegitimate crossing of the boundaries on the other hand can be a threat to the unity of the team and become a barrier to engaging in interdisciplinary research. Sue's actions in extract 10 demonstrate a transgression because she is seen as making an assumption and a claim. She illegitimately claims epistemic rights and is forced to retreat. The crucial difference between illegitimate and legitimate boundary crossing lies in whether or not a member transgresses the relevant disciplinary boundary by exceeding their epistemic limits. Where such limits are perceived to have been exceeded, there are serious interactional consequences. The power of Kogan's embedded identity is evident here. He defines embedded identity as being:

a member of communities and institutions which have their own languages, conceptual structures, histories, traditions, myths, values, practices and achieved goals. The individual has roles which are strongly determined by the communities and institutions of which he or she is a member. (Kogan 2000: 210)

So when Sue insists on her views, she is forced to retreat for failing to respect the other's embedded identity.

In her discussion of epistemic domains, Elgin (2012: 146) refers to 'the division of epistemic labor. Very roughly, a community of inquiry consists of those who share background beliefs, methods, standards, and goals.' When one makes an epistemic claim from another's territory, it threatens to undermine the basis of this sharing; it is a transgression, which has the potential to create tensions within the group. The members of a discipline act as legislating members of its epistemic realms, and, when one member violates the epistemic realm of the other's discipline, this triggers a quick response from members seeking to reassert their epistemic authority. Thus, unlike the legitimate crossing, which can serve as a resource to bind the team together, illustrated here through humour, transgressing threatens the unity of the team; while the dynamic of the former is centripetal, that of the latter is centrifugal.

6. Conclusion

Insights from this analysis of teams in systems biology demonstrate the importance of working together in boundary-crossing research. When involved in interdisciplinary work, academics must negotiate boundaries. The challenge is to ensure that the boundaries do not become barriers in their continuing interdisciplinary endeavours. This involves crossing boundaries in order to understand but also recognising and respecting those boundaries. The division between legitimate and illegitimate boundary crossings has given us insight into what constitutes a disciplinary boundary. A close analysis of the interaction between members involved in boundary-crossing research reveals how academics seem to be intuitively aware of where disciplinary boundaries lie despite the inherent ambiguities around defining what disciplinarity and interdisciplinarity are.

As interdisciplinary research increases, concerns about the cost-effectiveness of public- and private-sector investments in team-based science research will also grow. In order to attain a better understanding of how interdisciplinary teams work together productively, more work on the micro-level interaction of their research engagements is needed. This chapter has opened a window on this potentially productive area of research.

Transcription conventions

.	falling contour
œ	strong falling contour
,	continuing contour
?	questioning contour

⟩	strong rising contour
!	exclamatory delivery
:	lengthening
<u>underline</u>	emphasis
CAPS	loudness
-	cut off
° °	quieter than surrounding talk
> <	faster than surrounding talk
< >	slower than surrounding talk
(xxx)	untranscribable
(.)	micropause
(0.5)	pause of between (roughly) 0.3 and 0.9 of a second
=	latched turns
[	beginning of overlap (always at beginning of word)
]	end of overlap (always at end of a word)

Note

1. In Figures 11.2 and 11.3, the number of bars represents the number of contexts (nine in all).

References

Aderem, A. (2005), 'Systems biology: its practice and challenges', *Cell*, 121: 4, pp. 511–13.

Aldrich, H. J. (2014), *Interdisciplinarity*, Oxford: Oxford Scholarship Online.

Aram, J. (2004), 'Concepts of interdisciplinarity: configurations of knowledge and action', *Human Relations*, 57: 4, p. 381.

Bakhtin, M. (1994), 'Double-voiced discourse in Dostoevsky', in P. Morris (ed.), *The Bakhtin reader: selected writings*, London: Edward Arnold, pp. 102–11.

Baxter, J. (2011), 'Survival or success? A critical exploration of the use of "double-voiced discourse" by women business leaders in the UK', *Discourse and Communication*, 5, pp. 231–45.

Becher, T. (1989), *Academic tribes and territories: intellectual enquiry and the culture of disciplines*, Milton Keynes: SRHE and Open University Press.

Boogerd, F. C., F. J. Bruggeman, J.-H. S. Hofmeyr and H. V. Westerhoff (eds) (2007), *Systems biology: philosophical foundations*, Amsterdam: Elsevier.

Brew, A. (2008), 'Disciplinary and interdisciplinary affiliations of experienced researchers', *Higher Education*, 56, pp. 423–38.

Calvert, J. and J. H. Fujimura (2011), 'Calculating life? Duelling discourses in inter-disciplinary systems biology', *Studies in History and Philosophy of Biological and Biomedical Sciences*, 42, pp. 155–63.

Choi, S. (2016), 'The case for open source software: the Interactional Discourse Lab', *Applied Linguistics*, 37: 1, pp. 100–20.

Choi, S. and K. Richards (2014), 'Turns in interdisciplinary scientific research meetings: mapping interactional dynamics using R', in Thomas Schmidt, Kai Wörner, Sukriye Ruhi and Michael Haugh (eds), *Best practices for spoken corpora in linguistic research*, Newcastle upon Tyne: Cambridge Scholars Publishing, pp. 95–115.

Choi, S. and S. Schnurr (2014), 'Exploring distributed leadership: solving disagreements and negotiating consensus in a "leaderless" team', *Discourse Studies*, 16: 1, pp. 3–24.

Choi, S. and S. Schnurr (2016), 'Enacting and negotiating power relations through teasing in distributed leadership constellations', *Pragmatics and Society*, 7: 3, pp. 482–502.

Elgin, C. Z. (2012), 'Understanding's tethers', in Christoph Jäger and Winifrid Löffler (eds), *Epistemology: contexts, values, and disagreement*, Frankfurt: Ontos Verlag, pp. 131–46.

Finkenthal, M. (2001), *Interdisciplinarity: toward the definition of a metadiscipline?*, New York: Peter Lang.

Gardiner, T. (1993), 'Reaping the whirlwind', *Teaching Mathematics and its Applications*, 12: 4, pp. 149–53.

Garfinkel, H. (1967), *Studies in ethnomethodology*, Englewood Cliffs, NJ: Prentice Hall.

Goffman, E. (1981), *Forms of talk*, Oxford: Basil Blackwell.

Gray, B. (1989), *Collaborating: finding common ground for multiparty problems*, San Francisco: Jossey-Bass.

Gray, B. (1996), 'Cross-sectoral partners: collaborative alliances among business, government, and communities', in C. Huxham (ed.), *In search of collaborative advantage*, Newbury Park, CA: Sage, pp. 58–99.

Hay, J. (1994), 'Jocular abuse in mixed-group interaction', in Janet Holmes (ed.), *Wellington Working Papers in Linguistics*, 6, pp. 26–55.

Hollingsworth, J. R. (1986), 'The decline of scientific communication within and across academic disciplines', *Policy Studies Journal*, 14: 3, pp. 422–8.

Holmes, J. (2000), 'Politeness, power and provocation: how humour functions in the workplace', *Discourse Studies*, 2: 2, pp. 159–85.

Holmes, J. (2006), 'Sharing a laugh: pragmatic aspects of humor and gender in the workplace', *Journal of Pragmatics*, 38: 1, pp. 26–50.

Holmes, J. and M. Marra (2002), 'Having a laugh at work: how humour contributes to workplace culture', *Journal of Pragmatics*, 34, pp. 1683–710.

Hunt, L. (1994), 'The virtues of disciplinarity', *Eighteenth-Century Studies*, 28, pp. 1–7.

Huxham, C. (ed.) (1996), *In search of collaborative advantage*, Newbury Park, CA: Sage.

Jacobs, J. A. and S. Frickel (2009), 'Interdisciplinarity: a critical assessment', *Annual Review of Sociology*, 35, pp. 43–65.

Katze, M. G. (2013), 'Preface', in M. G. Katze (ed.), *Systems biology*, Berlin: Springer, pp. v–x.

Klein, J. T. (1990), *Interdisciplinarity: history, theory and practice*, Detroit: Wayne State University Press.

Klein, J. T. (1996), *Crossing boundaries: knowledge, disciplinarities, and interdisciplinarities*, Charlottesville: University of Virginia Press.

Klein, J. T. (2004), 'Interdisciplinary and complexity: an evolving relationship', *E:CO*, 6: 1–2, pp. 2–10.

Klein, J. T. (2008), 'Evaluation of interdisciplinary and transdisciplinary research: a literature review', *American Journal of Preventive Medicine*, 35: 2, pp. S116–S123.

Kogan, M. (2000), 'Higher education communities and academic identity', *Higher Education Quarterly*, 54: 2, pp. 207–16.

Kuhn, T. (1970), *The structure of scientific revolutions*, Chicago: University of Chicago Press.

Leitch, V. (2003), *Theory matters*, New York and London: Psychology Press.

Maza, S. (2006), 'Interdisciplinarity: (why) is it still an issue?', in G. J. Mallinson (ed.), *Interdisciplinarity: qu'est-ce que les lumières. La reconnaissance au dix-huitième siècle*, Oxford: Voltaire Foundation, pp. 3–17.

Pickering, A. (ed.) (1992), *Science as practice and culture*, Chicago: University of Chicago Press.

Price, D. J. de Solla (1963), *Little science, big science*, New York: Columbia University Press.

R Core Team (2014), *R: a language and environment for statistical computing*, R Foundation for Statistical Computing, Vienna, Austria, <https://www.r-project. org/> (last accessed 17 November 2016).

Repko, A. F. (2008), *Interdisciplinary research: process and theory*, Los Angeles: Sage.

Salter, L. and A. Hearn (1996), *Outside the lines: issues in interdisciplinary research*, Montreal: McGill-Queen's University Press.

Stokols, D., J. G. Grzywacz, S. McMahan and K. Phillips (2003), 'Increasing the health promotive capacity of human environments', *American Journal of Health Promotion*, 18: 1, pp. 4–13.

Thomas, J. (1984), 'Cross-cultural discourse as "unequal encounter": towards a pragmatic analysis', *Applied Linguistics*, 5: 3, pp. 226–35.

Wagner, C. S., D. J. Roessner, K. Bobb, J. T. Klein, K. W. Boyack, J. Keyton, I. Rafols and K. Börner (2011), 'Approaches to understanding and measuring interdisciplinary scientific research (IDR): a review of the literature', *Journal of Informetrics*, 5: 1, pp. 14–26.

Ylijoki, O.-H. (2000), 'Disciplinary cultures and the moral order of studying – a case-study of four Finnish university departments', *Higher Education*, 39: 3, pp. 229–362.

Index